DESTROY OR DIE

★ ★ ★ ★ ★ ★ ★ ★ ★ ★ ★ ★ ★ ★

DESTROY
OR
DIE

★ ★ ★ ★ ★ ★ ★ ★ ★ ★ ★ ★ ★ ★ ★

The True Story of Mylai

★ ★ ★ ★ ★ ★ ★ ★ ★ ★ ★ ★ ★ ★

MARTIN GERSHEN

ARLINGTON HOUSE   *New Rochelle, N.Y.*

Library of Congress Catalog Card Number 76-139887

ISBN 0-87000-102-7

MANUFACTURED IN THE UNITED STATES OF AMERICA BY HADDON CRAFTSMEN INC., SCRANTON, PA.

To my father, former Pfc. Hyman Gershen, a United States infantryman in World War I and recipient of the Silver Star for bravery. He was a gentle man who would get angry at us children only when we asked him to tell us war stories. He refused. Now I think I know why.

And to all United States infantrymen of America's wars. Your valor assumes even greater significance for refusing to burden the public with the weight you have carried on your shoulders, even when your packs were removed.

And, finally, to Charlie Company, 1/20, Americal Division. On behalf of the American people who failed you by refusing to hear your story, my humble apologies. But on behalf of most Americans, who are willing to accept the truth, I thank you and salute you for carrying the burden of your countrymen on your frail, inexperienced shoulders.

Contents

★　★　★　★　★　★　★　★　★　★　★　★　★　★

ACKNOWLEDGMENTS

★　★　★　★　★　★　★　★　★　★　★　★　★

Newsmen by their very nature and that of their profession are highly competitive and reluctant to share information with their colleagues. Yet, in their common search for truth, they will cooperate with each other, and I am indebted to many of them throughout this country for the help they gave me. I want to thank particularly:

Theo Wilson, New York *Daily News*

H. D. Quigg, United Press International

Frank McCulloch, Time-Life, Inc.

Arnold Markowitz and Gus Schuettler, *Miami Herald*

Hal Scarlett, *Houston Post*

Stan Redding and Zartow Frank, *Houston Chronicle*

Bob Fleming, *San Francisco Chronicle*

Jim Quint, *San Francisco Examiner*

Jerry Brydges and Jack Myer, *Niagara Falls Gazette*

Gary Hanlon, *The Independent* (Richmond, California)

Dean Theodore Peterson, College of Communications, University of Illinois

AUTHOR'S FOREWORD

★ ★ ★ ★ ★ ★ ★ ★ ★ ★ ★ ★ ★ ★

In mid-Novermber 1969, the story of Mylai (4) was splashed across the pages of the world press in all its horrible details. The stories in essence claimed an American infantry company had committed a massacre in South Vietnam. Nobody seemed to know why it happened nor were any reasons advanced.

An embarrassed Army hierarchy, aware for twenty months of that terrible tragedy of war, finally broke its silence to announce it had already charged one second lieutenant with murder. Then the Army set forth to pinpoint the blame for the tragedy on the company's enlisted men and low ranking officers, the traditional foot slogging infantrymen who are the pawns and the victims of all wars.

At the same time, the author set out to determine what indeed did occur at Mylai (4), why it happened and who the villains truly were.

In May 1970, the author's conclusions were published in a six-part series in newspapers around the world revealing for the first time the true story of Mylai. The series made one fact clear:

The American GI was not to blame for what happened in Mylai (4). He did not start the Vietnam War; he did not set policy; indeed he had no enthusiasm for this unpopular conflict.

But the Army legal machinery already had gone into motion and 12 soldiers, all enlisted men and low ranking officers were being charged with murder.

Another 14, all high ranking officers were being investigated on minor charges of withholding information.

By January 22, 1971, two enlisted men were found innocent at their courts martial of doing any wrong at Myali and charges against the rest of them had been dropped.

By January 29, 1971, the highest ranking officer involved in the Mylai investigation was told he did not have to stand trial and charges against him were dropped.

As the series had pointed out and as the Army hierarchy now realized the GI in the field could not be blamed for the mistakes of their leaders.

The Army was dropping the Mylai affair.

This book, an expansion of the series, relates the true story of Mylai. It not only tells what happened at Mylai, but most important, why the members of this hard luck company reacted as they did. It offers for the first time an opportunity for the innocent infantrymen to tell their side of the story.

It was written long before the Army saw the error if its ways and decided to let its people go.

PRELUDE

★ ★ ★ ★ ★ ★ ★ ★ ★ ★ ★ ★ ★ ★

"They have seen and done and felt things you cannot know."
                                                    ERNIE PYLE
A civilian combat correspondent and Pulitzer Prize winner, killed in
action in the final days of World War II as he was following his beloved
infantrymen in a battle against Japanese forces on Ie Shima.

★ ★ ★ ★ ★ ★ ★ ★ ★ ★ ★ ★ ★ ★

The tragedy at Mylai cannot be condoned. But the
Americans who were thrust into that situation cannot be
condemned. For if there was a failure it must rest with
the society that forced these kids to go to die in a foreign
land for a cause it refused to defend at home.

"If we're guilty, then everybody is guilty. And that's the
way I feel," Frederick Widmer, a member of the company
told me. In essence he sums up the attitude of most of the
members of Charlie Company, or for that matter most of
the servicemen in Vietnam.

The U. S. should have never gotten into the Vietnam
mess. Before the first adviser was committed there our
political leaders should have carefully considered the
consequences. Intervention in Vietnam should have been
discussed in the halls of Congress and argued in the columns of the press and opposed on the street corners of
America. But this nation remained strangely silent as
its leaders girded for battle. The protest should have

come before the battle not in its midst.

A war cannot be taken lightly, nor is physical combat a debatable subject. Therefore those members of our society who through conscience or cunning have protested this war are as guilty of what happened in Mylai as the soldiers they seek to condemn.

The time for talk and protest and argument is before physical violence occurs. One argues in a bar, then either walks out or fights. Nations accuse or defend each other in a world forum; then they either fight or resolve their differences. But once the battle is joined, once a fight begins, all the resources at a combatant's disposal must be used.

The old adage that all is fair in love and war still holds true. In both cases each party is seeking total victory, emotional or physical, and the means of achieving it assume secondary importance.

There are really no laws of war except those that are of mutual benefit to the combatants. Poison gas wasn't banned from the battlefield because of its horrible effects on a human being. If that were true, then mines and booby traps should also be banned. Poison gas was banned because neither side could control it perfectly, and a simple shift of wind could result in devastating effects even to the side employing this means of warfare.

The humanitarian treatment of prisoners of war and of civilians of warring nations at one time proved of mutual benefit to both sides in a conflict. Today war prisoners and civilians are used by the North Vietnamese in the same way as other weapons of war are employed.

If rules of war thus may arbitrarily be broken by one side, then there are no rules of war.

If proof is needed that war is hell then the tragedy at Mylai is a classic example. If proof is needed that the Vietnam War is more hell than other wars, then the Mylai affair is just another tragic incident of war—of far less significance, say, than the bombing of Hiroshima and

Nagasaki, or London or Berlin.

If the war in Vietnam is debatable, the debates should have taken place before the Gulf of Tonkin resolution. It seems unfair and unjust for a society to discuss the righteousness of a war in which it continues to send its young men to die. I wouldn't want to go off to die for a cause that I have been told in advance is worthless.

Would you?

Neither did the men in Charlie Company.

* * * * * * * * * * * * * *

Charlie Company, 1st Battalion, 20th Infantry, Task Force Barker, Americal Division, died in an enemy minefield on the morning of February 25, 1968.

The haunted, hollow-eyed, shell-shocked survivors who stormed Mylai (4) three weeks later were psychologically twisted, emotionally disturbed wrecks of the boys who had arrived in Vietnam three and a half months earlier —reluctant warriors in an unpopular war, but nevertheless full of the piss and vinegar usually attributed to American infantrymen.

The story of the company's destruction in the minefield went unreported because nobody gave a damn. But Charlie Company was as heroic and as scared and as awkward and as green as any group of civilian soldiers who served as United States infantrymen in America's wars.

This, then, is their story.

DESTROY OR DIE

★ ★ ★ ★ ★ ★ ★ ★ ★ ★ ★ ★ ★ ★

★ ★ ★

CHAPTER I

D-DAY

★ ★ ★ ★ ★ ★ ★ ★ ★ ★ ★ ★ ★ ★

"Until now, we were dying uselessly."

FREDERICK WIDMER
A member of Charlie Company

★ ★ ★ ★ ★ ★ ★ ★ ★ ★ ★ ★ ★ ★

When James Bergthold was shaken awake before the sun rose that morning of March 16, 1968, the young, heavy-set soldier, couldn't tell whether this would be a beautiful day or not. Nor was he sure he'd ever see another sunset.

The bunker at LZ Dottie where the men slept on wooden boards was dark as the night. Bergthold was luckier than some. He had an air mattress to buffer the discomfort of the sleeping slab. He lay a few moments in the dark, stretching comfortably, then suddenly his heart sank. He realized what was happening today and suddenly that wooden slab and air mattress became like an oversized double bed for a king. Would this be his last night's sleep? Would he live to see this wooden rack another night?

Charlie Company was going on that air assault to Pinkville this morning, Bergthold remembered. There would be a terrible battle there today, he thought, and his throat tightened in fear, a fear shared by every member of this decimated infantry company that day.

"I was scared. I didn't want to go, but I had to," remembers Bergthold. "Because if I didn't I'd probably get court-martialed. I'd rather take my chances out in the field."

Everybody in Charlie Company was frightened that early morning of March 16, 1968, remembers Herbert Louis Carter, a former rifleman. Some of the men hadn't gone to bed all night, he said, choosing to stay awake and talk or drink beer or smoke pot. Many members of Charlie Company felt that March 16 would be the last day of their lives.

"That night a lot of guys wondered if they'd be alive for another night," Carter remembers.

There wasn't anything they could do about it. "We're going and that's it," Bergthold told himself as he tumbled out of his bunk to get ready for the operation.

Outside it was warm and the light of a new day was slowly rising over the rice paddies. It promised to be a beautiful day. Down at the other end of the fire base where the men lived during the infrequent periods when they weren't in the field, the helicopter engines were already being warmed up for the assault.

There was an air of tension at the base that morning, an excitement stimulated by fear and depression, but it didn't keep Bergthold from having breakfast.

Despite the lousy chow in the Army, particularly in the field, Bergthold at 190 pounds had a weight problem. He tried to stay on a diet in the field and the guys kidded him about it. But there was no use missing chow at Dottie where you can get hot meals. Bergthold walked over to the primitive mess hall and sat down to a breakfast of orange juice, scrambled powdered eggs, toast and two glasses of milk.

"I never ate too much of that junk," he recalls.

Then he got his 90-pound pack and his weapon and double rations of ammo, which everybody would take, and walked out to the helicopter pad where the rotor blades of nine choppers were kicking up the dust and sending a

powerful wind blast screaming at the soldiers, who had to
bend forward to keep from being knocked backward.

There was the usual confusion, Bergthold remembers,
that occurs when the men got ready to go on a mission,
and he sought out the second squad of the first platoon, to
which he belonged. What worried him most about the
operation wasn't only the fact that twice before in recent
weeks Charlie Company had been bloodied in actions involving Pinkville. He was worried about what he would
do when the helicopter landed, how he would seek cover,
where he would seek protection from enemy snipers.

"I didn't mind walking into a place like that," said Bergthold, recalling the countless hamlets Charlie Company
had searched in the three and half months it had been in
Vietnam.

"But jumping out of a helicopter, you don't have too
much cover," he explains.

Bergthold soon found his platoon sergeant, M. Sgt.
Isaiah Cowan, Robert Maples, a machine gunner, and
finally his squad. He boarded a helicopter with them.
Bergthold's platoon was under the command of Lt. William Laws Calley, Jr., and he knew his unit would lead the
assault on Pinkville.

Charlie Company, under the command of Capt. Ernest
Lou Medina, was one of three companies belonging to
a bastard unit called Task Force Barker. It's commander, Lt. Col. Frank Akeley Barker, would be flying overhead in a helicopter—which is where the brass usually
stayed during an action—to supervise the operation in the
field.

While the two other companies would be serving in
blocking positions, Charlie Company had orders to sweep
the hamlet they were assaulting, which was supposed to
be the home of the 48th Light Force Battalion, an elusive
Viet Cong unit that fought well and had taken a heavy toll
of Americans. In the last few weeks Charlie Company
had lost 42 men killed and wounded to the 48th without

ever seeking the enemy. Now they were being given the opportunity to hit back.

The company was in a severe state of depression because of its recent losses, and it was suffering from war fatigue as well as fear.

"Let's put it this way," recalls Fred Widmer, one of Capt. Medina's radio telephone operators who was asked to describe the mental attitude of the company that morning. "Everybody wasn't natural. They weren't their usual self. And I mean everybody."

The assault would take place in two waves, both landing at a hamlet called Mylai (4) about 2½ kilometers from the South China Sea, from where the enemy already was fleeing.

The sound of a helicopter engine is similar to the chatter of a machine gun, and the rapid staccato of nine of them only served to further excite the men as they boarded the aircraft for the assault. Carter, also a member of the first platoon and one of the company's tunnel rats, climbed into the helicopter with Capt. Medina, Widmer and S. Sgt. David Mitchell, a squad leader in Calley's platoon who seemed to get along better with the lieutenant than Cowan did. Also aboard were two other RTOs, an artillery liaison officer and the company's chief medic.

"Everything was all mixed up in the choppers," Carter recalls. "All the platoons were mixed up."

LZ Dottie was only about five miles northwest of Mylai (4) but the assault wave did not fly directly to its target for fear of giving away its plans to the Vietcong. Instead the helicopters paralleling nearby Highway 1, flew south to Quang Ngai city, then northeast to Mylai (4), a nine-minute flight.

Looking out of his helicopter door, Medina recalled, "I could see the smoke and flash of artillery landing on Mylai." He remembers six helicopter gunships also pounding the hamlet with rockets and machine-gun fire.

"There were Cobras, Rattlers and Cowboys," Carter

remembers the names designating the gunships. "We came in with our M-60s blazing, even on our ship."

The nine troop-carrying helicopters landed in high grass about 150 meters west of the hamlet and the men tumbled out to secure the LZ as the choppers flew off to get the second wave. The grass was up to the groins of the troops as they stood in the rice paddies, getting organized into squads and platoons.

Medina and his headquarters section immediately raced to a small graveyard closer to the hamlet and radioed LZ Dottie, where the Tactical Operations Center was located, that the landing zone was cold, meaning he had received no ground fire coming in. But a helicopter, hovering over the scene, broke in and the radioman shouted, "Negative, negative, we are getting ground fire and we see VC with weapons. The LZ is hot," Medina remembers.

The Viet Cong living at Mylai (4), seeing what was coming, fled, leaving behind their wives, children and loved ones.

One of them, Nguyen Ngo, a deputy VC platoon leader, left his mother and three sisters and nephews to fend for themselves and ran into the woods to hide. Another, Pham Em, a VC tax collector, fled into a bunker where the VC kept their weapons and stayed there, unable to see what was happening. Another, Pham Lai, a VC security guard, crawled into a bunker with a bamboo top, leaving his wife, two daughters, ages four and eight, grandmother, uncle, aunt and cousin to provide for their own safety. And another VC security guard, Nguyen Bat, also took off for the bushes from where he could watch in safety what was happening.

On hearing the area was "hot," Medina immediately informed his platoon leaders to "move with extreme caution and to return any fire." Then he and his section moved to the east side of the landing zone, still outside the cluster of 31 huts that made up the hamlet.

In the meantime the second and final wave of helicopters landed and the company began forming up for the move into Mylai (4).

Calley's first platoon and the second, under command of Lt. Karl S. Brooks who was later to be killed in action, formed a line abreast. The third platoon, under Lt. Jeffrey LaCross, was held in reserve. The weapons platoon and attached demolition men were supposed to be with Medina.

Carter says everybody formed in a long line abreast, except for Medina and his headquarters section. Then the frightened company of men, holding their weapons horizontally at the waist in a firing position, began, grim faced, to move through the groin-high grass and muddy ground toward the hamlet.

The ranks were almost still.

"There was not too much words spoke," Carter remembers the advance on the hamlet.

"We knew we was there to be killed or to kill. A lot of guys thought this was the chance of revenge; the chance to clean Pinkville up."

It was a company of zombies, a company of psychologically destroyed infantrymen who were advancing towards their destiny. In their ranks walked the ghosts of their dead. In their minds they still saw the horribly mutilated bodies of their wounded. In their ears rang the screams of their dying. And in their hearts was the hatred they felt for all the Vietnamese who had destroyed them.

Suddenly, in the rice fields, a Vietnamese farmer saw the GIs approaching. He began running towards the advancing soldiers, shouting, "GI Number One, GI, Number One," a pidgin English term meaning "Americans are great." The soldiers had heard that phrase many times. They heard it from whores who wanted more money or from kids selling black-market beer. It was always said with tongue in cheek and never in sincerity.

Paul Meadlo of the first platoon remembers the scene this way: "There was one gook in a shelter, he was all huddled down in there—an older man. And Sergeant Mitchell hollered, 'Shoot him,' and so the man shot him."

Carter also remembers the scene, except the young tunnel rat says the old man was running towards the soldiers and waving and shouting "GI Number One," when the order was given to "shoot him."

"That's when all the mess started. That's when all hell broke loose. He was immediately annihilated," Carter remembers.

And once that volley of rifle fire began, it never stopped. What followed cannot be described in sequence. Each man saw only what happened in his immediate surroundings. Some still don't believe they did what they know was done. None of the men were sufficiently sound mentally to remember exactly what was happening. The situation was abnormal. So was the company.

Meadlo remembers that after the farmer was shot his squad, led by Mitchell, "started searching out the village and gathering up the people and running them to the center of the village.

"There was about 40, 45 people that we gathered in the —in, like I say the center of the village. And—and we placed them in there, and it was like, like a little island, right there in the center of the village . . ."

Those gathered were men, women, children and babies, Meadlo remembers. Bernhardt observes that he didn't see any Vietnamese of military age.

The villagers were forced to squat, Meadlo said, "and Lt. Calley came over and said, 'You know what to do with them, don't you?' And I said 'Yes,' so I took it for granted that he just wanted us to watch them. And he left and came back 10 or 15 minutes later and said 'How come you ain't killed them yet?' and I told him that 'I didn't think you wanted us to kill them; I thought—that you just wanted us to guard them.' He said 'No, I want them dead.' "

Meadlo said there were three or four others who heard the order. Then he said Calley "stepped back about 10, 15 feet and he started shooting them. And he told me to start shooting them. So I started shooting them."

Meadlo said he fired four clips of 17 rounds each into the crowd with his M-16 set on automatic, estimating he killed about 10 or 15 of the villagers.

Meadlo, not considered bright by his buddies, said that at the time he felt he was doing the right thing in carrying out Calley's orders.

"I lost buddies. I—I lost—I lost a good, damn buddy, Bobby Wilson. And it was on my conscience," Meadlo said. "So after I done it I felt good. But later on that day, it kept getting to me."

Carter also remembers the scene. He was standing watching, he said, when "Calley told the dudes to get rid of them. Nobody did nothing. He come back, he got rid of them. Calley was cool, man," Carter remembers.

"Once that gook in the field was down, it was open season. We'd been waiting for it for a long time anyway," Carter remembers.

"We went into that village with guns blazing. When the gooks heard the shooting they didn't know what to think. Maybe they thought the VC was drunk and raising hell. When they came out of their hootches they were shot down. Or they were gathered in a group and shot down.

"Cowan was nowhere around," Carter says of the platoon sergeant. "Because Calley and Mitchell actually gave orders to kill. Mitchell said, 'Help round everybody up,' " Carter remembers.

"I helped pull them out of the hootches and others reacted the same. Each was trying to outdo the other to prove he was a better man; that he could be rougher than the other guy. There was so much confusion that day nobody gave a damn. People were pulled out of their huts and kicked and beaten. If a woman looked good enough, she was raped, kicked and beaten.

After Meadlo and Calley had fired into the first group of villagers, seven or eight more Vietnamese were taken and thrown into a hootch.

"Then we dropped a hand grenade in there with them," Meadlo says.

Then a group of 70 to 75 people were gathered by a ditch, Meadlo remembers.

"Meadlo, we got another job to do," the soldier says Calley told him.

"And so he walked over to the people and he started pushing them off and started shooting. We just pushed them all off and just started using automatics on them," Meadlo remembers.

Michael Terry, who was in the third platoon, remembers hearing about this incident. The third platoon, being held in reserve, didn't get into Mylai until most of the shooting was over.

"The first platoon marched through and I guess . . . shot most of the people that they saw. A lot of the people evacuated the areas. They just ran along the trails and tried to get out as fast as they could. And they shot quite a few that they saw, I imagine, and I know one group, specifically, they had rounded up, oh, 20, maybe 30 people, and most of them were women and children, there might have been a few old men in the group. But they rounded them up just over a ditch bank and shot them all with a machine gun and left them in the ditch.

"I had a friend that, well, that told me about this one incident with this Lt. Calley. And he ordered one man, I believe his name was Torres, to shoot these—he was a machine gunner and he ordered him to shoot the people. And he shot about half of them, and he wouldn't do it any more. And so Calley grabbed the machine gun and shot the rest himself," Terry remembers.

When the group was ordered to the ditch, Carter remembers Calley ordering Mitchell to "get that bunch in the ditch too." Then Carter recalls "I think Mitchell was

pretty confused. The look on his face was should I do this
or shouldn't I?"

"Calley looked very pleased and proud of his work as he
killed," Carter says. "He never smiled, he wasn't that
type. I seen Calley kill guys by himself. I seen Calley kill
people in the group by the ditch. He acted like he was
doing the right thing."

Calley was taking orders from Medina. Carter learned,
and Bernhardt confirms this, that Medina had received
orders from Barker to "sweep" Mylai (4).

Then, Carter says, Mitchell turned to him. Carter was
standing with Harry Stanley and a machine gunner.
Mitchell ordered the three of them to carry out Calley's
order.

"I walked away and looked at them like they're crazy.
Stanley walked away too. You could look on the machine
gunner's face and tell he didn't want to do it. But he and
Mitchell did. There were about 35 or 40 people in the
ditch, boys too. And they were crying." At one time, Carter
says, when he was ordered to round up people, he saw two
villagers and waved them away, in effect telling them to
beat it.

Many of the Vietnamese, he said, showed no emotion,
but others did. The crowd being fired on by Meadlo were
weaping and pleading for their lives.

"Boy, he wracked up points that day," Carter said of
Meadlo. "Every time you kill somebody, that's a point."

After Carter walked away from Mitchell, he wandered
through the holocaust that was Mylai (4). Throughout
the village fires were burning and men were screaming, laughing hysterically, burning, looting, raping, killing. Young men crazed by an insane war had gone stark
raving mad.

Not all the people were killed.

Pham Em, the VC tax collector, said he heard of 100
villagers who begged, screamed and pleaded for their
lives.

"Then a white American officer waved the soldiers away. All the villagers ran into the woods, but 14 had been killed in the first shooting," he said.

Nguyen Ngo, the VC deputy platoon leader, said his mother and sister survived by hiding in a ditch into which dead bodies toppled. But another sister and three nephews were killed while he was hiding in safety. Pham Lai, the VC security guard, lost his grandmother, uncle, aunt, cousin and four-year-old girl as he provided for his own security by hiding in a bunker. But his wife and eight-year-old daughter survived.

Many of the inhabitants huddled in their huts, or in the tunnels that they call air-raid shelters, sweating out the artillery attack that preceded the assault.

Truong Van Vinh, a 71-year-old farmer who had two wives, sat in his hootch with his older wife while an artillery barrage continued for hours. His younger wife had gone to the market earlier that day. When the barrage ended, his older wife said she looked outside and saw shouting GIs coming towards her. The only words she could understand them saying were VC, VC. When her husband stepped outside, she says, he was shot. Then she said, "The soldiers came in and saw me and motioned for me to come outside. One of them lifted his rifle to shoot me, but another group of Americans sitting around the well shouted to him and he walked away."

Another elderly male survivor said he grabbed his two nephews and ran to the "family shelter" when he saw the helicopters land. He said he crawled into the five-foot hole first and his nephews climbed in over him. They were covered by thatch and a wooden pallet.

To GIs, any hole in the ground is a tunnel and a tunnel is where the VC hide and therefore must be destroyed. As the GIs passed the hole, one stuck a rifle inside and fired twice, a sound military tactic. He killed the two nephews.

Another old woman said she had just sat down for breakfast with 13 members of her family when the soldiers arrived. At other times, she said, Americans always brought candy and medicine. This time the family was ordered out and taken into the field. Then the soldiers began shooting. She and two of her grandchildren were the only survivors.

"If you hurt one of us, you hurt us all," Carter once explained the bond of brotherhood that ran through his company. The company had lost almost 40 percent of its men in a one-month period. It was hurt.

As the men raced through the village, their minds seemed to become numb.

"There was no expression on the American faces," remembers Ron Haeberle, the GI photographer who was on his first combat mission, after almost a year in Vietnam, to do a story for the Army press service. But he wasn't a member of the company, had no combat experience, and wasn't qualified to judge the infantrymen. For example, he wasn't around when the company lost 32 men in 5 minutes in that minefield 3 weeks before.

"I couldn't believe it. They were destroying everything," Haeberle recalls. "They were doing it all very businesslike. The Vietnamese saw the Americans but didn't run. They kept on walking until the GIs saw them and started shooting. Some of the people started pulling their animals off the road and hiding behind trees. The GIs were opening up with M-16s, machine guns and grenade launchers. The grenade launchers made a 'ka-PLOW' sound."

The company was very businesslike because they rounded up the people at Mylai just as they had done in scores of other villages that they had searched. Their reception in all the other villages had ranged from unfriendly to hostile. This time they were killing because they thought they were supposed to.

"Being nice to them proved out no good," one soldier recalls. "Maybe the people we helped weren't trying to kill us, but they were covering up for those who were."

And, Carter reflected later, "The people at Mylai, when they died, they didn't know why they were dying. And the people who were doing the killing, they didn't know why they were killing."

"I went in there and I killed," another soldier recalls. "And after a while we began to realize that this, that this is not right. It was like going through the minefield all over again. Something in your brain said that this wasn't the way it was supposed to be. It was like adding hurt to hurt. But that was after it was all over. Then your emotions ran away with you.

"Everyone was more-or-less doing something that they shouldn't be and way down inside they knew it wasn't right, and yet felt they were getting revenge, and, what we felt, we was destroying the enemy."

Vernado Simpson remembers the morning was getting warmer. He was with the second platoon, leading 25 men into the hamlet. They went from hut to hut, searching each. If the huts were empty they were burned. If people were found inside, they were taken back to the intelligence officer accompanying the company. If villagers tried to run they were ordered to stop. Those who didn't were shot.

At one time three people, one a man with a weapon, kept running from Simpson and his group. Simpson ordered them, in Vietnamese, to halt. They didn't.

"What else was there to do?" Simpson asks. "Run up and beg them to stop? I had orders to shoot anyone who ran. They were about 20 yards away. I couldn't see the child. I used my M-16 . . . I noticed it was a woman and child when I walked over. It's hard to tell what they are from the back . . . The man? He got away."

Long afterward Simpson would say, "Someone will always be pointing a finger at me and saying 'He was one of them.' I didn't like what happened. But I didn't decide."

Former Sgt. Charles West of the third platoon was leading his squad of 13 GIs down a sharply winding trail through the rice paddies. They were especially nervous about booby traps. They had just lost four of their close friends two days before to a booby trap.

Suddenly, as they turned a curve in the unpaved road, they saw six Vietnamese running in all directions, towards the Americans and away from the Americans.

"It's hard to distinguish a mama-san from a papa-san when everybody has on black pajamas," West reports. He and his squad opened fire. Then they continued towards the village, from where the sound of gunfire could be heard.

West, who used to visit a Vietnamese orphanage when he was off field duty and could recall when the company would share its C rations with kids it met on patrols, said he was feeling differently at Mylai.

"That day I was thinking military. I was thinking of the security of my own men. I said to myself this is a bad thing that all of these people had to be killed. But if I was to say that at that time I actually felt a whole lot of sorrow for the people then I would be lying."

West, who said he could not remember anybody actually firing at the Americans, nevertheless recalls that on the initial assault "everyone was scared going in. We thought there would be heavy enemy troops there."

When his squad arrived at the village, West says he and his men helped round up women and children. When a member of West's squad protested that he couldn't shoot the people, West ordered the man to take the villagers to Capt. Medina. On the way out of the village he says he remembers seeing the ditch filled with dead and dying civilians.

This might have been the same ditch that Tom Partsch described in his diary. The young soldier from the second platoon wrote: "Even when they were shot their legs and arms wiggled. It was horrible.

"I didn't shoot anyone," Partsch wrote in his diary. "Not even animals. I couldn't."

It is doubtful, based on my own investigations, that anyone killed out of pure, cold-blooded premeditation. All
were temporarily crazed. Some still are.

"To us, they were no civilians," Simpson recalls. "They
were VC sympathizers. You don't call them civilians. To
us they were VC."

Partsch and Bernhardt were moving in with the second
platoon. Partsch kept hearing Bernhardt saying, "It's
wrong, it's wrong." Partsch kept saying, he remembers,
"What can you do. They're higher up."

Those who didn't kill people killed animals; some to
avoid doing the former, but others with a vehemence that
didn't seem normal. They killed cows and chickens and
pigs and ducks and water buffalo, and they did it manually and with the knife, the bayonet, the rifle, the pistol,
the grenade launcher.

At first, says Partsch, the second platoon went after the
animals.

Pendleton who was in the third platoon says all he
killed were animals. "I heard people shouting 'Shoot the
people' and I thought those not doing it were disobeying
orders," Pendleton remembers. "We never did nothing
quite like that before," he adds. "We did things that were
littler.

"I kind of thought we were supposed to do it. But then,
in a way, I didn't. I killed animals. We burned down everything and killed animals. That was my job, kill animals
and burn down the village. I did my job."

Pendleton remembers there were two villagers that nobody around him had the heart to kill.

"Like one was a real little girl. But nobody felt like
doing it." Pendleton for a moment gave the impression
that he had to defend his decision not to kill any villagers.
It was as if he had been disloyal to the group.

"I didn't do it. But nobody saw me not doing it. So nobody
got on me," he says. "I wasn't in a position where somebody could come up and tell me to shoot. I didn't feel like

it. Because I could look around and see that they weren't
doing nothing," he says of the Vietnamese. "The GIs, they
didn't know who to hate. They were kind of mixed up
about what they had to do."

The third platoon got to the village late, he remembers.
It had first moved south, as a reserve unit, after getting
a report of fleeing VC. It moved half a mile south then
turned around and entered the village.

"When we got there everybody was already shot," he
recalls. I saw about 200 bodies. They were all over and
neatly stacked.

"There was two big groups that I knew of. There were
still some alive. They were moaning and crying. There
were probably more alive than you'd think. I was just kind
of wondering."

Then Pendleton remembers, "Some guys were still
shooting people who were running around the village.
The Vietnamese were running off and being shot by rifles.
Guys just picked up their rifles and shot."

Pendleton says he saw a boy standing among a group of
bodies. "I looked over and saw Medina shoot him. I don't
know why he did it except that there was a bunch of
bodies there—and I guess the boy's mother was one of
them."

Medina has denied Pendleton's charge. But he has told
of a villager who he killed. He received a report from a
helicopter that there was a VC with a weapon near where
he was standing. Medina went to the position marked
with smoke by the helicopter and saw a wounded woman
lying there without a weapon.

"I turned around and I started to walk away," he says.
"As I turned around, I saw movement out of the corner of
my eye . . . I instinctively, from my army training, turned
around and fired two shots. I assume that I did kill her."

Bernhardt remembers as his platoon started going in,
he saw helicopters dropping leaflets on the village, warning of the assault. As he was moving in with the platoon,

he remembers he was ordered to inspect a suspicious box on the ground. He dragged it back to the headquarters section and opened it. It contained medical supplies and a Sony radio.

Alone, Bernhardt headed back to Mylai to find his platoon. He remembers passing a quarry where villagers were being ordered into a hole and shot. "They were using the grenade launcher in the quarry," he says.

He remembers having to step over the ditch where Meadlo and Calley were ordering villagers to go. But he says he didn't see what happened. "I saw the bodies," he says.

Bernhardt says he never shot anyone. He felt the shooting was wrong and unnecessary.

He heard of one instance where a soldier had fired into a group of dying Vietnamese for no apparent reason except that they would get no medical attention and probably would die eventually.

Bernhardt wasn't critical of this action. "I didn't run into anyone partly alive. So I don't know what I'd do," he has said.

Michael Terry of the third platoon told how he and William Doherty arrived near noon in the village. Terry, a devout Mormon, had never slept with a girl because he felt premarital sex was immoral. He remembers there were few animals or people alive when he and Doherty arrived.

"Billy and I started to get out chow, but close to us was a bunch of Vietnamese in a heap and some of them were moaning. Calley had been through before us, and all of them had been shot but many weren't dead," he said, meaning that the first platoon had already been there.

"It was obvious that they weren't going to get any medical attention so Billy and I got up and went over to where they were. I guess we sort of finished them off."

About two years later Terry explained, "I did what I thought I had to do."

"He put them out of their misery," Terry's lawyer stated.

"Terry said a couple of times, 'I had to kill some people who were dying,'" recalls Pendleton. "I thought it was a good idea. I thought he used his own judgment.

"I saw religious people do it and patriotic people do it," Pendleton recalls. "But Terry, he did it because they were gonna die anyway."

When the first platoon moved into Mylai (4), Bergthold was ordered into the outskirts of the village to set up machine-gun security there. To get there, he remembers first going through the village.

"Some of the guys went in shooting, shooting first and asking questions later. There was a lot of yelling and cursing.

"I looked into a hut, there was a bunch of people there. I chased them out. I saw a man lying on the floor. He was about 60. He was shot in both legs real bad. There was a lot of blood. He was unconscious.

"I saw he wasn't going to live so I shot him to put him out of his misery. It was a mercy killing.

"I believe I was right in doing it," Bergthold says with all sincerity. "I could have let him alone. But I just couldn't see him suffering. So I looked down, pulled the trigger and walked away. I knew I hit him in the chest. But I didn't stick around to look."

Then Bergthold moved to the left flank of the hamlet and set up his machine gun, where he sat the rest of the morning listening to the shouting, screaming, shooting.

One Vietnamese woman, who had fallen among the bodies and was saved, recalls:

"All I remember was people being killed. There was blood all over. White Americans and black Americans both did the killing. Heads were broken open and there were pieces of flesh over everyone."

South Vietnamese killed their own countrymen too. West remembers seeing two Vietnamese males of military age running across the field about 500 meters away.

"I yelled, 'Dong lai, dong lai' (Vietnamese for halt), but neither of them stopped. At this distance we could have killed both of them, but we just fired in the air and then chased them about half a mile. Only one of them lived. The other one was killed by the interrogation unit. Some of the people told the interrogation unit they didn't understand what was being talked about. The men that didn't talk were killed by the Vietnamese that were doing the questioning, not by the Americans. There were, I guess, nine or ten killed before one of them started talking. I was told that the guys were saying that there had been Viet Cong and North Vietnamese troops there and that they had gone toward the ocean by underground tunnels."

Carter remembers many people were raping; some raped and killed. Men walked into hootches alone or in pairs, and Carter saw them come out smiling sheepishly, some still buttoning their flies; others holding their rifles in one hand and their packs in the other.

And it was a rape of anger, of contempt, not of lust or love. You hate a man you beat him; you hate a woman you fuck her. That was the attitude of these soldiers. That was how bitter the hate burned in their hearts towards these Vietnamese who had been killing them.

Some soldiers, not wanting to participate, or too shocked or dazed, or not knowing or wanting to know what was happening, tried to get away. They drifted off by themselves so there would be no one to order them. But they couldn't get away from themselves.

Sometime near noon it stopped. Some elements of the company remained at Mylai until 5 that afternoon. The rest moved out to join up with other companies of the task force. Medina reported 128 VC dead and 3 weapons captured.

Gen. William C. Westmoreland, remember Carter, Widmer and Shivers, sent a letter of commendation to the company for its action. Everything that occurred at Mylai (4) was immediately known throughout the command.

Not only was Barker overhead in a helicopter; so was Col. Oran K. Henderson, who took command of the 11th Brigade that day, and Maj. Gen. Samuel W. Koster, commander of the American Division.

One helicopter pilot, seeing civilians die, landed his aircraft and, ordering his gunners to cover him, moved in and rescued some of the children. He had to argue with Calley and Mitchell, who seemed to feel no one should be saved. The pilot reported what happened to higher headquarters.

The following day, while the company was in the field, Meadlo stepped on a mine and blew his foot off. Calley, behind him, was slightly wounded. They carried Meadlo to the hospital, where he was placed in a bed next to Carter.

Carter remembers that he heard Meadlo was arriving and asked that his buddy be placed near him but that the nurse didn't want to do it.

"He's white," Carter said the nurse told him.

"We're brothers," Carter answered, reminding himself that he was home.

"We never did get to Pinkville," Bernhardt would remember long afterward. The company did capture an NVA area commander later in the operation.

Back at the hospital, Carter remembers Meadlo kept talking of the punishment God had wrought on him.

He wasn't alone. Charlie Company never found favor with God. To this day its survivors are haunted with tragedy.

★ ★ ★

CHAPTER II

RAPE

★ ★ ★ ★ ★ ★ ★ ★ ★ ★ ★ ★ ★ ★

"By March 16, we were weary from the war."

ALLEN BOYCE
A member of Charlie Company

★ ★ ★ ★ ★ ★ ★ ★ ★ ★ ★ ★ ★ ★

And all around him they were shouting, the men were shouting and it was as if something had gone wrong with all of them—but mostly with their minds.

"VC bastards, you dirty VC bastards," and "Chalk one up for me," the men were shouting, and a grenade was lobbed into a thatched hut and the people ran fleeing and were shot down, and the fires burned and the machine guns chattered and blood splattered, and the soldiers took drags on their joints and it was heaven and it was hell.

Sometimes they ordered people from their hootches and sometimes they just set fire to the roofs and the people fled from their huts or ran into them, and it didn't matter for in either case they were slain.

"How many bullets does it take to kill a water buffalo," they asked each other, and then they found out one shot will do it. And they asked, "Can you hit a chicken with a .45 when it's running," and they found out that you can.

"And that's for Bill Weber," they said, and the machine gun fired, and here's one for the kid, Van Leer, and for poor Hendrickson, and Gus Rotger, who died screaming.

"Scream, you mother-fuckers," their minds cried, but the gooks wouldn't scream, and they wouldn't even cry and they just stood there and obeyed the orders of the Americans.

All except the group that Meadlo had thought he was guarding, until Calley came and ordered them shot. Then they wept, the old men wept and the women cried and the children looked about in fright as they died.

But Wilson was scared and he died, and Bell wept in pain when he burned to death, and they had to carry Foreman out screaming like a raving maniac, so "Cry, you dirty gook bastards, cry like you made us cry."

And Calley was in the middle of it all, and killing in Charlie Company was racking up points, and Meadlo was sure scoring this morning, Carter thought.

And Calley ordered his men to round up more gooks, but Carter wasn't having this, and he looked at Stanley and Stanley wasn't having any of this either, and the young black tunnel rat saw two gooks and told them to beat it and they fled.

And over at the second platoon Tom Partsch was alongside Bernhardt, who had always been the boat rocker in the company. "This is wrong, this is all wrong," Bernhardt was saying to Partsch, and "Man isn't this a smart-ass company," Stanley muttered derisively, and Haeberle, the Army's publicity man, was taking pictures in color and black and white because they might be valuable to him someday, and they were.

And then another group had been rounded up, and Calley ordered Torres, a grammar-school dropout, to shoot them down, Ridenhour told the congressmen, and the young soldier started to do it, but halfway done he threw his gun away in disgust because it was too much.

Then Calley reached down and picked up the weapon and finished the job. That's what officers are for, to set examples to the men, to teach them how to do things properly, and someone thought, "Man, that Calley is cool."

And Carter watched Calley, his leader; and the lieutenant was in his fatigues, his sleeves rolled down, wearing a pack on his back, a helmet on his head, and carrying an M-16 in his arm. And Sgt. Mitchell was right alongside Calley and his sleeves were rolled up, and he was only a squad leader. But nobody seemed to know what happened to Isaiah Cowan, the bible-carrying platoon sergeant who always wanted to convert guys and who had conveniently disappeared here.

And Calley ordered Mitchell to go round up another bunch of gooks, and the look on Mitchell's face, Carter thought, was "confused, very confused. But he's taking orders from Calley and Calley is taking orders from Medina." And who Medina was taking orders from nobody knew yet.

And the look on Mitchell's face said should I do this or shouldn't I do this, Carter noticed, but the sergeant came from the Old South in Louisiana where a black is still a boy, Carter thought, and the lieutenant was a white southerner and was giving the orders.

And Carter heard Mitchell shouting, "Help round everybody up," and he saw Cowan still wasn't around but it didn't matter because, Carter said, "Calley and Mitchell actually gave the orders to kill."

And Mitchell turned to Carter and to Stanley and to a machine gunner and he ordered the three to do as Calley had bid. And Stanley and Carter walked away contemptuously, and Carter looked at Mitchell as if to say "What's the matter with you, boy? You crazy or something?"

And then Carter looked at the machine gunner's face and he could see the man didn't want to do as he was told; but then Carter saw what he and Mitchell did.

And then men tried to outdo each other as they pulled villagers from their huts and lined them up to die, and kicked them and beat them. And if they looked good enough, the women were raped, then beaten and kicked and killed.

And soon Carter saw that Calley wasn't giving orders anymore. And he thought, "But why give orders when everybody is doing what you want them to do in the first place?"

And the fires of hell were burning in that hamlet and rifles and machine guns competed with each other for attention, and grenades barked and bodies dropped and Carter thought, "Calley looks very pleased and proud of his work," for Carter knew that usually the lieutenant was given hell by the captain for goofing up or getting lost in the field or doing things his way instead of the way he was told.

And then Carter thought, "Calley isn't acting like an officer. He's acting like an enlisted man. He's following suit."

Carter wanted no part of all this, and he was a tunnel rat anyway, which meant his job was to search the underground hideouts whenever the company entered a village, so he moved away and began to do what he was supposed to do. He went looking for tunnels, but he never found the ones where the VC were hiding; the VC who would later come out and tell the newspapers what they saw, but for the time being were letting their wives and little children face the wrath of a berserk company.

As a tunnel rat, Carter carried, besides his M-16, a .45 automatic, 4 grenades, TNT and other explosives. As he was approaching what looked like a tunnel, he saw a boy of about 15 dart by and he raised his rifle and shot him. Then he saw a man run out from a bunker.

"I opened up on that ass too with my M-16," Carter says. An Army rule of thumb in Vietnam says anyone seen running away or adopting elusive tactics is to be considered an enemy and should be shot.

For more than three months now, ever since the company had arrived in Vietnam, and for as long before that as each soldier had been in the Army training as an infantryman, the idea of killing another human being had grown like a cancer to torment and spread through the mind of every boy in Charlie Company. For war means to kill and to destroy, or die, and the infantryman is made aware of this most of all, because only he among all members of an armed force must commit these asocial acts in a personal confrontation.

And each man at one time or another wondered whether he could kill another man when that dreaded moment would finally arrive, and some in that company had already learned that they could, but most had never done it.

Now Mylai (4) had become the great target of opportunity. It was a free-fire zone, which is military terminology for shoot anything you see or fire at will, because these men had been told the night before that they would be entering an enemy headquarters and were expected to make a clean sweep of the area. The ambiguous orders, the men had decided the night before when they were drinking beer and smoking pot and watching a pornographic movie, meant they would have license to kill everybody in this morning's operation.

There were those who looked forward to this opportunity and there were those who rejected it completely, but the great majority were in between and didn't know what to do or whether they would do it. Killing an enemy had become too much of an obsession with this company; it was something that had to be done and it had nothing to do with being lustful or bloodthirsty, but it had something to do with being curious and confused and afraid.

Can I kill? was the thought that had gone through every man's mind, and how will I act when that moment arrives? And what does it feel like to kill somebody else? You're not a man until you kill, for in the infantry that is the sign of maturity—killing is when a boy turns into a man.

It was an understood fact in Charlie Company that the soldier who killed was a better man than the one who didn't. A soldier explained that one day to a newcomer.

"If I killed someone and you didn't, I wouldn't look down on you and you wouldn't act inferior to me. But deep in my heart I would know I'm a better man than you are and deep in your heart you would know I am too."

This has to be understood and it mustn't be condemned, and a man cannot be punished for developing a point of view that his army and his society and his country have demanded of him when they made him a soldier. For while killing may be instinctive in every human being and while man is capable of murdering his fellow man, given the right set of circumstances, most civilized human beings are brought up to believe it is wrong, abhorrent and punishable. Then in an eight-week course in basic training, young men are told that everything they have been taught was wrong, and that indeed their mission in life will be to kill.

It is difficult to adjust your thinking to accept mores that are completely contrary to what you have been taught. So you have to think about your new lessons, and the men of Charlie Company did their homework and thought carefully until killing became an obsession. Killing was something they would have to do sooner or later; it was a challenge they would have to meet if they would be accepted by their peers, and Mylai (4) was their moment of truth.

There was something wrong and there was something right about this moment of opportunity, and the men moved through Mylai as if drugged, which most of them probably were if smoking pot can do that to you.

But there was more to this. These were angry men, tired men, sick in body and sicker in mind from endless weeks of fatiguing field duty and frightening guerrilla combat, in which they had seen too much death and undergone too many emotionally shocking experiences that could easily have broken older, wiser men.

And now they were heavily armed in a face-to-face encounter with their tormentors and backed by vague orders from their superiors that gave them the authority to break every rule laid down by God and society in times of peace.

And so they cursed and they yelled and they laughed and they cried and they killed and they raped, and deep down in their hearts they felt it was wrong. But on another level of their minds they felt they were right and war is wrong and the death of their buddies was wrong and being in Vietnam was wrong and protesting the war in the States was wrong and who the hell knows what's right and what's wrong.

One GI wandered around the village and he saw the men and the dead and he felt sick and disgusted, and yet he felt compassion for the men. And he looked at them and he knew, as a brother knows, that they were feeling guilty, but the opportunity was irresistible and they couldn't stop. It was like the first time you masturbate. A GI tried to find a comparison to this feeling. You feel guilty because you think you shouldn't do it, yet somewhere you heard that it's perfectly natural and anyhow it's irresistible, so what the hell.

And it became irresistible and everybody was doing it, and Carter remembered thinking, "Every one of us is capable of doing anything, given the right circumstances."

Some Vietnamese who could have gotten away didn't. They were shocked into paralysis and froze where they were; one boy just lay on the ground in fear.

Soldiers were grabbing girls and taking them back into the huts to rape them and they came out alone, holding their packs in one hand and buttoning their flies with the other.

And there was a story of one officer who argued with a group of enlisted men—over who would get a woman first

—and the officer would not tolerate sloppy seconds, so the men acknowledged that rank did have its privileges.

Sometimes a girl or her mother resisted a soldier, but mostly the girls cooperated because they thought if they screw for the GIs they might live. And some did and some didn't.

And one soldier wandered around the village and he didn't know what was happening and what he was doing and whether it was right or wrong, and he was stunned. And he heard shooting and saw the raping and felt the heat of the burning, and he thought well, everybody is having a merry old time, but at the same time he looked into the eyes of his buddies and the men seemed to be in a daze.

And if they were having fun and scoring points for the body count, there was something unnatural in their actions and strange in their demeanor. It was as if each man was saying to himself, this is wrong and I shouldn't do it but what the hell we've gone this far and so I might as well.

And so the soldier wandered not wanting to participate and yet not wanting to miss anything, and he wondered where was the enemy fire. If this was a hot zone like they said last night, where was the enemy?

And the soldier was off by himself among the hootches and there was a girl and she was very pretty and her pale skin was delicate and unblemished and her hair was black and long and she wore the black pajama garb of the peasant. She was standing on what appeared to be a porch of a house and she was looking out to the center of the hamlet at the carnage, and she was frightened because of what she thought she was seeing, because she couldn't believe it was really true.

She saw soldiers pulling people out from the other huts around her, and the soldier wandering by himself saw her and she looked good and he came up to her. He carried his rifle muzzle down and he didn't say anything to her and he didn't smile, and she saw him and thought he would pull her out with the rest of the villagers.

He looked at her and he didn't like what was happening and he didn't hate what was happening, but she looked good so he pushed her back into her one-room hut. There wasn't a word said between the two and the soldier couldn't quite understand what he was doing for he had no feelings of lust. The whores at LZ Dottie always met his needs. He didn't understand the feeling that was coming over him because he was revolted by what he had seen in the village. But he knew what he was going to do and there was nothing to control him.

He thought of his friends who were killed and a feeling of pure spite came over him, now that this girl was in his power, and still no word passed between them.

And then he held his rifle in his left hand and reached up with his right to grab the pajama blouse that the girl was wearing. She made a slight motion in the darkened room to back away but he ripped off her blouse. She stood there impassively, just staring, making no effort to conceal her pretty young breasts, for she wore no brassiere beneath her blouse. And she knew what was going to happen but she showed no emotion and he sensed it, but she was mistaken if she thought she would only be raped.

He looked at her and thought she looked pretty clean for a Vietnamese, and then anger welled up inside of him and he thought maybe I'll make her blow me, but then he said, "C'mere bitch." He grabbed her and pushed her down to the ground and he grasped his rifle in his right hand and got down on top of her and ripped off her pants and she was wearing nothing beneath them.

And he thought you dirty bitch you killed Wilson and you killed Weber and Cox and Rotger and Bell, and you got me out here and look what you're making me do and look what my buddies are doing, and I hate this war and its your fault that I'm here. And he mounted her, never bothering to remove the heavy pack from his back or the .45 caliber automatic in a shoulder holster under his left arm.

She lay there silently, but quietly crossed her legs to resist him.

He switched his rifle to his left hand and hit her hard in her gut with his right fist, and she uncrossed her legs and didn't resist him as he inserted his penis into her vagina. Her legs now were spread and he was on her, his left hand firmly clutching his rifle and resting it on the ground, his right arm also on the ground, his helmet on his head and his pack on his back.

At first she just lay there, letting him do all the work, and then slowly she started to wiggle around, finding and joining his rhythm. Then she closed her eyes, but he kept his wide open because he wasn't taking any chances, and he looked down at her and he could see she was enjoying it. And slowly, hesitantly, she moved her right arm and placed it around his shoulder gently, and he could see she was pleased.

And he was disturbed and upset, because he wasn't making love to her; he hated her, but he was fucking her, he was doing this to show contempt for her; but her right hand squeezed his shoulder tightly, gently, passionately. And then he felt her moving her body quicker, quicker, quicker as her muscles tightened around him, and slowly the both of them came.

And he was mad and glad and all mixed up, and he got up, still holding the rifle, and he buttoned his fly and she reached for her torn clothes and scurried into a corner of the hut and covered her body modestly.

Then she looked at him and he stared at her and he knew what he was going to do and he could see she was not going to beg. Her eyes showed fear and arrogance and they seemed to say to him, please don't do it, but if you're going to, then go ahead and get it over with. And he raised his rifle, pointing it at her chest, and pulled the trigger once, and with his left hand reached into his pocket for a cigarette lighter.

And he was shaking and frightened and confused and couldn't understand it, because he knew he hated these people and he didn't know why he was doing it.

And then he stepped outside the hut and set fire to it with his cigarette lighter, and then he went and sat down by himself and smelled all the dead bodies that were burning in all the huts. And he trembled.

And somewhere another soldier saw a little boy with one arm shot off, and the little boy was walking in a daze as if he didn't know what was going on and couldn't believe it. The soldier, who was not too much older than the little boy, was also walking around in a daze as if he didn't know what was going on and couldn't believe it. And the soldier looked at the little boy and said to himself, "This little boy must be the same age as my sister."

The soldier had his rifle cocked and he thought to himself, what if a foreign army was in my country and a soldier was looking at my sister just as I'm looking at this little boy.

"Would that foreign soldier have the guts to kill my sister?" the GI asked himself, and he looked at the little boy and the little boy looked at him, and the American kept asking himself would a foreign soldier have the guts to kill his sister if the positions were reversed.

"Would he kill my sister, would he kill my sister, would he kill my sister?" the soldier kept asking himself. "If he'd have the guts then I'd have the guts." And then he pulled the trigger and killed the little boy, and he knew the answer.

"At one point it was just to prove something to myself," he said later.

There were VC hiding and watching as the American company was running berserk, and the guerrillas knew that most of their comrades had fled successfully because these Americans came in so noisily with helicop-

ters and bullhorns announcing their arrival and leaflets telling the people not to flee. And as long as these
Americans fight as stupidly as they do, which will be
forever because of their sense of fairness, they will never
win, and if the Vietnamese hold out long enough, they
can't lose.

Meanwhile the shooting and the looting and the burning continued, and machine guns roared and blood ran all
over the hamlet. And the GIs did everything they had ever
wanted to do, killing water buffalo, and chickens with
grenade launchers, and one soldier unsheathed his knife
and chased a duck.

And Pendleton looked and he didn't know what to think,
and he thought the GIs don't know who to hate, and Pendleton was afraid to kill and afraid not to kill, so he shot
animals.

And many men there were afraid not to kill and afraid
to kill and afraid of being killed, and that's why the
GIs didn't know why they were killing and the Vietnamese didn't know why they were being killed. It was a
clash of peasants from two cultures, and neither had hate
or love for the other, but both had to die, for in war it has
always been the peasants who die while the kings and the
wise men debate in the people's name. And there were no
racists in Mylai (4) that day, for man's fear of his fellow
man transcends all colors, and at Mylai it was proven that
ignorance begets fear and fear is the father of hate and
the offspring of hate is death.

For West remembers that South Vietnamese killed
their brothers in the village to make them tell where the
Viet Cong had gone. And the blacks and the whites for a
change were joined in a mutuality of interest and bound
by a common fear. They proved that all men are equal
and are equally capable, and proof lay in the hamlet's
death. The message was spread in the rivulets of red that
moved through Mylai (4).

A soldier removed the bayonet from his rifle and

stabbed a calf over and over and over again, and the calf tried to go to the mother cow and the GI wouldn't allow it and just stabbed it over and over and over again while others watched or joined in the slaughter. And the animals all died, and the fowl died, and the wells were fouled by the blood of the people who died, and then the hamlet died.

And religious people killed, and patriotic people killed, and stupid people killed, and bright people killed, and responsible people killed, and weak people killed, and, given the opportunity and the right circumstances, wouldn't all people kill?

And some killed out of curiosity and some out of compulsion, and some felt they had orders, and some wanted to kill and some were too ignorant not to kill, and some sought revenge and some didn't want to let the company down, and others wanted to be accepted in this militant society in which the only qualification for membership was to kill, kill, kill, as the drill instructor at basic training had taught them to do.

And all the men were crazed because of the frustrations they had felt and the horror they had seen and the bitterness in their hearts for being in this terrible place and fighting a war that even their countrymen at home could not understand and refused to accept.

Everywhere there were groups of Vietnamese dying, and some soldiers even killed the dying, out of compassion they said, and they really believed it.

Carter was sitting next to a group of dying people and he was feeling sick because he knew, and Bernhardt knew, that the company had been misled into Mylai by the selfishly ambitious, higher-ranking officers who had made them believe they would be fighting the VC. A young soldier came up and asked Carter for his .45 and Carter gave it to him and the soldier tried to fire it but it jammed. He handed it back to the tunnel rat and told Carter to clean the barrel. Carter tried to unjam the .45

by cocking it and uncocking it, and suddenly a round went off and hit him in the foot.

Some people thought Carter had deliberately shot himself in the foot, but he didn't. It was a terrible accident, and considering the condition of the men that day it was a perfectly understandable mistake. For Carter was high on pot that morning, as were many of the men, and after he was shot Widmer gave him another joint, and now Carter was really grooving.

And then the amateur photographer who was to earn $40,000 from the tragedy of Charlie Company took pictures of Carter, and if he will look closely someday he will find that Carter is smoking a joint. The photographer told the public, later, that Carter deliberately shot himself, and the photographer's buddy, the army reporter, verified it, although both men had never been in combat before so weren't really qualified to pass judgment on fighting men. The reporter said he knew Carter shot himself purposely because "he looked happy even though he had shot up his own foot."

Not only is every infantryman happy to get out of combat, but the smile was extra broad on Carter's face because he was so high on pot and still had half a joint to go.

And soon the horror of Mylai (4) was over, and the company withdrew and returned to the field where they stayed for 60 days.

Widmer remembers the company was acting very unnatural that morning at Mylai (4) and they seemed to be doing things at one level of their minds that at another level they knew they shouldn't have done.

"After it was over you were faced with what you did." Widmer remembers the anguish of the company; for these had been sick men with unsettled minds, grown worse after Mylai. And he remembers men talking to each other and asking, "What did I do? What did I do? I'll hate myself for the rest of my life."

The next day Meadlo stepped on a mine and blew his foot off and screamed, "God punished me for what I did yesterday," and then he turned to Calley, who had been near him and was slightly wounded, and he said, "You'll get yours," and then a helicopter came and took him away.

The whole company had heard what Meadlo said and they knew that March 16, 1968, would be in their lives forever, and that for them the war in Vietnam would never end.

CHAPTER III

* * *

THE COMPANY FORMS

★ ★ ★ ★ ★ ★ ★ ★ ★ ★ ★ ★ ★

"When I took over the company, it was in a sorry state of affairs."
CAPT. ERNEST L. MEDINA
Commanding Officer,
Charlie Company

★ ★ ★ ★ ★ ★ ★ ★ ★ ★ ★ ★ ★

Charlie Company was stillborn on July 1, 1966, in Schofield Barracks, Hawaii, as part of the 11th Infantry Brigade, which had hurriedly been activated to replace the 25th Infantry Division, an old-line outfit rushed to fight the escalating war in Vietnam.

A brigade is hardly a replacement for a division, but from all indications the Army started to panic a little at the time the 11th was formed. The Vietnam war was increasing in ferocity and intensity, and manpower needs were rising faster than they could be filled.

Manpower wasn't its only problem. The Army lacked proper training facilities to indoctrinate the troops going to Vietnam. For example, the jungle warfare training center, located on the east range of Schofield Barracks, had deteriorated after the 25th Infantry Division left, and one of the chores of the 11th was to rebuild it.

In Charlie Company's 17 month history in Hawaii, the Army never got around to preparing its men properly for

the role they would have to play as infantrymen diplomats in Vietnam. Its training was vague on how to take
and search a village, and how to treat the inhabitants in
Vietnam. In a censored report on the Mylai affair, issued
by Lt. Gen. William R. Peers, it was indicated that Charlie
Company underwent an "accelerated training program
for the oversea movement" to Vietnam.

"During this instruction little emphasis was placed on
the treatment of civilians and refugees or the responsibility for reporting war crimes or atrocities," the Peers report notes.

Even this very limited training was further reduced in
effectiveness, the report says, because the company was
ordered to Vietnam one month ahead of schedule and
about 50 percent of its personnel were bodies assigned to
it at the last minute.

Of course, the Army would argue that the men who
joined Charlie Company in July 1966 could not be expected to go overseas 17 months later. The company that
left for Vietnam did have a number of men who had been
with it for at least 8 months in Hawaii. But an entire
platoon, totalling 40 of these men, was kept behind at the
last moment to form the nucleus of a new company.
These training men were replaced by rookies and worse.

The 11th Brigade ran into personnel problems right
from the start, and when it was redesignated a Light Infantry Brigade, just before going overseas, its problems
increased. It went to Vietnam 700 men short of its au-
thorized strength, and it could not provide sufficient
experienced soldiers to wipe some of the greenness
off Charlie Company. If the 11th had problems, therefore,
Charlie Company had to have problems.

The company ranks in the beginning were filled with
wounded Vietnam veterans and with soldiers returning
from Guam, Okinawa and Korea, as well as with other
Army short-timers who could care less because they
weren't going back to the wars. It also faced a critical

shortage of experienced officers and noncommissioned officers, cooks, supplymen and infantrymen, a problem that was never alleviated until its dying day.

Its death came on February 25, 1968, when the company as a combat unit was wiped out in a minefield near the hamlets of Lac Son (4) and Lac Son (6). Those who weren't killed or mutilated physically were destroyed psychologically.

Eight days later, on March 4, 1968, as it lay dying, the company's wounds were rubbed with salt by a Viet Cong mortar attack on its fire base, LZ Dottie, when all personal possessions and links with home were destroyed.

And the coup de grace was administered to the company on March 14, 1968, two days before the Mylai affair, when an overly protective sergeant held in high esteem by the young enlisted men was killed by a Viet Cong booby trap and three men horribly maimed.

The kids who landed at Mylai (4) that terrible morning were mere shells of the once ordinary, although mostly underprivileged, American boys who had the bad luck to be drafted into the Army infantry to fight an unpopular crusade in Vietnam.

The story of March 16, 1968, has been told and retold, often with relish, sometimes with glee. What has never been told is what happened to Charlie Company from the day it was formed and why its members went berserk on March 16. It is difficult to understand why the press, so eager to describe Charlie Company's sickness, never showed any interest in finding out the cause of its psychosis.

Charlie Company's story is tragic, certainly no less gory than the events at Mylai (4). For the men who walked into that minefield and landed at that hamlet were for the most part unprofessional, unskilled, unschooled soldiers, with no motivation, little direction, inadequate leadership and no indoctrination as to what the war was all about.

Charlie Company was a microcosm of the nation it represented and a manifestation of that country's ailments. It was truly representative of the American state of mind at that period in history. To understand this unit of inexperienced fighting men, it could help to know something of the basic ingredients in its composition and the underlying problems that remained with it until its death.

The company was a closely-knit, fiercely loyal tribe of boys, lacking in experience and with little sophistication and limited education. Its loyalties were to its own members only. A prevailing attitude among members of Charlie Company was the feeling that they were alone and forgotten—overworked in the training fields of Hawaii, overexposed to the physical and psychological rigors of guerrilla warfare in Vietnam. As part of a three-company, free-wheeling counterguerrilla task force in Vietnam, the men never came in touch with other Americans—not even with members of the other two companies. They had no sense of belonging to the Army or to a division or even to a battalion. Charlie Company was cast off in an enemy sea—or at least that's the way its members felt—and left to drift for itself.

Most members of the company were reluctant draftees. At least two were dragged into the Army by the FBI. At least one had a history of emotional problems before going into the Army. One changed his name twice to stay out of the Army. Some had minor police records. The average educational level of the company was somewhere between grammar-school dropout and high-school dropout. Many have been unemployed or worked as unskilled menial laborers. According to one Army report, the draftees of this company were better than average in infantry aptitudes but "had less education and were less trainable than the average soldier of that period."

Between 8 and 12 percent of the company (probably more, but the Army is keeping the figure secret) had below normal IQs, scoring between the 10th to the 30th percentile in the Armed Forces Qualifications Tests. Anyone could score in the 20th percentile by just guessing at the answers. These were part of the replacements for the trained platoon the company lost in Hawaii. On its squad and fire-team levels, the company had no noncommissioned officers and Medina had to place low-ranking PFCs and Spec 4s in charge of other PFCs and Specs 4s.

Hardly anyone in the company knew what he was fighting for. The men's Army indoctrination never went much further than basic infantry training. The company never knew its mission in Vietnam. A recurrent complaint from its members was that nobody ever told them what to do.

Feeling thus abandoned by the nation they served, abused by the Army that had inducted them, ignored even by the rear-echelon soldiers the men occasionally met, the company naturally turned inward toward its own. It became, as one member recalled, a family of brothers. When the family was destroyed, Charlie Company was finished, and that happened with its psychological annihilation on February 25 in one of the bloodiest and bravest, most fruitless and frustrating, and least known and least understood episodes of the war.

Michael Bernhardt, a former member of Charlie Company, once summed up the history of the unit by observing that "everything miserable that could possibly happen to you over there happened to us—the company. We weren't spared anything."

One good thing about the company was that it had no racial problems. Somewhere between one-third to one-half the company was black. There was a healthy representation of Mexican-Americans and Puerto Ricans in the company, as well as one Filipino, one Hawaiian, at least one American Indian and three South Vietnamese army interpreters. Two of its three rifle platoon sergeants were black; the third had a Spanish surname.

Its commander, Capt. Ernest Lou Medina, was a Mexican-American who came out of poverty, was intimately acquainted with prejudice, and had risen by his own bootstraps from nothing to a bright young star in the Army's officer corps—until Mylai.

Nobody in the company had combat experience to speak of. Except for Medina, all of the officers were inexperienced. One, 2d Lt. William Laws Calley Jr., a platoon leader, earned a commission despite failing out of junior college in his freshman year. In little more than six months, Calley led two different platoons of the company. He didn't get along with either of his platoon sergeants. He was so unpopular with the troops that at one time they placed a $150 price tag on his head.

An infantry company has four platoons. Three are made up of riflemen; the fourth is a weapons platoon consisting of mortars and their crews. Charlie Company's fourth platoon never went into the field until the Mylai affair. Hence the burden of the company effort was carried by the three rifle platoons and Medina's headquarters section, together never totalling more than 105 men B. C. (before casualties).

Despite its heavy casualties, the company never received replacements from the time it went to Vietnam in December 1967 until well after the Mylai affair.

The company was poorly motivated, but then so was just about everybody in Vietnam by early 1968. Most members of Charlie Company were less concerned about serving their country than surviving their year's "penance" in Vietnam, so they could get back to "the world" alive and unscathed—a dream they would never realize.

To understand this lack of motivation among many servicemen in Vietnam, it is necessary to understand about the one-year-only policy. Nobody in the Army was expected to remain in Vietnam longer than one year. While this was great for troop morale, it did little to help achieve military success on the battlefield. Just about the time a soldier learned how to fight a guerrilla war, he was ready to go home. Even more important, the fact a soldier only had one year in which his life would be at stake made him tend towards caution in combat.

It was a subtle thing, this inclination towards being careful. Certainly many men have taken brave risks in the Vietnam War and many brave men will not be coming home. But when you know on arriving in Vietnam the day you're scheduled to leave, you're inclined not to take that little extra chance, even if it might mean the difference between victory and defeat, because it might also mean the difference between your life and your death.

A complaint heard frequently by members of Charlie Company was that the brass, meaning the colonels and above, were seeking personal glory in Vietnam at the expense of the foot soldiers. The men have charged that higher-ranking officers flew over them in helicopters but would never dare to land in the field where the men were on patrol.

This is understandable, too, considering the peculiar nature of the Vietnam war and the type of professional soldier fighting it. For the young professional, like Medina, Vietnam was a land of opportunity. If he was any good, he needed a war under his belt to prove his worth, so the rest of his military career would flow smoothly. For the old-time professional who never quite made it, Vietnam offered a last chance to distinguish himself on the field of battle and get that big promotion that would put him in a higher pension bracket. But for the average professional, the kind the draftee derogatorily refers to as a "lifer," Vietnam was a necessary evil.

The lifer is the civil servant in uniform, the man who keeps his nose clean and doesn't rock any boats and has stayed in the service for its PX privileges and its retirement benefits.

Under any army policy all professionals had to go to Vietnam for at least one tour before retiring.

THE TRUE STORY OF MYLAI

The lifer who had already bought that farm, or had grown children, or had fought his war and done his time and was close to retirement, didn't look forward to combat duty. But if he had to go, he couldn't be blamed for trying to play it safe.

Junior professional combat officers like Medina of course didn't mind going. There were so many of them, however, that the combat tour was reduced to six months with the second six months reserved for staff job assignments. Thus an ambitious officer, young or old, had only six months, or at most a year, to prove himself in combat. The trouble was that Charlie Company felt the proof was being made at the expense of the privates on the line.

Also, the one-year policy was not working out well in terms of achieving a military solution to the Vietnam war. Nobody wanted to take any unnecessary risks. Vietnam certainly wasn't worth dying for, particularly since half the nation at home was opposed to the war anyhow. Another problem with the one-year-only policy was that it caused the quality of the troops in Vietnam to decline. The complexities of the Vietnam War called for a professional soldier, highly disciplined and motivated, who could tell the difference between the good guys and the bad guys among civilian guerrillas.

Until President John F. Kennedy originally escalated the war in late 1961, the one-year-only policy could have continued indefinitely and the troops in Vietnam would have been the best America could muster. Before the escalation there were 700 military advisers, all professionals, to whom Vietnam was just another routine assignment. Kennedy increased the military commitment more than 20-fold when he ordered 16,000 troops into Vietnam—combat men complete with all the paraphernalia of war.

It was even possible to continue the one-year-only policy by 1965, when the troop strength was 75,000 men.

Then, in July of that year, President Lyndon B. Johnson

ordered the forces in Vietnam raised to 125,000 men and
the draft more than doubled from 17,000 to 35,000 a
month. The increases continued, so that by 1967 there
were more than half a million troops in Vietnam. A manpower problem was developing.

How could the one-year-only policy continue? Who
would replace the professionals? The Army's optimistic
approach to the war was having a devastating effect on
its manpower.

The assumption seemed to be that we could fight this
war single-handed because the enemy was just a collection of barefoot guerrillas. The U. S. was whistling in the
dark; it was involved in a far more serious war than it
thought.

Still there was no declaration of war, no call-up of re-
serves, nothing to relieve the professional army whose
ranks were spreading thin. The only solution appeared to
be the inexperienced civilian soldier, the draftee, America's traditional reluctant warrior. And that was the problem Charlie Company was facing as it formed in Hawaii.
Its ranks would slowly fill with draftees who didn't want
to go to war, and couldn't be blamed in view of the attitude towards Vietnam by the public at home.

Considering the complexities of Vietnam, where a soldier was expected to befriend a villager in the daytime
who may be a guerrilla at night, only a highly trained and
dedicated professional could be expected to do the job
properly. When the first army was fielded in Vietnam, it
consisted of such experienced professionals, well-disci-
plined, highly motivated men willing and able to understand the difficulties of guerrilla warfare. But all that
changed as the war dragged on.

By 1967, for example, the Army was having difficulty
finding helicopter pilots. Under the one-year-only pro-
viso, those who had once been in Vietnam did not have to
go back. And helicopters were becoming a booming civilian service, so pilots were much in demand. Soon the

Army was trying to make the pilots go back, but they quit for the much better paying and safer civilian jobs. The Air Force, too, was having a problem and was forced to drag out its pot-bellied, middle-aged World War II pilots to fly all sorts of planes in Vietnam. The Marine Corps had already set a 13-month minimum tour of duty in Vietnam instead of 12, and was beginning to make its professionals go back for a second round.

When the Army's most outstanding professionals began returning home from their one-year tours, the second- and third-best had to move out, and with them the draftees. The caliber of America's front line of defense had declined.

Soldiers either were resentful because they had to go to Vietnam, or officers had more ambition than talent and limited time to prove it. Men who thought they were budding Eisenhowers or MacArthurs or Napoleons would have a chance to test their theories. However, the tendency towards caution would mean that the lowly enlisted man would be put to the test while his leaders flew overhead in command helicopters.

The helicopter was rediscovered in Vietnam and proved a marvelous weapon of war. The brass could enjoy the comfort of an officer's club and fly out to combat for a few hours to slum with the men.

And that was one reason why Charlie Company's motivation had little to do with God and country. The men just wanted to live; it didn't matter what they did to survive. And they couldn't be blamed for feeling the way they did. Hardly anyone in this country was overly enthusiastic about Vietnam and its people.

Indeed Bernhardt has said he once heard a rumor that Gen. William C. Westmoreland didn't want the 11th Brigade to come to Vietnam. Bernhardt doesn't explain why, but if Charlie Company was typical of the brigade, Westmoreland's concern was understandable.

The brigade officers weren't too much to rave about.

They were men, for the most part, whose last contact with combat had been in World War II or Korea. One of the officers the men really disliked was their battalion commander, Edward D. Beers, who had had 6 months and 13 days of combat experience, all in World War II; he had 25 years in the Army, had two silver stars and lots of other medals, and was still a lieutenant colonel. At one time there was a price on Beers' head too. But he and Calley were the only two officers associated with the company who so enraged the men. The troops felt Beers overworked them for his own self-aggrandizement.

So until Dec. 19, 1966, Charlie Company was a flop. It was so bad that not only couldn't its men pass any of their field tests but the company couldn't even win a ball game in the intramural events. Then on December 19 Medina was assigned as the new company commander. He was a rising young star in the Army, bright, ambitious, hard driving, a human dynamo. The men feared and revered him. But even his severest critics conceded he was an outstanding field officer. He was the only officer Charlie Company respected. Charlie Company was Medina's first command, a job coveted by Army captains as much as sea captains want their own ships.

One of the problems the company had, Medina thought, was that the previous commander didn't know how to get along with the 1st Sergeant, Harry F. Hobscheid. But the 31-year-old captain had spent most of his military career as an enlisted man, starting with the National Guard when he was 16. He had an affinity for enlisted men, particularly the hard luck guy, the school dropout, the poverty class, the minority group. And as an old sergeant he knew the trick of getting the top kick on his side, an art that is essential to the smooth operation of an infantry company, or any military unit for that matter.

Then, by coincidence, Medina ran into Master Sergeant Augustine Hoaeae, a Hawaiian who was a battalion cook. When Medina first went into the army, as a KP, Hoaeae had been the captain's boss. Now he prevailed on Hoaeae to join his company as mess sergeant. Thus he had a top kick and a top cook working for him, so he couldn't possibly go wrong.

But he still had an absolutely demoralized company; the best word to describe the entire brigade in those days was "confusion."

One of Medina's favorite expressions is "good grief."

"Good grief, that company hadn't done anything since the day it was organized," he remembers. It hadn't passed inspections, its dayroom and classroom were down at the heels, its mess hall wasn't fit to eat in.

One of the first things Medina did was to make his company different, to distinguish it from the rest. The company liked to call themselves the "Charlie Cats." So he gathered them together one day and asked them if they wanted to have sweat shirts with a distinguishing insignia to set them apart. They did. And Charlie Company either had a great sense of humor or the men were clairvoyant. Because they voted for their own insignia on their sweat shirts—an alley cat atop a garbage can. The words "Charlie Cats" were printed atop the trash can, while below was the unit designation—1st Battalion, 20th Infantry.

Slowly Medina instilled pride and purpose into his Charlie Cats, and gradually they began to respond. Before long they were not only passing inspections but coming out on top.

"My soldiers took the Soldier of the Month award more times than anybody else," Medina remembers proudly. The company also took the Driver of the Month awards, Best Vehicle awards and U. S. Army Pacific Leadership awards. They came out on top in sports competitions and they were number one in the IG inspections.

"Good grief, when the battalion was having its reorganization day, we had been on a training exercise and got back at 2:30 in the morning," Medina recalls.

"We went to sleep, woke up at eight, participated, and walked away with all the trophies," he remembers fondly.

That wasn't all. Medina and his men redid the company dayroom and its classroom. They remodeled the mess hall and put curtains in the squad bay. The company threw its own beach barbecues and beer busts; it took the volleyball and basketball trophies; in short, it developed more espirit de corps and had higher morale than any other unit in the brigade. Medina was building a fighting team out of a ragtag collection of draftees.

He succeeded so well that Charlie Company became the best in the brigade of 12 infantry companies. It took all awards in the training field and on the sports field. When it was time for the 11th to deploy to Vietnam, Medina's company was selected as the only one to go with the advance party. It was quite an accomplishment for Medina, considering the tools he had to work with. The Army says 60 percent of Medina's enlisted men were draftees. Medina says it was more like 92 percent. The difference is probably the fact that many of the volunteers joined because they were going to be drafted anyway.

It is doubtful whether there was a single volunteer of the old-fashioned school of patriotism in the company. Certainly the kids of this war weren't fighting for Mom's apple pie; in all probability Mom had joined the Women's Strike for Peace and was using everything in her power to keep junior out of service.

Indeed the mother of one of the members of Charlie Company remembers urging her son to try for the Navy or Air Force so long as he had to go. But the youngster, who seemed a little on the passive side, didn't want to fight the system. Not only were enlistments in the Navy and Air Force for longer periods, but it was too troublesome to try. He decided to let things take their "natural" course.

The men entering the Army when Charlie Company was forming came in against a background of dissension at home, a rising antiwar movement and a tendency to treat draft dodgers and deserters as heroes. By 1967 there were at least 2,000 young Americans living in Canada because they didn't want to go into the Army, and the rate of desertions and AWOLs in the armed forces was spiraling upward.

Officially a deserter is anyone *a*bsent *w*ith*o*ut *l*eave for more than 30 days, but the military was reluctant to classify anyone as a deserter. Usually AWOLs who were apprehended were sent back to their units, many times without escort. Punishments were mild; recidivists just jumped the fence again. There was no stigma attached to a draft dodger or deserter. Even his own neighbors didn't seem to care.

Since it was not mandatory for everyone within a given age group to serve, only the dumb, the poor and the passive went. A young man could ignore the armed forces and still get a job or blend in with an indifferent society. Indeed in some circles a man out of service enjoyed higher status than a boy in uniform. On the domestic political front, President Johnson was coming under increasing attacks for his Vietnam policies; students demonstrated against ROTC programs on campuses that traditionally provided the armed forces with an intelligent officer corps, and more and more reknowned public leaders were coming out against the war and for the war protesters. With bright kids remaining in college and post graduate schools, or going abroad, and with not-so-bright kids going into the Navy and the Air Force, the draftees ending up in the Army were the unlucky ones who didn't have the brains, the money, the pull or the audacity to stay out.

Even in the Army, anyone with any kind of "smarts" was able to make it to one of the many support services, like logistics or medical or artillery or military police or

PX salesmen. Those who ended up in the infantry were really at the bottom of the heap. The Army had become a dumping ground for the poor blacks and the poor whites and the less intelligent and the unskilled and the unschooled and the unlucky. And the infantry had become the Army's garbage can.

These were men who could hardly be expected to understand the complexities of the Vietnam war or to undertake the responsibilities entailed in serving there as soldier-diplomats charged with winning the hearts and minds of a people. Indeed it would not be facetious to say there were probably some men in the company who didn't know where Geneva was, let alone what the Geneva Conventions were.

Yet when the story of Mylai finally broke in the world press, the nation's self-righteous segment expressed outrage and indignation over what it thought happened, given the very limited facts then made known. Charlie Company immediately was charged with racism, cold-blooded murder and unprofessional conduct.

Only the last of the three might have an element of truth in it. The men were very unprofessional soldiers. Racists they weren't. Cold-blooded murderers hardly.

Medina always felt he was given too many men who had below-normal IQs. Such men are known as McNamara's 100,000. The Army says the company only had 13 men like these. But it refuses to allow anyone to confirm its claim. It would be very simple to determine who these men were by looking at their serial numbers; certain digits identify men with low IQs. Although even the enemy is entitled to know an American soldier's serial number, the Army refuses to make this information available on members of Charlie Company. The official Pentagon lie is that soldiers no longer have serial numbers. They are identified by their social security numbers. While this is true, it is a recent innovation; the members of Charlie Company all had serial numbers.

McNamara's 100,000 would normally not have been allowed to enter the Army because of their low IQs. But they were enlisted under a special program instituted by former Secretary of Defense Robert S. McNamara. It was McNamara's contention that such men could be retrained and reeducated in the service and thus would come out of the Army as better citizens.

But the Vietnam war interfered with this theory. When the Army needs live bodies for the infantry, as any veteran knows, it just grabs anybody handy who can breathe.

Before Charlie Company left for Vietnam, it was assigned a group of McNamara's 100,000 who had not had the special retraining to upgrade them. The company, after all, was short of men.

"They rushed a whole bunch in at the last minute," remembers Medina, describing the contingent as men who "couldn't make the IQ test in the Army." Medina took what he could get but he wasn't happy about it.

"Guys like that might possibly create problems." He remembered his first reactions, explaining that such men would have been satisfactory for armies "in the sword-and-spear days." Those were the days when a strong back and a powerful right arm more than compensated for a weak mind, and indeed were the prerequisites for a good foot soldier.

"They didn't have the Geneva Conventions then," Medina observed. "An individual today," said Medina, speaking of the dream GI, "is an ambassador and a diplomat and is supposed to make decisions and act accordingly."

Charlie Company wasn't particularly interested in serving as ambassadors of good will. All the men wanted to do was live. And it didn't matter what they had to do to survive. No man likes to give his life or his limbs for any reason, but sometimes he can be convinced that a cause is worthwhile. There was nothing convincing about Vietnam, certainly not when there was such a vociferous

difference of opinion at home. So far as Charlie Company
was concerned, these men's primary objective in the war
was to go home. And if they tried harder it was only for
the reason—to survive.

And how do you survive in the infantry? By remembering what they taught you in basic training where the infantry drill instructor shouted to the rookies:

"What's the spirit of the bayonet?"

And they roared back in unison:

"Kill, kill, kill."

"And what's the spirit of the infantry?"

"Kill, kill, kill."

Medina was aware of all his personnel problems,
remembers Fred Widmer, who then asked:

"What could he do about it? You got to use every man
you got out there."

★ ★ ★

CHAPTER IV

THE COMPANY (2)

★ ★ ★ ★ ★ ★ ★ ★ ★ ★ ★ ★ ★ ★

". . . My hat's off to the Army, the poor bastards . . . Since hearing some of their stories I've been down on my knees every night thanking God I was smart enough to enlist in the Navy . . ."

A sailor interviewed by Ernie Pyle in World War II

"The GIs, they didn't know who to hate. They were kind of mixed up about what they had to do."

RICHARD PENDLETON
A member of Charlie Company

★ ★ ★ ★ ★ ★ ★ ★ ★ ★ ★ ★ ★

Charlie Company was reborn the day Capt. Medina took it over. He was from the young, ambitious, eager, dedicated category of the professional Army. Not many of the men joining the company in the months following its rebirth shared Medina's enthusiasm. But they accepted his authority and their fate and did what was expected of them.

That was the underlying characteristic of the company. They did what society demanded of them, without an argument. Had they been any different they wouldn't have been in the infantry—not for the Vietnam War anyhow.

They participated in amphibious operations on the island of Molokai, climbed and reclimbed and wandered the Kahuku Range in the Pohakaloa training area—and prepared for that dreaded war in Vietnam. Medina worked them hard and if he could be faulted for anything it might be overtraining. But he was getting them physically toughened for the duties that lay ahead.

Slowly he weeded out the men who wouldn't be going with him, and began to train the company he would lead in Vietnam. He built an award-winning company out of a lackluster group of draftees.

Members of the company always thought about Vietnam. And predominant in their thoughts was the idea of killing. For they knew that one day, as infantrymen, they would have to shoot someone. And it bothered them. Rumors would come back, rumors filled with fact, about free fire zones in Vietnam, which meant that in certain areas you could kill anything that moves.

And there would be stories of the body count, of how the sign of success is killing Viet Cong, much as a fighter pilot had to shoot down a certain number of planes to be called an ace.

The only trouble was they never quite knew what a Viet Cong was. All they knew was that you couldn't trust them.

And the men talked about Vietnam and how would it be out there? Would it be dangerous? Who could you trust and who couldn't you trust? And what would happen when the time came to kill a man? Could you? And who will get killed and who will make it back?

Medina once, long afterward, tried to explain the difference in the outlook towards fear and death between someone like himself who has accepted war as a profession and the men in his company who hadn't.

He recalled the fear he had on the morning of March 16 when he led his company into Mylai (4), or Pinkville as it was commonly called.

"Pinkville was fear," he said using the common expression for that area. "I was sure we wouldn't all come back."

But he believed the men were more frightened than he was.

"If you're not a professional, ready to lay down your own life, you'd be even more scared," he said.

Of course not all the soldiers in the company were indifferent to the war or reluctant about going out there. Bernhardt, a New Yorker, joined the Army because he wanted to experience war and because he had a slight feeling of guilt that people his age were going to Vietnam while he was going to college. He wanted to be a helicopter pilot. He had attended a military academy during his high-school years. He had two and a half years at the University of Miami when he quit to enlist in the Army. While at the university he was active in ROTC affairs.

Terry of Utah, the devout Mormon, was a student at Brigham Young University who sort of willingly let himself be drafted. He had been planning either to go off as a lay missionary for his church for two years or join the Army. When the Army took him, he didn't fight it.

James R. White Jr. had been going to college in California and working in a mortuary, which he didn't like. He also knew he was going to be fired from the job, information that didn't exactly depress him. He had had a falling out with his girl. White was indifferent to the war in Vietnam. "I didn't know what was happening either way," he said. He didn't want to study anymore and he wanted to get away from home. But he also knew he couldn't kill. So he volunteered for the Army on condition they place him in the medics. They did and he became a hero in Vietnam, although it cost him part of a foot.

Robert Shivers was born in Lexington, Mississippi, but was raised on military posts around the world as the son of an Army sergeant. His father was stationed in Germany when Bob graduated from the Munich American High School. On his return to the U. S. he was drafted. It was just something one accepted in his circles. Shivers had a hometown sweetheart, an American girl with whom he had attended school in Munich. She was the daughter of a civil servant. Shivers was assigned to Charlie Company in April 1967; in October he went back to the States to marry her, then returned to go overseas.

Frederick Widmer was attending Slippery Rock State Teachers College in Pennsylvania but he didn't like it. He was aware of this and when he began to see his friends being drafted, he volunteered.

Robert J. Van Leer was the son of an Air Force sergeant. He had a brother in the Marines. After his mother passed away his father remarried. Bob joined the Army at 17. He joined Charlie Company in July 1967, a real old-timer. Van Leer transferred out of the company in October because his brother was in Vietnam. Army regulations say two members of a family are not required to be in Vietnam at the same time. But the youngster felt an intense loyalty to the company. And even after he was out, he would come around every day to watch the men pack for Vietnam.

Finally, he could take it no longer and requested a transfer back to Charlie Company in time to go to Vietnam. Three months later he would lose a foot out there and be medically retired at 19.

David Mitchell joined the Army in 1960, one year after graduating from Dawson High School in St. Francisville, Louisiana, a black community. He was the product of segregated schools and one of 15 children of the Rev. and Mrs. Isiaiah (sic) Mitchell. He had a brother who had been in the Air Force 10 years. Rev. Mitchell headed the little Raspberry Baptist Church for 25 years.

David Mitchell tried working around the town where he was raised, but there just weren't that many opportunities.

"He worked around for a lot of these white people, cleaning their rooms and waxing their floors," his mother remembers. Then she added sadly, "It's hard for a young colored man to get a good job." The town only has a sweet potato canning plant and a paper mill. It also has a huge billboard near the post office that says, "The Army teaches over 300 skills. See your local recruiter." The Army offered Mitchell what his hometown couldn't give him. Then the Army charged him with assault with intent to commit murder in Mylai.

Herbert Louis Carter comes from a family of ten children. Three are veterans of Vietnam. The others aren't old enough to go yet. Carter was born in Georgia but raised in Arizona and Washington. His is a warm, close family now living in a black ghetto in East Palo Alto, California. His step-father worked in a factory until he lost his right arm at the shoulder in an industrial accident.

Young Carter always liked to do his own thing, says his mother. He always moved by himself and drifted away from his family. He was a ninth-grade dropout when the Army drafted him. But once in the Army he qualified as a paratrooper. He was in Hawaii when he heard Charlie Company was leaving for Vietnam in two weeks. He volunteered out of curiosity. He became the company's tunnel rat and was admired as a good field soldier by his buddies.

Richard Hendrickson of California was a high-school dropout who joined the Job Corps and then joined the Army. He is not sure why he volunteered, but he liked the Army. At 19 he was medically retired after losing one limb, his eyes and his ears to a booby trap. He was one of the casualties the company sought to avenge at Mylai.

Richard Pendleton from California was a draftee who was working as a gas station attendant when the Army got him. He might have tried to get in the Navy or Air Force but he didn't want to buck the system. Besides the Army was only a two-year hitch, shorter than the period in the other services, so why fight it. And once in the service he didn't attempt to manipulate, preferring to do what came "naturally." So when they put him in the infantry, naturally he went.

"The boys in our school who go to Vietnam are dropouts, immature or not making it academically." Thus observed a counselor at the Pinole Valley High School from which Rick got a diploma. When Rick was asked why he fought in Vietnam, he replied quite candidly: "I don't know why and nobody bothered to tell us. I don't think nobody knew theyselves."

James Bergthold of Niagara Falls, New York, could easily have walked across the bridge from his hometown and gotten out of the war by taking residence in Canada. He had no desire to go into the Army. But he really had no desire not to go into the Army, either, and so one day he was drafted and he went. His parents had separated; his family was poor. His mother, a native American, is illiterate and said she didn't know what happened to Charlie Company when its infamy was blasted across the front pages of the world until someone read her the story in the local newspaper.

Bergthold dropped out of the eighth grade when he was 16. After he quit grammer school, Bergthold remembers, he couldn't make it on the meager earnings of his mother, a hotel maid, so he drifted from one menial job to another. He took a job moving furniture, he worked for the local poverty program cutting grass, and he was in the Youth Corps working for the Department of Parks as a plumber's helper when the Army drafted him.

Being an eighth-grade dropout in Niagara Falls isn't unusual, observed Bergthold's school principal, William L. Sdao (sic). The neighborhood where the youngster lived was poor-white, and on the fringes of the black ghetto. "We're among the economically deprived," Sdao explained.

Following the Mylai affair, America's intellectual handwringers expressed shock and indignation over Charlie Company's failure to show the proper sophistication in winning the hearts and minds of the Vietnamese peasants. Sdao was asked whether, perhaps, society was expecting to much from boys like Bergthold. "We're asking a lot of any of these youngsters in turning them out to society," the school principal said.

Niagara Falls appeals to industry; it is a factory town. And factories need a pool of manpower. However, even factory hands must have better qualifications than Bergthold had. His education just wasn't good enough to get any kind of decent job. But the Army had a good job for Bergthold. It made him an infantryman-diplomat and sent him to Vietnam with the idea of winning friends for America.

Like so many members of Charlie Company, Bergthold fatalistically accepted what happened to him. "I went where they put me," he explained. So they put him in Ft. Carson, Colorado, where he was placed in the infantry because what else are you going to do with an eighth-grade dropout?

And he adjusted and made the best of a bad thing.

"I didn't really want to go into the army, but then I figured as long as I was in, I might as well make the best of it," the heavy-set ex-soldier recalled. At Carson, Bergthold developed an enthusiasm for Vietnam together with a bunch of the other trainees, and they volunteered to go.

Why did he want to go to Vietnam? Who knows? Maybe basic training was boring. Maybe Vietnam sounded exciting. Anyhow some of the volunteers were sent directly; others, like Bergthold, were sent to Hawaii first. There he was assigned to Charlie Company.

Training with Bergthold at Camp Carson, but in a different platoon, was Allen Boyce of Bradley Beach, New Jersey, another resort area. Boyce quit high school at the end of his third year because he didn't have the money to continue. He volunteered, he said, "to get my obligation over with." Since he was just married four months he hoped he could stay in the States. But he was sent along with Bergthold to join Charlie Company in Hawaii. He too had no desire to be an infantryman.

"See, like I really didn't want to go into the infantry. But they put everybody into the infantry and that's where I stayed. I made no big effort to get out," Boyce explains.

Although newlyweds, neither Boyce nor Shivers had their wives with them in Hawaii. Boyce felt he couldn't afford it. Instead he would write his wife every other day. And just before the company left for Hawaii he got a home leave back to New Jersey.

Paul David Meadlo from Indiana also was a newlywed and he brought his wife out to Hawaii. Widmer remembers that Meadlo was always worrying about his wife, particularly after the company was in Vietnam. "He never kept his mind on what he was doing. He was all bummed out about his wife," Widmer says. "He was just like Wood. Wood saw his wife two times, then got his ass blowed away," Widmer adds sadly.

John Wood, a close friend of Widmer's was another low-ranking enlisted man with a wife in Hawaii. Wood married her in September 1967, remembers Shivers. But he never had time to see her much because of the field duty. The men remember that Wood had opportunity to see his wife twice before the company shipped out. He was killed 20 days before he was due to return home.

Medina had his wife, Baerbel and his three children with him in Hawaii. So did his first sergeant, Harry F. Hobscheid, whose wife, Reiko, was there. And Sgt. George J. Cox had his wife, Brigitta, with him. Brigitta, like Baerbel, was a German girl. Both had met their husbands when the men were stationed in Germany.

Mrs. Medina remembers proudly how her husband would work in Hawaii until two in the morning and come home dog-tired. At 4 somebody would call him on company business. At 5 he would begin a new day by driving the 45 minutes from his home to where the company was quartered. It was a typical day, and Medina drove himself and everybody connected with him like a typically successful American executive. He was much older than his troops because he had been an enlisted man for so long. But he sure set the pace and he made those kids follow him.

That's how he got the name Mad Dog Medina, a nickname that has been misunderstood by the public and used against the captain by his enemies.

There was nothing mad about Ernie Medina—unless it's deranged to be professionally dedicated. The name came because of Medina's conscientiousness and the rivalry between his company and Bravo Company, commanded by Capt. Gerald F. Shelton of Raleigh, North Carolina, who would be so badly wounded in Vietnam that he would get a medical discharge. Curiously enough B Company members also have been accused of murder in Vietnam, in connection with the Mylai assault, but have been acquitted.

It was always a tossup as to which was the best company in the brigade, B or C. Once during a night exercise in the Pohakaloa training area, two battalions of the 11th Brigade were arraigned against each other. Dark had fallen and Charlie Company had set up night defensive positions before going to sleep. Then Medina decided to move out. It was an aggressive act. In doing so, Charlie Company overran a platoon of Bravo Company.

Shelton started the expression after that. "Old Mad Dog Medina. You can't keep him down. You never know what he'll do next."

"There's Mad Dog Medina," Shelton would say at the officers' mess; and the name stuck. It might just as well have been Eager Beaver Ernie. It was a compliment to Medina's drive and enthusiasm. He knew he drove his men but he had his reasons.

"I think I was very demanding on the men. But I knew when we left that I wouldn't be able to bring everybody back. This concerned me. When someone is killed it's like having your own son killed," Medina said.

Despite his gruffness, Medina had a fondness for his

troops which he tried not to show. Perhaps it was the fact
that he had had no parents to raise him. "I missed the love
of a mother and father," Medina once said. Then becoming embarrassed, he went on: "I really don't know how to
put it. Teachers have lots of kids but I wasn't looked after
by any teachers but one and I can't remember the name.
I grew up by myself.

"I got a lot of values from my grandparents: to be hon-
est, to keep a good name, to work hard. But they were
unable to give me advice and counseling. They weren't
interested in living in my world. They didn't go to sports
or the plays."

Medina's men undoubtedly sensed his concern for
them. That is why they instinctively trusted him as a
leader, although they resented his drive. "That Medina
was quite a guy," remembers Terry. Most thought Medina
was pretty good. They followed him. He had a temper, but
the guys respected him. "In the field Medina always was
the last one to eat. The platoon leaders ate after the men.
Medina made sure the men ate first. He got them fresh
clothes."

Then Terry thought a moment and added: "Medina was
gung-ho, but the men didn't resent it."

Field training in Hawaii was pretty difficult, remember
Boyce and Bergthold.

"Eight months in those kahukus on the island of Oahu
and we were out most of the time. I think sometimes the
training there was more rugged than in Vietnam," Boyce
said.

Thus the men had little time to enjoy the pleasures of
America's tropical island state. They only made infrequent trips to Honolulu, because their days were too filled
and their wallets too empty. "We used to get drunk a lot,"
Bergthold remembers. "But it cost too much to get laid. It
cost $25. I couldn't afford that."

A good part of the drinking was at the enlisted men's
club on post, where half the company would go on any

given night when they weren't in the field. Here the men would slop up the beer and shoot the bull. And here, probably, is where they got their indoctrination on Vietnam, where war stories would be swapped and warnings made about the deceitfulness of the Vietnamese, regardless of their age or sex.

The men got their indoctrination not only in the barrooms but at the bedsides of the wounded.

Bergthold remembers visiting the Army's Tripler General Hospital in Hawaii, where the wounded veterans of Vietnam were recuperating. The war veterans, Bergthold says, would show the rookies pictures of young Vietnamese boys or women and warn the GIs that these people are sneaky, that they concealed grenades on their person, built booby traps, laid mines and sniped at Americans.

You just couldn't trust nobody in Vietnam and the only good gook was a dead gook. That was the lesson Charlie Company learned in Hawaii. It was like kids learning about sex in the streets. But it was the only place they could get the information. Their elders were too busy or too embarrassed to give them the facts of life.

Boyce, a tall, lanky, tough-talking kid, remembers his training platoon sergeant in Hawaii and apparently was impressed.

"He had a "ski" at the end of his name . . . Novajewski or Novajowski or something. He had been in Vietnam a few times. He really knew what he was doing," Boyce remembers.

"He never talked too much. He wasn't a guy who said 'clean the barracks.' But in the field he got down to business. Like one time a guy was falling down. He had his rifle slung down on his shoulder. 'Better not have it at sling arms,' the sergeant said. He always said, 'Don't underestimate them. The enemy. Don't underestimate them.' That's what he always told us," Boyce remembers clearly.

   And that was the extent of Charlie Company's briefings
on Vietnam while they were training in Hawaii. And even
this indoctrination was diluted by half when 50 percent of
the company ranks were filled with newcomers just
weeks before it left for overseas.

   Members of Charlie Company laugh sarcastically
when anyone mentions anything about winning hearts
and minds. They don't know what you're talking about. If
there were fine points of distinction between a guerrilla
and a civilian, the men weren't told what they are.

   The main thrust of the field training in Hawaii seemed
to be to toughen them into a skilled, hard-nosed infantry
team that would react in concert to the drum Medina
played when the going got rough.

   Critics have charged Medina with not being too concerned over the discipline of his troops in the field.
Medina had a favorite expression, remembers Van Leer:
"If you put a quarter in the juke box you gotta dance to the
music." Medina set the pace, and he had his tune, and he
wanted his men to know it, and he didn't give a damn
about the enemy. And if his men had poor indoctrination
from the Army and didn't know what they were fighting
for, Medina knew he was heading into a guerrilla war.
His responsibility was increased because his men were so
unprofessional and the Army didn't have the time to train
them.

   Medina was going into a guerrilla war as the commander of an infantry company and the lives of a lot of
kids were on his shoulders. He wanted to bring them back
home alive, and as long as they danced to his tune he
didn't give a damn about how they dressed or what they
thought of the Vietnamese or anything else. And he
shouldn't have. And like Novajowski or Novajewski, it
didn't matter whether the men shaved or said "sir" or
shined their shoes or took a bath. It did matter that they
were comfortable and had physical endurance and that
they were obedient. For they would be constantly sur-

rounded by the enemy and each man would be dependent on the other if the company would survive.

Medina's concern was the survival of the company. The welfare of enemy civilians was not Medina's concern, for he was a simple infantry officer and not an ambassador. And in guerrilla warfare, anybody who is not with you is against you. If the U. S. Government wanted to hold the hand of the Vietnamese peasant class, then it should have sent out a company of sociologists or psychologists or chaplains trained in holding hands, and not a company of unskilled school dropouts trained to fight and kill. Or the Army should have found the time to train and to indoctrinate these young draftees for their secondary role as heart-and-mind-winners.

Instead they learned that killing is all right as long as it's the Vietnamese who die, because you can't trust those gooks anyway. Not even the mama-sans and the papa-sans and the baby-sans, or even the South Vietnamese Army who won't fight, and everybody out there is Viet Cong who will either steal your money or kill you when they can.

The Army was having enough difficulties just keeping its ranks filled with bodies, anybody's body. It apparently had no time to concern itself with the psychological subtleties of the Vietnam conflict. At least the infantry had no time. It must be difficult to train a boy raised under the Western Judeo-Christian concept of "love thy neighbor" to kill thine enemy. It calls for a complete reversal of values, and that's what infantry training is all about. So to ask that same boy not to kill the people he is being taught to kill would be enough to drive a simple mind into confusion.

In the military all complex matters are reduced to their simplest common denominator. It would probably be near impossible in a short period of time to explain to an eighth-grade dropout that he is supposed to win the hearts and minds of people in the daytime but blow their brains out at night. If he's going to be in the infantry, it's much simpler to prepare his mind to accept killing an enemy, and to accept an uncomplicated definition of who an enemy is.

"The company was psychologically conditioned to kill," Doc White explained at one time. Although he never approved what happened at Mylai (4) he agreed that it was explainable. "When the opportunity presented itself," he continued, "they were unable to distinguish the fine line between right and wrong." The thought of killing, just a matter of discussion in Hawaii, was to become an obsession with Charlie Company in Vietnam.

Carter once tried to explain it when he asked a friend, "Do you know what it means to kill? Do you know what it means when you get angry and tell somebody 'I'll kill you?' Do you know what it means to actually kill somebody?"

It is something to think about, particularly if you're in the position of an infantryman who will have to do just that; and in all probability in an eyeball-to-eyeball confrontation, where you see the enemy whom you must slaughter. It is much easier for the navy gunner to fire over the horizon, or for the Air Force bombardier to push a button when the numbers on his computer match, or even for the helicopter door-gunner to fire at running figures down below who are being "elusive" and therefore suspect.

But if an infantryman is a murderer, so are they all, all murderers, every man who wears the uniform of the country he serves and every civilian who stands behind him.

Indeed the infantryman should be credited for being braver than other servicemen, mentally as well as physically. For when he kills, it is with the full knowledge of the consequences of his act. When the helicopter gunner kills, the artilleryman or the bombardier, the result of his action is not seen. If these long-distance fighters err and miss their targets, they can always dismiss the thought from their mind. For they never see the results of their acts.

Thus Medina built a family of physically toughened men out of a collection of soft, reluctant civilian soldiers. He gave disgruntled draftees pride, he gave boys a sense of manhood, he gave his inexperienced leaders inspiration, he gave his company esprit de corps. He just never gave them motivation or an explanation. It wasn't his to give. And the Army was too busy.

And the company got to know each other and trust each other and depend on each other. That isn't to say they were a company of angels, because they weren't. The men liked to have a good time, and there were always a few AWOL each week, remembers Shivers. One man could never stay out of jail everytime he went into Honolulu. He would get drunk and be jailed, and someone from the company would have to go into town and bail him out. But once back in the field, remembers Shivers, this man was an outstanding soldier.

Then there was one squad who had a girl named Rita. She was known as the squad's slut because that's what she was. All eight members would visit town to gang-bang her on a fairly regular basis. There's nothing to bring men closer to each other than sharing a common experience. And it was good training for Vietnam.

Generally however the men didn't hit town too often. Van Leer recalls that some of the guys would go into the city once a month, on payday, when they would buy a bottle of wine, sit quietly and drink it, then go back to the barracks and the field.

And there would be company parties occasionally. Sometimes Hoaeae would fix teriyaki steaks, his specialty, Japanese-Hawaiian style or there would be beer busts on the pleasant Hawaiian sands. Doc White remembers one party on the beach where Hoaeae was brought in to cook his luscious teriyaki steaks in a preparation that

Mrs. Medina, even now with all her troubles, remembers with mouth-watering delight. Everybody got a little drunk that night, and some guys more drunk than others. Richard Lane, who Doc White says was dubbed "Night Train Lane" because he always slept with his finger in his mouth, apparently had a little too much to drink, the medic recalls.

Doc White didn't like Medina too much. It might have been a personality conflict or the fact that Medina gave Doc a hard time when the medic tried to get a leave to the States from Hawaii. He got the leave but it was coupled with a tongue-lashing from Medina.

Doc thought Medina was "standoffish." He conceded, however, that Medina "put up a facade that a leader must." Doc felt Medina had no patience with men on sick call. Medina considered them all malingerers.

Doc White, at 6 feet, was a little taller and, at 23, a little older than the rest of the company, and the men respected and loved him. Medics are always popular with combat troops. But he was upset by Medina's brusqueness. Medina, on the other hand, always felt that a commanding officer shouldn't get too familiar with the men. If he had to lead them into battle where some would possibly die, it was no good getting too friendly.

Medina, of course, also had a love affair going with the Army. Once during a training exercise in Hawaii, Medina and Doc were talking and the captain asked the medic what he planned to do when he got out of the army. Doc said he planned to return to school. Medina was an astute officer and a good salesman for the Army, but he might have been a little unpolished when it came to dealing with college men. Yet he certainly recognized the talents of his senior medic.

"You ain't nothing but a goddamn hippie," Doc said Medina told him. "You're too goddamn stupid to go to school. Why don't you reenlist?"

Relating this story, Doc White still felt hurt by Medina's

attitude. What may not have dawned on him was that being invited to reenlist in the Army, to join Medina's family of career soldiers, was a form of flattery coming from the tough old former sergeant.

Doc concedes however that Medina's gruffness was not all mean. "I realize," he reflects, "that half Medina's pressure on me was to make me a good medic and the other half was because of personal conflicts."

But Doc remembers when Night Train Lane didn't have enough steam to get him back to bed after that beach party. When the affair was over the men were being bussed back to their barracks. When they arrived Night Train Lane couldn't move.

"Medina carried that kid from the bus to the barracks. Then he put him to bed," said Doc White of an episode that was hardly in the line of duty of a company commander.

It was these little acts of Medina that endeared him to many members of the company. Medina tried basically to be a hard man and in the field he might have been a terror. But there was nothing he wouldn't do for his men. Van Leer remembers the time he had a problem after he had undergone an operation for varicose veins on his left leg. He was walking back to his tent one day when suddenly the leg began "spitting blood."

The CQ (Charge of Quarters) hastily summoned Doc White, who saw the spurting blood and immediately ordered an ambulance to whisk Van Leer off to the hospital. Then the CQ notified Capt. Medina.

Within the hour after the incident occurred, Medina was in the hospital at Van Leer's bedside. He had rushed there from his home and Van Leer remembers the captain was in civilian clothes, wearing a loud orange-print Hawaiian shirt.

"Are you all right, kid?" Medina asked the youngster.

"Yes, sir, I'm all right," Van Leer told the captain.

"It was the first time I sensed any compassion in him.

Capt. Medina was concerned. He was always concerned about us," Van Leer remembers.

"Medina was a hard-nose," Carter was to remember a long time afterwards. "But one thing you can't take from him," recalled the former soldier, who was then an unemployed farm laborer in the Southwest. "Medina did take care of his men. His men were just like his own kids. That's the way he treated us."

That was the one thing about which the company could be fairly certain as it prepared to leave for Vietnam, a month sooner than expected. At least Medina knew something about what was happening, even if the men didn't.

Besides White, others too got themselves home leaves when they heard the company would be leaving for Vietnam at the end of November instead of the end of December.

One who didn't was Widmer. Instead his mother came out to Hawaii to visit him. She is young-looking, slim and pretty, and the guys couldn't get over that. They would let him know about it long after the company left for Vietnam and he would write home and tell his mother that.

Bergthold also went home on leave, and again he could have walked over the bridge to Canada. But the thought never entered his mind. He ran out of money at home and went looking for an Army agency in Niagara Falls to help get him back to Hawaii. He was helped; then he had to repay the Army $242.42 for the plane ticket. But he earned $190 a month in Vietnam, he says, so the debt was soon erased.

To people like Bergthold, the idea of going to Canada for any reason other than to have fun just never comes to mind. It is not uncommon for young men living in Niagara Falls to cross the border on drinking forays. But to desert, no.

Now with all the pressures on the former members of Charlie Company, Bergthold may be thinking a little differently.

"Canada? I don't know. I might go there myself. One thing is for sure. I'm not going to jail," Bergthold told a visitor shortly after the Mylai affair was made public.

It looked as if one member of the company, Gustavo Rotger, wouldn't be going overseas with the company. He was in the stockade, remembers Medina, and was due to remain there until after the company left. Rotger gave Medina trouble in Hawaii. But the young soldier didn't want to leave the company. He begged Medina to let him out, so he could go along to Vietnam, and Medina relented and freed him.

Besides McNamara's 100,000, there were many other newcomers to Charlie Company who arrived at the last minute. Tom Partsch was among a group of ten who joined the company on Thanksgiving day, three days before it departed. He volunteered because he heard Charlie Company was leaving by air. That would beat the long miserable voyage on a troop transport. Carter joined just before the company left, too. He heard it was going to Vietnam, so figured what the hell and went along. Carter didn't like Hawaii. He claims the people were prejudiced against blacks. Bernhardt came into the company just a couple of weeks before it departed. He was among a group of some dozen paratroopers who joined the company when their own unit was disbanded.

The unit was the 70th Infantry Detachment (Long Range Patrol). It is known in the Army as "Lurps"—for Long Range Reconnaissance Patrol (LRRP). Its men, all highly trained paratroopers, are taken behind enemy lines for intelligence reconnaissance purposes. They are supposed to return back with the information they gather. They are not supposed to engage the enemy in firefights. Despite the obvious dangers involved, many ordinary infantrymen would rather be Lurps. Lurp patrols are only for periods of several days. When the Lurps aren't on patrol, they stand down, meaning they can go swimming on the pleasant Vietnamese beachs, go to beer halls, generally relax.

Another member of the Lurp detachment was Ronald Ridenhour, an Arizonian. But he wasn't assigned to Charlie Company; he was made a helicopter door-gunner. Ridenhour was the ex-soldier who filed the complaint of Charlie Company's alleged misdeeds at Mylai (4). The complaint ultimately brought the entire affair to light.

Ridenhour says he didn't get along with his sergeants in the helicopter company to which he belonged. He felt he only had to take orders from the pilot officers, whereas the sergeants wanted him to take orders from them. So after four months or so, apparently through mutual consent, he transferred out of the helicopter company in April 1968 and went back into a Lurp unit attached to the 11th Light Infantry Brigade. Here he met his former buddies from Hawaii, including Charles (Butch) Gruver, Terry, William Doherty and Larry LaCroix. The four had transferred back to the Lurps from Charlie Company in April 1968.

Gruver was the first man to tell Ridenhour about the Mylai affair the month before. It apparently was almost a nonchalant conversation. Maybe Gruver was trying to get something off his mind and was talking to a buddy he thought he could trust. At any event, Ridenhour began to track the story down, calling on other former members of Charlie Company now back in the Lurps, including, Terry, Doherty and LaCroix. Ridenhour devoted the rest of his tour in Vietnam tracking down the story.

When he left the service, Ridenhour continued his one-man crusade, which ended when a letter he sent to government officials resulted in the story being blasted around the world, a story that incriminated some of his former buddies. It is unclear why he went through so much trouble. He said he didn't do it for money, although he did ask a literary agent to try to peddle his story, after he had written to the government. The agent failed.

His reasons for pursuing the story are not within the province of this book. He may have had his own feelings of guilt, as every combat soldier has, one psychiatrist suggested.

Once, when he was asked why he went through all the trouble he did, Ridenhour answered, "I believe in America, the Bill of Rights and all things America is supposed to stand for." At another point he said he did what he did because "I don't condone murder and that's murder." He was referring to the action at Mylai.

It is difficult to understand how anyone believing in the America of the Bill of Rights could condemn a person for murder before anything has been proved. The America Ridenhour says he believes in considers a man innocent until he is proved guilty.

Ridenhour didn't seem to have much patience with the members of Charlie Company. Of course he is much brighter than the average infantryman; he went on to become a literature major at Claremont College for Men, a West Coast Ivy League school in California. Some years later he went back to Vietnam to write about it for a little known anti-war news agency. He feels if the men were told to win hearts and minds they would have won hearts and minds.

"If they would have put the stress on winning hearts and minds to Calley, instead of on killing gooks, then he would have done it. Because Calley did what he was told," Ridenhour once said.

Maybe Charlie Company didn't know the difference between hearts and minds and hearts and flowers, but as infantrymen they felt ready to fight. "If they wanted me to be a mechanic, they should have given me a monkey wrench instead of a rifle," Carter said two years later.

Perhaps the Army should have made Charlie Company mechanics. Vietnam is a different war in a different age and Charlie Company wasn't ready for it.

★ ★ ★

CHAPTER V

MEDINA

★ ★ ★ ★ ★ ★ ★ ★ ★ ★ ★ ★ ★ ★

"I always liked Medina. I liked what he stood for. He took care of us."
RICHARD HENDRICKSON
A member of Charlie Company

★ ★ ★ ★ ★ ★ ★ ★ ★ ★ ★ ★ ★ ★

You have to be a first generation American, preferably not a WASP, to understand a man like Ernest Lou Medina. You've got to be a Jew or an Italian or a Greek kid who grew up here, and whose parents could hardly speak English, to understand Ernie. It wouldn't hurt if you were a Negro too, or an American Indian of any generation, or a Chinese to understand the cross that Ernest Lou Medina carried as a Mexican-American American.

You've got to say that twice, Mexican-American American, because it must sink in that Ernest Lou Medina was an American. That's what he wanted to be, that's what he wanted to prove, that's what he is, although sometimes even he forgets it.

Medina is a short stocky guy; the temptation is to call him swarthy, which is what Medina is, but that's a bad word because it's reserved for dark, Latin-type people and it has bad connotations in these days of racial sensitivities. His friends all call him Ernie. So does his sister and her children, who call him Uncle Ernie, and who, until this mess happened, sat at his feet and worshipped him and waited for his letters from the far-off places to which he was assigned, and heeded his words of advice.

And his advice always emphasized the same theme. Study, study, study—you can't get enough of education—Uncle Ernie would tell the kids. And that's why his niece Terry, the beautiful one and the eldest of his sister Linda's 3 children, is a nurse, and Kenny, who is 20, is going to college and Russell, who is 15 will go to college.

There is heartbreak in the simple home of Don and Erlinda Lovato, Ernie's brother-in-law and sister, over the cruel twist fate has taken, and the children are hurt and their parents don't understand what happened. For Linda was more than a sister to Ernie; she was ten years old when he was born in Springer, New Mexico to an ailing mother who, it is believed, contracted blood poisoning after having a tooth extracted in the last months of her pregnancy.

Paula West was the daughter of a deputy marshal in Springer who achieved a small measure of fame when his picture appeared in National Geographic in a real western scene back in the 1930s. Paula herself must have been a very daring young woman in those days, considering her background and all, when she announced to her father that she was marrying Sam Medina, a Mexican sheepherder.

"My mother's father never approved of Dad," Linda recalls with a slight smile. "Mother was his favorite. She could hunt, shoot and ride a horse better than most men. My father was a cowboy, a sheepherder and he used to break horses. Grandfather resented the fact that Mother was marrying my father."

But Paula married Sam and they lived on a farm in New Mexico. Her first-born was Erlinda and her second-born was a girl who died at birth. The third was a boy who was stillborn and her fourth was Ernie, who almost died as an infant from the same blood poisoning that his mother had contracted.

Before Ernie's birth and his mother's death, remembers Linda, the family lived in a house provided by the ranch where Sam Medina was a cowhand, in an area now known as Cimarron where a huge Boy Scout ranch is located. It is the only one of its kind in the country offering kids the chance to become men by taking two weeks of the most rugged camping trip in their young lives.

"Dad says we were real poor," Linda recalls, "but we lived on a farm and had all the food we needed, and mother used to sew for us, so I really don't know that we were poor."

As a cowhand, Ernie's father was never around much. Cowboys are like sailors, except they range the fields instead of sailing the seas, so Sam Medina wasn't much of a domesticated man. That, by modern standards, would make him a typical American father.

After Ernie's mother died, Ernie and his sister were sent to live with an uncle, Claude Medina, in Ocate, New Mexico. Claude and Sam had been given a farm in Ocate by their father, Joe A. Medina, who then went to Montrose, Colorado, to live out his retirement. But Sam, the perpetual wanderer, couldn't settle on a farm, and he took off to Colorado too to seek work, leaving Linda and the baby Ernie with their uncle Claude.

Montrose, Colorado, might not have been the best place in the world for a Mexican-American family, but it beat New Mexico and Joe Medina turned his house into a home for children of the family. He had between 12 and 18 children living there at one time or another, all members of the Medina clan who for one reason or another needed help.

Probably the main reason he brought the children up to Colorado was because the opportunities for an education were better there than in New Mexico. And Joe Medina was a bug on education. He was a bug on education and on protecting the family name. If there was one thing he always harped on, it was to keep the Medina name good and clean and honorable and respected, and the way to do that was to get an education so you could move up in the world.

Right after Ernie's birth, when he began to be quite sick and it looked as if he were going to die, it was decided to bring him and his sister up to Montrose, Colorado, too. It was at this point that Erlinda became more a mother than a sister to her baby brother. For at ten years of age she had become responsible for his very life, and she still remembers the frightening ride in an old car, with a dying baby in her arms, from New Mexico to Colorado. At nearly every town they would stop and rush to find a doctor, but finally they made it to Montrose, and eventually Erlinda nursed Ernie back to health.

Erlinda and Don Lovato, also a Mexican-American from Colorado, now live with their three children in a neat one-story home in Pico Rivera, near Los Angeles. Their home is in a middle-class area on a street just across the highway from a huge factory. It isn't a Mexican neighborhood, but Mrs. Lovato says there are a few Cuban families living there. The family is fairly comfortable, although Don, a draftsman, has known being out of work, because when a factory loses a contract people have to be laid off.

Don served overseas in World War II and is an active member of the Veterans of Foreign Wars, and Erlinda participates in the activities of its women's auxiliary. Indeed it was Don's post, the Lt. Ray L. Musgrave Post, Auxiliary 7734 (Pico Rivera), that was active in sending books, magazines, cookies and other goodies from home to Charlie Company when it was in Vietnam.

Mrs. Lovato, seated at the little dining room table of her neat home, looks like the typical mother—the old-fashioned kind, not the modern one—whose life has been devoted to the raising of children and the juggling of limited finances to keep the family operative. Still a good-looking woman at 44, Erlinda Lovato's eyes nevertheless are tired and wrinkles have begun to form on her motherly face.

"I always had a happy childhood." Mrs. Lovato was recalling her years in New Mexico as well as Colorado, although one of her greatest chores was the raising of Ernie Medina until he was 9 and she was 19. "He was more my responsibility than my grandmother's. I raised him for nine years." Linda said proudly.

"I spanked him too, because grandmother never would. She thought the world of him. She just couldn't bring herself to punish him. But grandfather was very strict. Grandfather had very high principles. His reputation meant more to him than anything in the world," Mrs. Lovato continued in impeccable English with no trace of a Spanish accent.

There was always a strong attachment between brother and sister in that home of so many children where the only adults were the elderly grandparents.

In Colorado in those days you were either from the landed aristocracy, which means you owned a ranch or had other financial attributes, or you were poor working class. Medina's father was poor working class. He couldn't be around his family much because he had a job setting up camps and cooking for shepherds.

"We seldom saw father," Erlinda recalls, then adds hastily, "but we never lacked for anything. I had a car. I was the only girl in high school who had a car. And we were the only Mexican family on the block. The others were Americans."

It is in that last word, said inadvertently, that Mrs. Lovato reveals the insecurity of the minority group in America. "The others were Americans."

What are you, Mrs. Lovato? A Himalayan? You were born in New Mexico, raised in Colorado, settled in California, married to a man who served his country in World War II. You're at least a third-generation American and in your veins flows the blood of the peoples of the New World long before it mixed with that of the European newcomers. What are you, Mrs. Lovato? What else can you be but an American?

Ernie Medina makes the same slip of the tongue. Ernie Medina, the man whose company was accused of being racist by stupid people who don't understand the meaning of words, but who pay lip service to a political dogma called Liberalism that they can mouth but do not practice in their personal lives. Ernie Medina accidentally gives himself away.

Ernie Medina remembers the Morgan School in Montrose that he attended from kindergarten to sixth grade. "One day it was over a luncheonette, the next day it was next to the firehouse." It was a segregated school. The kids were all Mexicans."

Medina gets touchy talking about such things because Ernie Medina is an officer in the United States Army. He has been integrated. He has arrived. He is as American as apple pie or hominy grits—or tequila. But it wasn't always like that.

"Sure there were places in Montrose that didn't serve Mexicans," Medina concedes, "but I never had that problem. It was in the '40s when I was growing up. There was World War II, and a lot of attitudes were changing. I lived on the Southside across the street from the high school. All the other kids were Americans."

There goes that word again. "All the other kids were Americans." Ernie Medina is interrupted as he reminisces about his childhood. What does he mean that all the other kids were Americans? And what is he, a Mongolian?

Medina laughs, a little self-consciously, a little in embarrassment, a little in annoyance at himself. He tries again. "The neighborhood I lived in, it was . . . what do you want me to call it . . . white people?"

Medina becomes embarrassed. That's not the term

either. "They were non-Mexicans," he says with finality.

Ernie Medina wanted so badly to be an American. If Ernie Medina didn't understand prejudice and the closed mind of the racist and the hypocrisy of white America, then Martin Luther King was the secret leader of the Ku Klux Klan.

Medina attended the Montrose Junior High School and went on from there to the Montrose County Senior High School, and he went in for boxing, basketball, wrestling, football and acting in the school plays. "I did everything I could," he says. He was a Boy Scout and an Explorer Scout, he sold newspapers, he shined shoes, he worked with leather, he ran a lemonade stand.

"Oh, he tried everything," Linda remembers with a smile. "In high school he was always trying."

He tried working in the rodeo, Mrs. Lovato recalls. "But he came out ahead of the horse one day and that ended his career as a cowboy," she said, still laughing over the idea of her brother, the wild-West star.

But even before high school, Erlinda remembers, her brother was a driver, worker, leader. "He always had a way with boys. He would talk; his friends would do the chores. He did the talking; they did the work."

Ernie had a little girl friend when he was nine years old. It was the type of small-town friendship that would endure even into his army days when both were happily married and had families of their own. Actually, Medina was close with both Danette Hilliard and her brother Howard. But Howard, said Mrs. Lovato, didn't like a girl hanging around and would always invent tricks to get rid of his sister.

Ernie was protective of Danette. "He didn't want her hurt," Mrs. Lovato said, so he would always tip her off to the tricks her brother was planning. One day, Howard dug a hole and covered it, camouflaging it neatly so it would be a trap into which he wanted Danette to fall. Ernie knew about the plot, and his dilemma was that he was a close friend of both the brother and the sister. What should he do?

He tipped off Danette but made her promise to go through with her brother's plan to entice her to walk over the trap and fall in. "Act surprised when it happens," were Ernie's words of advice.

And Danette went through the whole scene. She even wore her new white dress and her new shoes, because her brother had expected that. Then she came to the hidden hole and carefully, she let herself fall into it.

"Oh, did her mother have a fit," Mrs. Lovato laughed.

From as far back as he could remember, Ernie Medina had been fascinated by the military. Part of it undoubtedly came because he was growing up in the war years in an exceptionally patriotic nation and in a small western town that was even more so. And part of it undoubtedly was because the military represented the United States to this boy torn between two American cultures, and so eager to prove that he was part of the country into which he was born.

And part of it undoubtedly was because Jerry F. Medina, one of the young relatives living with Ernie's grandparents in Montrose, had joined the old depression-days CCC, a quasi-military, make-work program. Later he switched to the Army; during the war he was in the Army Air Corps and now is a retired Air Force warrant officer.

To work for the United States Government—even better, to be an officer in its armed forces was to grandfather Joe Medina's mind, as it was to the minds of millions of immigrants in America at that time, the highest of attainments, on a par even with being the President of the United States. Jerry Medina was always used as the example in the Medina clan. Ernie's grandparents had raised Jerry and would always point to their pride-and-joy and say: "Look what Jerry did. Why don't you study hard like Jerry? Why don't you become like Jerry?"

"My grandparents didn't speak much English," Ernie Medina recalls. "They hadn't gone to high school themselves. Their only guidance was for me to be good, to study hard and to keep a good name.

"I think the proudest thing that ever happened to my grandfather was when I joined the Army. He could point with pride and say 'My grandson is in the Army. My grandson works for the American government.'"

Ernie always had a thing about the army, even when he was a little kid. One time, remembers Mrs. Lovato, they were having a Fourth of July celebration over at the National Guard armory and Ernie wanted to get in to see the soldiers. So he and Danette decided they were going to bake a cake and bring it to the soldiers and that's how they would get in. "I baked them the cake," Mrs. Lovato said, and they got in and they talked to the soldiers.

The Medina grandparents were very devout Catholics and this rubbed off on all the children in the household. Ernie was an altar boy at St. Mary's R. C. Church from the time he was in fifth grade until he was 16.

These were the World War II and Korean War years, and Ernie remembers once when the body of a soldier came home from a far-off battle front and there was a combined military funeral and Catholic service held at his church.

There was something that grabbed Ernie during the moving ceremony, especially out at the cemetery. It was listening to the mournful sounding of Taps by the army bugler, and the three volleys fired over the casket of the deceased hero, and the gentle folding of the American flag by the escort officer, who then handed it to the widow, and it all got to Ernie and he knew that one day he would be a soldier himself.

Who knows what it was that made him feel this way. The Army, after all, does offer a home to the homeless, security to the insecure, a mission and a purpose in life, and an opportunity to serve not only one's fellow man but one's country. Maybe it sounds corny and unsophisticated and probably a little naive to express such thoughts today, but those were the forties when a nation was fighting for its life on the battlefield, just as a few short years before it had been fighting for its economic life during the great depression, which left one third of the country hungry and the whole country marked by the indelible scar of insecurity.

The army represented a safe haven, a form of security, to a man, just as a ship represents home to a transient seafarer and as the church represents love and security to the restless religious man.

At one time Ernie Medina thought seriously of becoming a priest, so it was understandable that he would think too of becoming a soldier.

Perhaps Ernest Medina expressed his feelings most vividly once when he told a friend, almost inadvertently, while trying to describe his youth, "It was a happy childhood." He hesitated, then added, "Other than not having a father or mother."

But this is not to suggest that Medina was an unhappy, lonely boy. How can you be lonely, growing up in a household with at least a dozen other children around. And while Montrose might have been somewhat aloof to Mexicans, neither Medina nor his sister indicate that it was unfriendly. Indeed his childhood friendships remained through his adult life. He still remembers fondly the Ponsford family. Mr. and Mrs. Harry Ponsford now live in Tucson, Arizona, but then had a hardware store in Montrose.

"Mr. and Mrs. Ponsford took me under their wing," Medina remembers. "They would take me on family outings. I was like a second son. And they would give me guidance and counsel, too." When he graduated from high school, Ernie went to work in the Ponsford hardware store as a Culligan man, selling water softener.

After Medina's troubles in Vietnam were splashed

across the pages, a newsman interested in his background sought an interview with him. The captain agreed only after receiving approval from his attorney, F. Lee Bailey. That was because the Army, in its questionable wisdom, had clamped a lid on all interviews with members of Company C on the grounds that it would be prejudicial to the GIs should they be court-martialed for the tragedy at Mylai (4).

The weakness in the military reasoning, of course, was that they had closed the bag after letting out the cat. The story of Mylai (4) in all its horror had already been told. Now, as writers sought to find out what kind of men these soldiers were, the army refused the researchers permission. Were these soldiers men—or monsters as press stories indicated? Nobody knew, and the army wasn't saying.

But Medina agreed to an interview, with his attorney's permission. However, he requested the reporter not come to his home at Ft. Benning, Georgia, where he was living in a state of limbo, not yet a prisoner of the Army but about to become one. Ernie Medina didn't want his three young children to be aware of what was happening. Later, when the reporter was invited to his home, Medina made him promise to allow himself to be introduced as an old friend of the family, not as a newsman seeking information on the sensational story of Mylai (4).

In the beginning Medina traveled to a motel room outside the vast Ft. Benning establishment. Here, after removing his beribboned jacket, the powerfully built Army officer would reminisce about his childhood.

When told that the men of Charlie Company, even his critics, spoke well of Capt. Medina the army officer, he mumbled something like: "That's too bad. I didn't want them to love me. I was deliberately rough on them for their own good. I wasn't trying to be popular."

Of course he is right. No good leader, especially one whose men may be expected to follow him to their deaths, can expect to win popularity contests. That was the difference between a professional like Medina and an amateur fresh out of OCS school.

Michael Bernhardt, a member of Medina's company and one of the captain's critics, once was asked whether he thought 2d Lt. William Laws Calley, Jr., a platoon leader in Charlie Company, was a good officer. Bernhardt said he didn't think Calley was a good officer, nor did he think the young lieutenant was capable of keeping his platoon functioning. Well what kept Calley's 1st platoon together, Bernhardt was asked.

"I figure the platoon was held together more by just the mystical presence of Capt. Medina," Bernhardt answered. "When he wasn't there he even seemed to be there."

Richard Hendrickson today can't see, can hardly hear and is barely able to walk as a result of the wounds he suffered in Vietnam with Charlie Company. But he swears by the man who led him.

"As far as I'm concerned he was a great guy. I like what he stood for. He'd risk his neck as much as we risked ours. He took care of us," Hendrickson said.

That was Medina, always concerned over the welfare of others. "He took care of us" were the words echoed or the thought expressed over and over again by the men in his command. He was the last to eat in the field and he made sure his men got at least one hot meal a day, no matter where they were. He drove them hard, but he demanded that they be cared for properly in the way of clothes and as much creature comfort as a man in the field could have.

Ernie Medina was loyal and preached loyalty. His "mystical presence" cemented a company of individualists into a fighting team, cast into alien surroundings to fight a guerrilla war for which the United States was not prepared. Medina forged a counter-guerrilla force. The whole world could be against them but Charlie Company knew that they could trust each other.

"The guys got along. We were all for one and one for all.
But I think what made that company was Capt. Medina,"
Hendrickson reflects.

Medina thinks back to his small-town upbringing, to the
times he went hunting and fishing, to the picnics and the
outings and to the many extracurricular activities in
which he was engaged. "Good grief, I was always busy."
A smile came over the worried countenance of the infantry officer; then he thought for a moment. "Everything I
did, I did myself. Everything I got, I got myself."

Ernie Medina, the little boy in the big land of opportunity, didn't covet riches or fame. His world would be
one of service, service to his country. Maybe, that's corny,
but not the way Medina explained it.

"When you live in a small town, it's different than the
big city.

"I can remember a wall and on the wall a plaque with
the names of all the men who were in World War II and
Korea. I remember Veterans Day and Armed Forces Day
and the parades and all. It was a patriotic town, Montrose," Ernie Medina recalls nostalgically. "There was
just a lot of patriotism there. During World War II we had
a victory garden; a lot of families had victory gardens.

"On Armistice Day the church would have a service.
And then the American Legion and the VFW would get
out and have a ceremony. And they would lay a wreath in
the canal for the Navy dead too. They would lay a wreath
in the canal that went by the cemetery.

"Good grief, I remember we used to have a rodeo once
a year. And everybody who could walk would participate.
The flags would be out in front of all the stores. There was
a lot of flag-waving patriotism in our town. I guess you
don't see that any more.

"And every Friday night our whole family would go
down to the court house to listen to the concert. Everybody in town went to the court house on Friday night to
listen to the band. Good grief, where could you find a

concert by a high-school band with amateur musicians where everybody in town would go down to listen." Ernie Medina remembers the simpler days of America.

When he was 16 and a high-school junior, Ernie joined the National Guard. He had to lie about his age to get in, but the military was his thing and it was time to get started. He attended weekly meetings and summer programs, beginning first as a radio operator, although he couldn't handle the set because he was too small and the 65-pound pack he had to carry was too heavy. So he became a cook, and then went into heavy weapons, but mostly he used to march with the color guard in parades and at football games.

However, Ernie was serious about the national guard and by 19, one year after graduating from high school, he had risen to the rank of E6, one step from the top for enlisted men. He had also been sent to Ft. Benning, Georgia, to attend the advanced heavy-weapon NCO course.

After graduating from high school, Medina went to work in the forestry service, then he was a yardman for a lumber company, and of course he was the Culligan man at Ponsford's hardware store. He also worked for Gerald Dome as a soda jerk in the town's popular Busy Corner Drug Store and he was a cashier at a Safeway grocery store.

But Ernie Medina knew what he wanted to be ever since he was a child, and in 1956 he joined the Army.

"My grandfather was so proud when I joined the Army," Medina, the captain in trouble, remembered. And if you're a first-generation American fighting for your place in this society you could understand the pride.

Once in the army, Ernie Medina, the perfectionist, started all over again. He wanted none of the rank he had earned with the National Guard. He wanted to make his own way, so he started as an E2, just one step above recruit.

But Ernie Medina was cut out for army life and there was no stopping him. He took his basic at Ft. Carson, Colorado, where he was made a heavy-weapons squad leader, and then he was shipped out to Germany just as the Hungarian revolution broke. From there he was rushed to the Czechoslovakian frontier as a member of the 28th U.S. Infantry Regiment of the 8th Infantry Division. Then he was transferred to the 2d Brigade of the 12th Infantry and transferred from Heilbron, Germany, to Baumholder, then to Fuerstenfeldbruck.

Ernie rose quickly in the Army, becoming an E5, which is a staff sergeant, by his 21st birthday.

He bought himself an old 1939 Mercedes and would wander Germany, "staying off the GI path," and visiting, instead, monasteries and churches and learning about the German people. He learned German too, so that today he can boast that he speaks, besides his native English, German, Spanish and "altar-boy Latin." He remembers once picking up a hitchhiking German soldier who invited the American sergeant to his home on a farm.

Then he met Baerbel, a tall, willowy, blonde German secretary from Leiman, near Heidelberg, and Ernie Medina was in love.

At about the same time, Medina was offered the chance to take an examination for West Point. He turned it down.

"I was in love. Going to West Point then would have meant staying single for the next six years," Medina explains. Instead Medina married and seven years later, when he was offered the opportunity to go to Officers Candidate School, he accepted.

Back to Ft. Benning he went and, after graduating with honors as a battalion commander of his cadet class, Medina was made an instructor at OCS for two years, then assigned to Hawaii as an assistant staff-planning officer (S-3) with the newly forming 11th Infantry Brigade. Then he was moved up to division planning officer

(G-3) with the Americal Division, but what any young officer wants is his own command. And on December 19, 1966, Ernie Medina was named commanding officer of Charlie Company.

★ ★ ★

CHAPTER VI

CALLEY

★ ★ ★ ★ ★ ★ ★ ★ ★ ★ ★ ★ ★ ★

"Calley tried to be a junior Medina."

MICHAEL TERRY
A member of Charlie Company

"Medina . . . could trust the company to all junior officers but Calley."

MICHAEL BERNHARDT
A member of Charlie Company

★ ★ ★ ★ ★ ★ ★ ★ ★ ★ ★ ★ ★ ★

Robert Joel Van Leer, who stands six feet, three inches tall, remembers when Lt. William Laws Calley, Jr., who stands five feet, three inches tall, joined Charlie Company. It was in September 1967, the same month that Calley had been commissioned a second lieutenant in the United States Army. It was about two months after Van Leer had reported to the 11th Brigade and had been assigned as a private in Charlie Company.

At that time Medina already was there and Van Leer remembers there was a Negro lieutenant who was one of the platoon leaders. He also remembers being afraid of Medina. That was his first reaction.

"He was stern. I was afraid of him. I was afraid of my father, too," young Van Leer recalls of Medina.

Calley reported into the training room of Charlie Company, a ramrod-stiff little lieutenant, immaculately attired in his new officer's uniform, looking almost like a toy soldier because of his size and the perfection of his dress. "Calley seemed sharp as a whip to me the way he dressed and the way he carried himself," Van Leer remembers. "When I first saw him, I combined him and Medina both as the same type person."

Others who knew them have also remarked about the similarity between the two. It wasn't their looks. Medina is short and stocky, and handsome in a rugged way. Calley is shorter, but slight and handsome in a cute way. It was perhaps that Calley aspired to be what Medina was, a professional soldier, self-sufficient, capable and knowledgeable. Calley, from all indications, wasn't any of these things, but apparently tried to become what some soldiers would later describe as a "junior Medina."

Months after he had had an opportunity to observe the lieutenant, Van Leer decided that "Calley was not as good as Medina.

"Calley was a hard-nosed little man who made his share of mistakes and Medina cursed him out," Van Leer was to recall, echoing but understating the opinion of other members of the company.

There were some men in the company who thought that because of his size and slight build Calley had the classic Napoleonic complex of the little guy. But Van Leer disagrees.

"I used to think his height was a complex," Van Leer says. "But really he was just average and he wanted to be above average." And that's probably the best one word description of William Laws Calley, Jr.—average, an average American, a very average American.

"That's why he became an officer. He should have been an enlisted man. But to be above average he had to be an officer," Van Leer said, emphasizing the word "had." "He strived to be outstanding."

Van Leer thought Calley hero-worshipped Medina, that

the lieutenant set up the captain as an idol whose image
he coveted. "Calley respected Medina a hell of a lot and
Calley was looking for a goal. The goal was to be better
than average. And Captain Medina was better than average," Van Leer once observed.

Putting it another way, Van Leer explained: "The other
lieutenants would have tried to climb a wall because of
their respect for Medina. But Calley would have tried
harder." Yet try as he would and hard as he tried, Calley
didn't seem to hit it off with his commanding officer—or
for that matter with his troops.

According to members of Charlie Company, Medina
was always yelling at Calley. The young lieutenant apparently had difficulty reading field maps and was getting
himself and his men lost in the woods during the training
period in Hawaii. Or Medina would tell Calley to carry
out a maneuver one way and the lieutenant would decide
to do it his own way, which might be described as showing
initiative, but which apparently was the wrong thing to
do.

If Medina was the most respected officer in the company, then Calley was the least liked man, although the
young lieutenant tried hard to pattern himself after the
captain.

"He tried to do what Medina would like," Terry remembers, adding, however, that "Calley was unpopular with
the troops. He was willing but he really didn't know a
whole lot. Maybe it was something you sense. They didn't
have confidence in him. He wasn't a model leader."

Apparently one of the lieutenant's faults was that he
was too GI. Unlike Medina, Calley tried going by the book,
and if there was one thing this company didn't like it was
the book.

Calley, who ended up leading the first platoon, never
got along too well with his platoon sergeant, Isaiah Cowan, a bible-carrying black master sergeant who was
well liked by the men. But Tom Partsch remembers that

before Calley took over the first platoon he had the second platoon, and couldn't get along with his sergeant there either.

The platoon sergeant of the second was Jay A. Buchanon, a veteran of almost 20 years in the army, described by the men as a good leader, particularly in combat. Buchanon had a deep booming voice that the men remember could be heard for miles.

"He was an old colored man," recalls Van Leer," and we had no respect for him in Hawaii. But under combat conditions he would run from a secure position to help others by putting himself in a position of being shot."

"The whole platoon didn't like him in Hawaii," another soldier recalls of Buchanon. "But in Vietnam opinions changed. He stuck up for the guys getting in trouble."

"Calley," says Tom Partsch flatly, "was dumb and you couldn't tell him nothing. Buchanon wouldn't tell him anything because he knew Calley was dumb. The squad leaders would tell him and he'd say 'I'm the lieutenant.'"

Of all the members of Charlie Company, Calley seems to be the least known and the most universally disliked. A Miamian, Calley flunked out of junior college in his freshman year, getting four Fs, two Cs and a D. But his official Army statement of service credits him with one year of college.

He lived with his mother, father and three sisters in the El Portal section of Miami, which was a well-to-do, upper-middle-class residential area of homes ranging in the $30,000 to $40,000 class. A neighbor remembers that Calley had his own den, a "little sitting room" she called it, with a television set, books, assorted trinkets and souvenirs, where he could go to study. There were also, she remembered, little banners from football games. The den was set aside from the rest of the house.

William Thomas, dean of boys at Edison, perhaps knew Calley better than most teachers there. The youngster, called Rusty by his friends because of his reddish hair, was a student volunteer who "ran errands" for Thomas. Being a monitor or volunteer for the dean of boys, Thomas explained, was holding an "in" position in the school from a student's point of view. Thomas' office was a seat of student power or prestige at Edison High School.

"He could have been a messenger for others," Thomas explained, but the most power was in the dean of boys' office. "Volunteers are more popular," among other students, he said, and the dean added that "Calley was responsible. If you had a job to do, he'd do it."

Calley moved with the swingers and the operators and the wheels of the school, Thomas said, because the youngster also was a member for two years of the popular Mike and Masque Club. This was supposed to be a dramatic club. Its purpose, as listed in the 1962 high-school yearbook, was "Service with the development of dramatic talent." In practice, however, it was a social organization. A student had to perform a skit as part of the entrance requirement and had to be voted into the club. But once in, members of Mike and Masque seemed more devoted to fun than to theater.

Still it wasn't an easy group to join and those who belonged to it were "in." "The fact that Rusty was a member would indicate that he was accepted by his friends," Thomas said.

Rusty Calley belonged to Mike and Masque in his second and third years of high school according to the year book. Somehow he vanished from the extracurricular scene in his senior year, without explanation.

Despite his size, Calley's friends insist he had no hangups over his slight, small build. "This kid was so nice there wasn't anything wrong with him. He had no reason to have any complex," remembers Mrs. Sharon Hobbs Thorpe, who knew Rusty when both were students at Edison.

Mrs. Thorpe's mother and Rusty's mother were friends when the two high-school kids were growing up. The two families lived across the street from each other. A staunch defender of Rusty Calley, Mrs. Sharon Thorpe became angered over an article in the Miami Herald written after the young lieutenant was charged with murdering Vietnamese civilians. According to that article, written by David Nelson and Tom Smith, Calley was described by neighbors as "a character, not a model son." The article also reported that according to neighbors, Rusty wouldn't go to bed without kissing his parents goodnight even when he was a teenager.

A next door neighbor, Mrs. Shirley Zaret, described Rusty Calley as "an ordinary average boy. He was quiet, got into a little trouble and didn't have many friends." Mrs. Zaret also said that Calley liked to play the "tough guy" role, "but he was always respectful to adults."

The article also quoted an official at Palm Beach Junior College as saying that Rusty was "a poor student."

Tracing his history after his one-year college experience, the article noted that Calley worked as a hotel bellhop and a dishwasher before taking a scab job as a switchman and later train conductor for the Florida East Coast Railway. Calley's employment record with the railroad, according to the article, "shows several negative markings, including tardiness and failure to fill out required forms. He picked up 15 demerits when he permitted several cars to run free from an engine, hitting a loading ramp." As a train conductor, Calley was twice involved in weird situations that made the newspapers. He was arrested in 1964 for blocking traffic in downtown Fort Lauderdale at 5 train crossings for 22 minutes. Three months later he did it again, this time for 55 minutes. He was acquitted both times.

Summing Calley up, the article observed, "The Miamians who knew Rusty Calley, who watched him grow up, all agreed on one point: He was a well-mannered, respectful boy who did what he was told to do."

Mrs. Thorpe objected to the Miami Herald article in a

letter to the editor questioning the neighbor's observations that Calley was "a character, not a model son," "tough guy," and other comments she considered derogatory. Wrote Mrs. Thorpe: "Rusty was and still is a well-mannered young man who associated with peers of an equally good background." She questioned the right of the press to delve into Calley's school and work records and family affairs. And she ended the letter by praising Calley as a patriotic American "fighting to help the Vietnamese."

In return she received a rather nasty letter from David Nelson, the Herald reporter. "Dear Sharon Hobbs Thorpe," he wrote, "I was thoroughly disgusted after reading your letter of November 17, 1969. Not only was it flawlessly written, but it flawlessly displayed the kind of ignorance and stupidity on the part of a large segment of society which only helps keep things screwed up.

"It is beyond my imagination how you arrive at the conclusion that a man charged with killing between 100 and 500 Vietnamese civilians is helping those same people.

"Also, I might point out that Lt. William L. Calley, Jr., led those gallant men through 'Pinkville.' He gave the orders.

"However, I cannot bring myself to condemn you for making an obviously human mistake in terms of both perspective and judgment."

That same eveing, however, the reporter had second thoughts and wrote Mrs. Thorpe a second note offering to interview friends of Calley. "It seemed to me the problem in presenting a true picture of Rusty, balanced and in perspective, was simply that when the big news broke, people sharing your viewpoint didn't make themselves or their thoughts known to news media," Nelson wrote. He asked Mrs. Thorpe to get friends of Calley together so he could do a second story.

A second story, based on interviews with Calley's high-school friends did appear in the Miami Herald and was a more sympathetic study of the boyhood of the young lieutenant charged with mass murder. But sympathetic or not, the picture that emerged of Rusty Calley, as painted by his friends, wasn't too different from the portrait developed by his neighbors in the first article. And in subsequent interviews with members of Charlie Company and other neighbors, teachers and friends, which I conducted, similar patterns of the original painter's brush were discernible.

The page-one headline of the word portrait of the young Miamian in the second story that splashed across all eight columns of the Herald read, "Rusty Calley: The Man Remains a Mystery." And a mystery is what Rusty Calley appeared to be to everyone who attempted to know him —his friends, his teachers, the soldiers who served with him and those who loved him, perhaps even his family.

Calley, the article revealed, had an ulcer in 1962 at the age of 19, and a 1Y draft deferment, generally given for medical reasons. That would be the year he went to junior college, from which he flunked out.

At this time, tragedy struck the Calley family. They had lived in a lovely white stucco home in a fashionable part of Miami, just across from Miami Beach. By 1964, Calley's mother was dying of cancer. His father had become ill with diabetes and had also come on hard times financially. The family, which in addition to its Miami home owned a boat and a summer place in Waynesville, North Carolina, had lost everything. They moved to the wooden cabin in Waynesville. Calley stayed behind working for the railroad.

But in 1965 he bought himself a brand new car and headed west to California. He dropped from sight and soon a rumor spread that Calley was dead as a result of his ulcer condition. However, he ended up in Albuquerque, New Mexico, where he enlisted in the regular army on July 26, 1966. He was an enlisted man for about one year, then was appointed to Officer Candidate School and was commissioned a second lieutenant on Sept. 7, 1967. That same month he was assigned to Hawaii to join Charlie Company.

Calley had enlisted one month before his mother's death. Perhaps the rumor of his death was mixed up with his mother's passing away. The point is his friends accepted the rumor of Calley's death and apparently nobody attempted to confirm it—or showed any interest. As far as his friends in Miami were concerned, William Laws Calley, Jr., died in 1965.

Then, near Christmas 1968, he suddenly reappeared. He arrived in Miami attired in Army fatigues, called his friends and was joyfully invited to a Christmas party that same day. It is unclear why he wore fatigues, since no one in service, particularly if he is on leave, would wear his work clothes while traveling. Indeed, in this war servicemen don't even wear their dress uniforms if it can be avoided.

Meanwhile, Calley's father and youngest sister, Dawn, had returned to Miami and were living in a trailer camp in Hialeah. But Calley didn't spend much time with his family. However, he seemed in good spirits and gave no indication of any concern over the Mylai affair, which still was unknown publicly and had happened in March of that year.

The folks back home always described Calley as a cheerful happy kid, but the pictures that appear in the high-school yearbook all show him unsmiling—one might almost say sad. But everyone says that he didn't seem to have any hangups as a teenager. He was one of the smartest, most fashionable of dressers, he had a car in high school and he liked to tinker with it and to go to the auto races. In short, Calley was average. That's the term Thomas uses. It's the term almost all who knew him use to describe him.

"He was average," Thomas said. "But did he realize it?

In high school he had acceptance, but it could have been insecure to him." When Thomas was told that Calley had once been described as a man who would climb a wall to please Capt. Medina, the high-school dean showed no surprise.

"Climb a wall? It doesn't surprise me," said Thomas. "He would lean over backward to please someone he respected. He was seeking acceptance. He never quite knew he had it."

Carter once made a similar observation about his platoon leader. Carter, a tough little kid who stood five feet, six inches and knew the ways of the street, always felt he was envied by Calley. There were times, said Carter, when Calley seemed to outdo himself in an effort to win acceptance by the enlisted men, particularly the so-called tough guys.

"Calley was trying to get our friendship. He thought I was tougher than he. I believe, in Calley's earlier life, everything he did in his neck of the woods was best. Now he found guys who could outdo everything he could name," Carter said.

Doc White, made a similar observation. "Calley was a yes-man. He liked to show off to me."

According to White, the men did not have a "spontaneous" respect for Calley. "He tried to be buddy-buddy with the men—and just couldn't make it."

White also said Medina would always yell at Calley. "Calley had to be prodded sometimes. Like sometimes he couldn't make it up hills. Medina was forever on Calley's tail. The guy was not performing. He was either lagging behind or he was too far ahead or he was late to meetings."

Calley seemed to get along well with girls back in Miami. He was considered cute and a gentleman. One girl remembers back in her high-school days when Calley took her out Christmas Eve to the fashionable Eden Roc. Then, right after the dinner was placed on the table, she became ill. He paid for the dinner and left. That's all there was to it.

Rusty apparently had one steady romance while in high school, with a girl named Pat, who is now married, has two children of her own and has left Miami. Pat still is a very attractive, short, dark-haired young woman, with a slim, girlish figure. She fondly remembers her "childhood sweetheart." Pat is a serious and religious young woman and Calley was her "first love," she recalls. To her it was a serious romance and it might well have been to him. His ulcer came after their breakup.

Pat was about a half inch taller than Calley and six months older, and was a senior at Edison when Calley was a junior at the time they first met. She explained Calley lost a year of school because of time he had spent in the Georgia Military Academy. Pat met Rusty when she was going with another boy whom she described as "a real good friend" of Calley's. She found herself attracted to Rusty because he was "soft-spoken, friendly and had pretty eyes."

"He talked a lot. He was always happy. He always had a smile on his face and he got me out of bad moods," Pat remembered.

She said Calley would be late many times on dates, which made her angry. He would explain he was out with the boys. But he would always talk her out of her anger. "He'd have me laughing before we got in the car," she remembered.

The couple went steady in November and December of 1960 and in January and part of February 1961, then decided to date other people. But in April they were back together again and Calley took Pat to the main high-school functions of the season, including the senior prom. Pat graduated that June of 1961; Calley still had a year to go. In the summer of 1961, she remembers, he went to work as a construction man for an uncle in either Boca Raton or Pompano, Florida.

But the two sort of broke up. In September Pat went on to Florida Christian College, a school run by the Church of Christ and described as having "a strong religious atmosphere." Pat was very religious and belonged to this denomination, which held services on Wednesdays and Sunday nights.

When they were going steady Pat would try to get Rusty to come to church with her but she said he refused. Instead he would meet her after church on Sunday nights and have ice cream. They would also go out on Friday or Saturday nights, never both. Her parents wouldn't permit it.

"We'd have conversations on the Bible, but he liked to argue about it. He teased me about it," Pat said.

Pat saw Rusty again during the Christmas vacation of 1961 but she was already engaged to the man she would soon marry, a fellow student at the college. Their breakup was amicable.

"I think I was more in love with him than he with me. He was too young. There was a lot ahead for him. He was very carefree. I guess he had a lot of living to do," Pat remembers. She remembers that the Calley family was "close. They didn't want for anything but I wouldn't consider them wealthy. Rusty went to football games with his parents, and his sisters were crazy about him."

Although it had been about eight years since Pat had been Rusty's steady, she still remembered him fondly and laughingly told of how her husband kidded her for knowing a man who had become "famous." Remembering Calley, Pat said "I don't think he had ambitions or goals. He fooled around a lot in the Mike and Masque Club. He enjoyed that. But I don't think he really had ambitions then. He never talked of why he went in and out of military school."

Pat candidly says she would have liked to keep dating Rusty but she doesn't think she would have married him. "I didn't want to marry Rusty because he wasn't a member of the Church. I don't think I'd ever marry anyone who wasn't a member of the Church," she explained.

When Pat came home from her first year at college in the summer of 1962, her aunt told her Rusty had called to ask if she was coming back for the Easter vacation. She wasn't. "It was the last I heard of him," she remembers.

It was in 1962 that Calley was supposed to have developed his ulcer.

But Pat did ask about him and heard he was working for the railroads. And, she concedes, "It seemed like I heard something about him dying."

Pat says she thinks Rusty broke up the romance because he was afraid "it was getting too serious. I would have just liked to have kept on dating him." Rusty was the only boy her parents approved of, Pat remembers. "And my father was pretty particular."

When he'd call to take her out, "he was nice to me and sweet to them. He'd come in the house and if I wasn't ready he'd go out and talk to my parents and clown with my mother and ask about their bicycle shop." Pat's father operated a bicycle repair shop. The couple would go to a movie or out to eat or to a party, and Rusty was always gentle.

"We would pet a little, but not much; not as much as most people. We'd kiss and things like that but he wouldn't go too far. He respected me too much for that," Pat remembers. "He was my first love. I think he liked me a lot, but I don't think he was in love with me."

Pat says the girls always liked Rusty Calley.

"He was cute. I liked his eyes. He was nice, sweet, considerate. He would always open the door for me. He was always polite. He never cursed. He never tried anything with me. He never got rough.

"A lot of boys smart-talk about their girls; cut their girls down. I don't think he did that to me," Pat said.

Pat concedes that she would give Calley a bad time. But she thinks it was because she was in love with him and he wasn't serious about it. But he never got angry.

"I'd pick on him a lot about being late, about being with the guys a lot. I guess it was because he wouldn't go steady. He just told me he wasn't ready to settle down. That he liked me and wanted to date me steadily but didn't want to go steady. I told him I loved him and he said it back, and I don't think he meant it. I liked him a lot and tried to get him to settle down," Pat recalled.

The first time the couple broke up, it was because Calley thought things were getting too serious and broached the subject with Pat. But when they were separated, she remembers, "we missed going out with each other. So he called up and we started going together again."

In school, said Pat, Rusty was "obedient and respectful. He was not really a leader but I wouldn't say he was a follower either. I always felt he could do a lot with his life. When we talked about things he always had an opinion."

She doesn't know what happened to the Rusty Calley who was a kind, considerate, gentle, average boy, respectful to his elders and who never took advantage of girls. "I don't think he knew what he wanted. Maybe he wanted to sow wild oats," she guesses. She thinks too that perhaps the death of Calley's mother must have come as a shock to the young man.

Car racing was Rusty's big thing, Pat remembers. He didn't read a lot or play a musical instrument. He didn't seem to have much of an interest in going to college, but she insists college wasn't important to the kids when she was going to high school.

When the stories broke in the papers that Rusty Calley was charged with the murder of 109 Vietnamese, Pat heard about it from her mother, who called her to read the news over the telephone. She couldn't believe it. Not Rusty, the first and only boy she had ever dated seriously until she met her future husband.

"My first reaction was he didn't do it. It's still hard for

me to believe that he did, if it happened at all," she said.

Then, after thinking a while, she added: "I really just don't think he did it, really. It's just hard for me to think that he could have done it. I guess now it's gonna be nailed down to whether he was ordered to do it."

Towards the end of her talk with a writer, Pat hesitantly asked whether the troops under Lt. Calley liked him. When told he wasn't too popular she said: "It's hard to realize. I can't imagine anyone who didn't like him in school."

Then Pat asked whether Rusty had a girl at Ft. Benning, Georgia. When told that the rumor was he sees a girl in Columbus, Pat seemed pleased. "I hope he does. I enjoyed him. He had so much to give. Maybe he should have got married." Then she added, "I'd like to talk to him; to let him know at least I was behind him."

It was difficult getting any of Rusty's other friends to talk about him, particularly after the Miami Herald story. Some of those friends told Time Magazine they would talk for pay but Time would not go along with this.

Calley himself doesn't talk to anyone. His lawyer, George W. Latimer, a former Supreme Court justice in Utah, once considered allowing an interview with Calley, but only for a price. He was turned down.

But apparently some writer did pay the price for an interview because, in the spring of 1970, a prominent paperback publisher in New York was approached and asked if he was interested in buying a book on Calley's life. The publisher turned it down.

Later, however, Calley reportedly did sell his story for a six-figure sum. But it is not known what portion he received and what went to his biographer and legal staff.

Mrs. Zaret, the Miami woman criticized for describing Calley as a loner, became afraid of the press after his friends objected to what she said. She engaged the services of an attorney who apparently advised her not to talk to anyone.

But Dean Thomas still agreed to discuss Calley and so did Mrs. Thorpe, who is terribly hurt over what she considers the bad publicity Calley received in the press.

"The least we can do is stand by our soldiers," Mrs. Thorpe says with some justification. "We send them over there and tell them to be killers, and then we make them all scapegoats."

But the picture that emerges, even from his friends, is that Calley did seem to be strange, if not a loner. And while he got along with his peers, he was no leader. "I think he had leadership ability but he wasn't a leader. He wasn't regarded as one by his friends," Mrs. Thorpe said. And Thomas said the same thing.

"He kind of fit into a little hole. He was an average-type kid, so average," Thomas said. His marks in high school were just average. But under a family order, Calley's records are not available to the public. However, the school principal, William Duncan, said Calley's academic average was C and that the subjects Calley took were debating, Speedwriting and typing, no foreign languages. "He didn't set the world on fire in anything," said Duncan kindly. "He did best in physical education."

"Rusty had status in high school," said Thomas, "but he was not a leader. He was obedient, a follower. He was polite, clean-cut, well-behaved. Among his friends I don't think he was a leader." When Thomas was asked whether he felt Calley was officer material, he answered: "He didn't appear to me to have that type of leadership in high school. He shouldn't have been an officer."

In the debate between Mrs. Thorpe and David Nelson of the Miami Herald, both appeared to be right and wrong.

Mrs. Thorpe was right in feeling that only the worst picture of Calley had been depicted in that first interview. Still, in subsequent interviews and in talks with members of Charlie Company, Calley emerges as something of a loner, a strange man, who did try to act tougher than he really was in the Army and who was a mystery to his own friends.

Nelson, on the other hand, perhaps reflecting the feeling of many newsmen at the time the Mylai story broke, was ready to write off Calley as a murderer, without qualifications.

Herbert Carter, a member of Charlie Company, once expressed the opinion that Calley would have made a great enlisted man but was not officer caliber. Still, the fact Calley strived to be an officer cannot be held against him. And if indeed he was a poor leader, he cannot be blamed for that either. Not everyone is born to lead. The failure, in part, rests with the Army for permitting someone of Calley's caliber to be commissioned. But even the Army cannot be blamed entirely.

For the Army must find its leaders among the manpower made available to it. Apparently the Calley-type officer is the best available currently. College graduates don't go for military careers these days and aren't encouraged even to consider them. The army made do with what it had, and the nation suffered, and society must accept its portion of the blame for what happened at Mylai.

That is why Mrs. Thorpe, despite the righteousness of her cause, is wrong in feeling that the press had no right to probe into Calley's private life. If Calley had been a private citizen then what he did was of no concern to the public—unless it affected the public in some way. But as a commissioned officer of the United States Army, Calley's alleged actions reflected on every American citizen. And whether or not the allegations are proved true, the public has a right to know, indeed a duty to learn, everything about one of its fellow citizens who has accepted the responsibility of representing the United States to the world.

★ ★ ★

CHAPTER VII

PATROLS

★ ★ ★ ★ ★ ★ ★ ★ ★ ★ ★ ★ ★ ★

"Anonymity of the person to be attacked greatly facilitates the releasing of aggressive behavior."

KONRAD LORENZ
On Aggression

"All them villages looked the same to me."

RICHARD PENDLETON
A member of Charlie Company

★ ★ ★ ★ ★ ★ ★ ★ ★ ★ ★ ★ ★

Every unit in the armed forces likes to think of itself as the best damned outfit in the service, and Charlie Company was no exception.

It even had proof that it was good. Not only did it take all those awards in Hawaii, but here it was getting ready to leave for Vietnam with the advance party of the 11th Light Infantry Brigade. The men were in the only infantry company among the 12 in the brigade so singularly honored, and they took this tribute as a sign of recognition for their outstanding achievements in the training field.

But they didn't know the real reason they were selected. Charlie Company was picked not because of its men but because of its commander, Capt. Ernest Lou Medina. Everybody agrees, from the lowliest private to the top-

ranking brass, from his greatest critics to his most ardent
admirers, that Medina was a soldier's soldier when it
came to leading men in the field.

He proved it in Hawaii by welding a fighting force out
of a ragtag collection of draftees. But when the company
was ready to go to war, only about half of its original
personnel were coming along. However, as long as
Medina would be there, the brass felt it had little to worry
about.

The company wasn't told that the reason it was picked
to go to Vietnam first was that a labor force was needed
to do the dirty, menial and backbreaking chores so necessary when a new unit moves overseas to establish itself
on a permanent basis. Lt. Col. Edwin D. Beers, Medina's
battalion commander, said he would have picked any
company, as long as Medina commanded it. The captain
was that good. He could get work out of a dying mule.

"Medina was selected because I considered him the best
company commander," said Beers. "I had to consider the
job and what would be done in the first three weeks [in
Vietnam]."

The 176 men departed Hawaii November 30, 1967, on a
commercial 707 jet chartered from Braniff International
(or Pan American World Airways). The men aren't sure
which. All they recall is that it was a momentary pleas-
antness in an otherwise unhappy situation.

Most armies march off to most wars to the accompani-
ment of brass bands, cheering throngs and waving flags,
giving soldiers about to die some feeling of purpose, or at
least a suspicion that the people are behind them. Charlie
Company left for war with one part of the nation silently
watching, another part prayerfully watching, and a vociferous part, including some national leaders, telling them
not to go.

The men carried their brand-new M-16 rifles, issued
just before they left. They were attired in their new jungle uniforms and they dragged their green duffle bags

behind them. The men had to travel light because they were going by plane. And Doc White remembers that Terry, the devout Mormon, left some of his clothes behind so he could carry a voluminous amount of religious literature that he preferred to take with him.

There was a band playing "My Country, 'Tis of Thee," remembers Carter. "Everybody laughed," he recalls dryly. There were five stewardesses on the plane, two black, two white and one Japanese. "Man, we gave them a rough time," Carter said, with a laugh. "We were a company of hard-nosed infantry, and we were going right from the field to Vietnam. We had no finesse," he explains —proudly.

But Tom Partsch doesn't remember the departure as very much of a big deal, particularly for the lowly enlisted men who sat in the equivalent of tourist class and weren't allowed any of the drinks associated with commercial air travel.

"On the plane, the big brass sat up front. They wouldn't serve us drinks," Partsch says. He was with the second platoon, which was being led at that time by Lt. Calley. He doesn't remember being given any instructions about what the mission of the company would be in Vietnam.

"I don't remember anything about winning hearts and minds," he said. "Calley was supposed to brief us. He didn't say too much. All we were told is when we get over to be ready for action; to secure the 11th Light Infantry Brigade area."

Van Leer also recalls the luxurious trip over—with a tinge of sarcasm. "They sure did have stewardesses and everything," he agrees. "But we couldn't do much. Lipscomb was up in the front seat." He was talking about Brig. Gen. Andy A. Lipscomb, the brigade commander, who was travelling first class with the rest of the brass.

This is the first war where men have been sent off to die eating lobster or steak dinners in de luxe accommoda-

tions aboard commercial jet airliners with pretty stewardesses waiting on them.

The plane stopped in Okinawa where the men, just like
American tourists everywhere, bought postcards to send
home to their families. Then they were taken to Danang,
in South Vietnam, where they arrived December 2, 1967,
although some thought it was December 1 because they
didn't realize they had crossed the international dateline.
"The stewardesses cried when we got off," remembers
Van Leer, still sarcastically. "It was probably SOP with
the airlines: 'All stewardesses will cry as the passengers
debark.' "

Shortly before leaving Hawaii, remembers Van Leer,
the men had heard of an outbreak of rioting in the U. S.
over the Vietnam war. "We wondered. Why fight in Vietnam when they're fighting at home?" he said. And Carter
remembers there was a protest against the GIs going on
in Danang when the company arrived.

"What the hell are we doing here in the first damn
place," he remembers thinking.

Partsch expected a warlike atmosphere when he arrived in Vietnam. Instead, Danang didn't seem any different to him than any military base he had seen at home.
"Everybody walked around just like here," he recalled
after he came home.

Danang was headquarters for I Corps, one of the four
American military areas into which South Vietnam is
subdivided. It is the northernmost of the military subdivi-
sions, bordering on the demilitarized zone that separates
North from South Vietnam. At that time it was under the
control of the U. S. Marine Corps. "We slept in Marine
tents that night," remembers Partsch. "Then we went by
truck to Duc Pho."

The company stopped first at Chu Lai, headquarters of
the Americal Division to which the 11th would be attached. Somewhere along the line they were given a lecture on the pacification program, recalls Widmer.

"We're supposed to be in there helping the people. We're supposed to be their friends and not win them over through brutality." Widmer recalls the lecture with sarcasm. "We didn't buy that line; everyone thought it was a joke. You're in the Army and you resent that. Then you resent the fact you're out there. Right away it was all a big joke."

Of course other planned orientation courses were cut to the bone because of the early arrival of the company. So the only thing they paid attention to was the emphasis that all units there in Vietnam placed on the body count, on killing Viet Cong. As for pacification, the company would rather believe the advice they had heard in Hawaii that cautioned them not to trust any gook.

The philosophy of winning hearts and minds in the daytime and killing gooks at night may have been a little too much to expect from eighth-grade dropouts. But perhaps the Army was counting its blessings. It did have a company that could master the limited requirements of an infantryman. And these men were here right now to build a brigade headquarters. So nobody bothered to indoctrinate the men on the complex purposes of the Vietnam war. It would have taken a whole hitch in the Army to learn that.

Chu Lai would be out of this world as a vacation resort. It is located on the South China Sea and the officers' club is built on a gentle incline coming up from the calm blue waters. If there was a war going on in this area you couldn't tell it in Chu Lai.

But there was a vicious war going on in this area which, including Mylai (4) further up the coast, was part of Quang Ngai province, among the northernmost regions of South Vietnam. It is here in Quang Ngai province that the seat of the rebellion in South Vietnam is located. It was here that the Viet Minh organized to fight the French, and here that the Viet Cong launched their war against Saigon and the Americans, and here that Communist revolutionaries still operate in force. Indeed, the Prime Minister of North Viet Nam, Pham Van Dong, came from Mo Duc, a little coastal town between Duc Pho and Quang Ngai city.

One of the first guerrilla units to form in South Vietnam was organized in the mountains of Quang Ngai province by a peasant now known as Tran Nam Trung, who leads all the Viet Cong in the country and is defense minister of the Communist National Liberation Front in South Vietnam. The people of Quang Ngai province, more than anywhere else in South Vietnam, are the Viet Cong, are controlled by the Viet Cong, are relatives of the Viet Cong, are sympathizers of the Viet Cong or are afraid of the Viet Cong. Certainly, therefore, no one in Quang Ngai province could be described as innocent of the knowledge of the historic Viet Cong presence there, except foreigners. And hardly anyone could be described as a civilian in a region that has seen a total population engaged in war for at least a quarter of a century.

Charlie Company was the only group of innocents in Quang Ngai province.

This peaceful-looking area, made up of rice paddies bounded by the sea to the east and the Annam mountain range to the west, was perhaps the roughest, meanest Communist stronghold in all South Vietnam. To call Quang Ngai province unfriendly is to be diplomatic. The people here hated the Saigon government and its American allies.

Long after the Mylai affair, a South Vietnamese Army general in Danang was asked by a reporter whether he felt the people in that area would turn to Communism as a result of what happened there. "Turn to Communism?" the general asked incredulously. "They are Communists."

Indeed a legend has even developed about women from Quang Ngai province. According to this story, wealthy South Vietnamese women in Saigon will not hire girls from Quang Ngai province as maids unless they could be physically examined. Communist girls, according to the legend, grow no pubic hair.

Of course Charlie Company didn't know any of this because of their vague orientation. One has to have been in the Army to understand the indifference with which indoctrination courses are given and received by GIs. Charlie Company was told something about stopping Communism and preparing for action. And as conventionally trained infantrymen, they were ready for a shoot 'em up, bang-bang type of war. They were not ready for what the Viet Cong had in store for them.

Poor Charlie Company. The enemy they had come to fight had been in the field before most of these kids were born. These little boys had come with their rapid fire M-16 rifles and M-60 machine guns, with grenade launchers and mortars and small artillery pieces, convinced that in a knockdown-drag-out confrontation with the enemy, they would fight well and emerge victorious. In some respects the company had the attitude of a bunch of children. Van Leer even expressed that feeling once when he recalled: "It was all like a game. Here it was just a few short years since I finished playing with toy guns and I had a real one in my hand."

No one could fault the company for their enthusiasm. But they didn't begin growing up until they were knocked down. That's when they realized that the Viet Cong weren't going to give them the opportunity for an eyeball-to-eyeball firefight, the kind they were taught to expect in infantry school.

Why should the VC fight the Americans fair and square when they were outnumbered, outgunned and physically outsized. The VC would use the enemy's strength against him, they would teach the Americans the Vietnamese version of battlefield karate.

When a boy moves to a new block or enters a new school, sometimes the other kids are going to torment him, especially if he is a wise guy or a bully or bigger than

they—until he shows what he can do. They might surround him in the school yard and someone behind him
will slap him on the back of the head, but when he turns
around he'll stare into a sea of impassive faces and he
won't know who did it. And while he tries to figure it out,
some other kid, now behind him, will ping him on one of
his ears. And when he turns in that direction, a third kid
will ping him on his other ear.

And the new boy will be thus tormented by the gang
until he learns his place or loses his cool, until he cries or
just goes into the gang swinging blindly so that they beat
him up—because he has lost his self-control. You just
can't fight a whole gang of kids if you're an unwanted
newcomer. The tormented child may finally put up his
fists to show his manhood and challenge any member of
the group to fight him "like a man," or "fair and square."
And the other kids will laugh or walk away. And the new
kid will have been put in his place.

Charlie Company was the new kid on a strange block.
But the members of the company didn't realize that yet.
They considered themselves first-class infantrymen in an
award-winning company recognized for their skills by
being picked to lead the advance party of the 11th Light
Infantry Brigade to Vietnam. And there was nobody in
their company—no combat veterans—to warn them of
their unrealistic outlook. They were all green. They were
good in theory, but in the cold, hard facts of Vietnam they
were living in a fantasy world. They told each other how
good they were and they came to believe it.

In Duc Pho, Charlie Company was quartered in an old
Korean Army base, and here they met the 3rd Brigade of
the 4th Infantry Division, whom they would relieve. The
4th had been under the command of Maj. Gen. William R.
Peers, who as a lieutenant general one day in the future
would be charged with the investigation of Charlie Company's conduct in an area for which he had once been
responsible.

One of the first moves at Duc Pho was to dispatch Lt. Calley and his second platoon to Qui Nhon, a lovely coastal city where the men remained for three to four weeks guarding the docks and awaiting the arrival of the main body of the brigade and its supplies, which were coming by ship. Qui Nhon seemed to be a fun assignment. Partsch said Calley would "disappear for a week or so. He'd come back drunk or with a can of beer. If you didn't salute him, he'd say you got to salute."

But for the rest of the company Vietnam was no beer bust, not even those first few weeks. It was the job of the remainder of Charlie Company to build the brigade headquarters at Duc Pho. This meant digging and constructing semiunderground bunkers, laying tar paper and sandbags over them, after first filling the sandbags individually by hand, setting up permanent-type tents and mess halls, working without letup in a grueling heat that sometimes sent the mercury bursting through the tops of thermometers. And for a break the men were sent off to guard bridges or the perimeter of the new headquarters. Occasionally they practiced air mobile assaults or went on patrol to nearby hamlets that the GIs called villes or villages.

"Nobody in the company was getting more than a couple hours sleep a day for 18 days," remembers Bob Shivers. The men were shuttled back and forth from where they slept at LZ Bronco to the hill that they were turning into a headquarters.

"We had our own 81-mm mortar section and the 4th division tanks. But the hill was turning into a brigade-size base camp and one company was doing it all," recalls Shivers.

"It was rough. We were going 24 hours a day," agrees Medina.

At night, recalls Medina, there would be some incoming sniper fire, as the VC probed this new unit, testing its strengths and weaknesses, its aggressiveness and defense

capabilities. The VC were taunting the new guy on the
block. But it was only a start. Because, relatively speaking, the first seven weeks in Vietnam were fairly safe for
Charlie Company, even when they went on operations
from nearby LZ Carentan or Fire Base Charlie Brown on
Gilligan's Island, a pleasant coastal spot filled with palm
trees and supplied by barge.

A fire-support base, or fire base, is a forward area, usually of primitive but lasting construction, where an infantry company locates its headquarters section and
weapons platoon and where artillery units are stationed.
The men live in underground bunkers, sleeping on
wooden boards, or if they are lucky, on air mattresses
between their backs and the wooden boards. Some fire-
support bases have mess halls and showers; others do not.
Compared to an infantry division headquarters, a fire-
support base is the front lines; compared to an infantry
company on patrol, a fire-support base is heaven. Other
servicemen may live at modern air bases, artillery bases,
supply bases or naval bases. But the best place an infantryman can expect to see during his year's tour in Vietnam is a fire-support base.

Entertainers, politicians and other visiting firemen
usually never go beyond a fire-support base when they're
in Vietnam, and then come home telling about their tour
of the front lines.

A fire base is called an LZ (for Landing Zone) because
helicopters may land and take off from here. When a
company is on patrol and needs a helicopter to remove a
wounded or dead man or to bring in a replacement or hot
chow, it first must clear an LZ. Vietnam is dotted with
such temporary LZs that mark the paths of infantry companies on patrol. The more permanent ones are at fire-
support bases that can handle many helicopters. LZ
Bronco was a permanent fire-support base. It was headquarters of the 3rd brigade of the 4th infantry division.

While LZ Bronco was kid stuff compared to what was in

store for Charlie Company, the men were understandably nervous their first night there. "We didn't know it was secure," remembers Terry, who despite his harrowing experiences in Vietnam thinks he was most scared that first night because he didn't know any better. "I pulled guard that first night and I kept waiting to be shot at. In the beginning we were all real extra cautious. That first night I hid in the weeds instead of staying in the bunker. I thought it was safer."

Early one morning, remembers Shivers, shortly after the men had arrived in Vietnam, he and some other men who were awake heard noises at their perimeter. The nervous youngsters looked into the first morning light and saw "four or five women" coming towards them.

"One woman had a pole across her shoulder with a sack at the end of it," Shivers recalls. "We had been in the country less than a week," he said, explaining the reason for the nervousness. "We tried to scare them off. We didn't shoot at them but we shot in the air. They didn't run. They just kept coming towards us."

Lt. Col. Frank Akeley Barker, Jr., then the brigade's staff-planning officer (S 3) drove up in a jeep and immediately ordered a squad leader to send two men out to meet the women and keep two men behind with weapons at the ready. The two GIs stopped the women and demanded to look inside the sack. There was a little boy inside the sack, remembers Shivers.

"It was hard to tell his age. I'd say he was about six or seven. His face and his hands were all messed up. It looked like he had been shot with a shot gun. We called Ron Grzesik. He went to interpreter school in Hawaii and could speak Vietnamese. They said the kid had been shot. Col. Barker called for an ambulance and they took him away. It looked to me like the kid had fragmentation wounds," Shivers said.

The story that circulated, and it had a basis in fact the company learned, was that the kid had been trying to set a booby trap and it exploded on him. Hadn't the veterans back in Hawaii warned Charlie Company not to trust anybody in Vietnam, not even kids? Here was proof. How could a kid get all messed up like that if he wasn't playing with fire?

Van Leer also remembers seeing a child "who had his fingers blown off his hand." It may have been the same youngster. It is difficult for members of Charlie Company to remember all events chronologically of a tour in Vietnam that they want to forget and that happened "so long ago." "The talk was that he tried to put together a booby trap," Van Leer says of the child he saw with fingers missing.

The guys began early to look differently on children. They still gave away soap bars and candy and chewing gum, but it wasn't with the same abandon that GIs of other wars have been known to befriend children.

"The guys were told in Hawaii to watch out for kids," remembers Van Leer. Now it appeared as if those warnings were being borne out. "Once we bought cokes from a little girl in Duc Pho," Van Leer said. "Some guy told us only to buy canned cokes, never in bottles. Bottled cokes have ground glass or bamboo shoots in them," that was the warning of veteran combat soldiers.

"Psychologically, at least to me, it meant watch out for children," Van Leer says.

Medina recalls he had heard reports of women and children picking up weapons and running with them. "The Australian advisers said don't trust children." Medina recalled his chats with Aussie soldiers working with the South Vietnamese 2d Division that was responsible for the area in which Charle Company operated. "They ask for candy but all the time they're counting soldiers," Medina said the Aussies warned him.

It must come as a shock to the Western-oriented public that places its children on a pedestal even above its women to hear that little boys and girls can be dangerous.

Long after his Vietnam service, Herbert Carter was talking to an interviewer in a rundown bar in Houston, Texas. Hesitantly he recalled his experiences in Vietnam, a duty which like other members of Charlie Company, he found difficult to discuss. Then suddenly he looked at his interviewer, reflected silently for a moment, and said: "This is a hard thing for a man to say and I shouldn't say it . . . but it's the truth . . ."

Then he hesitated again as if debating whether or not he should make the admission. Then he decided to say it.

"I don't like kids anymore. I can't stand them. I was in a mental hospital in Japan after Mylai. They handed me a doll. I threw it down."

Just before Christmas, 1967, the men had their first experience searching a village, and their first encounter with death—that of a Viet Cong suspect.

"We hit the village in the middle of the night," remembers Van Leer, "and we found a lot of rice there. But the men didn't know enough to look underneath the bin for a false bottom. The men had nothing to go on. There was no ten- or eleven-month vet telling a first-month vet what to do."

The company was awkward, firm but polite, in that first village but they were never quite sure what they were really supposed to do there, a feeling that always seemed to be with them in Vietnam. Suddenly, remembers Van Leer, "someone screamed 'cockadai GI, cockadai.' That meant 'slit your throat GI' in Vietnamese," Van Leer explained. Then whoever was yelling started to run.

"They killed him," remembers the tall, lanky ex-soldier, "and a report went out on the radio that someone had arrogantly told a GI to slit his throat and was killed."

Then the body was searched and the men found they had killed a woman. She had been carrying a sack and the men searched that too. Inside, says Van Leer, they found band-Aids, bandages, gauzes and a hand grenade. "The guys were pretty upset that they killed a woman," Van

Leer remembers. "But on the other hand she was a VC just as much as a man. She had been running from the men, her hair was hidden and she was carrying medical supplies.

"There was a conflict in me that women here are killers. In the U. S. only men go to the wars. Sure we heard about it and were told about it. But to see it is different."

The men left the village; they never did destroy the rice supply. They had done a clumsy job. They were bloodied now and upset. They hadn't done anything wrong, but a life had been taken, a woman's life. But this was a guerrilla war. A guerrilla war involves men, women, children —and babies. The VC set the ground rules for the war in Vietnam—not the Americans.

Sometime soon after their arrival in Vietnam, Charlie Company suffered two mishaps of its own. Two members of the company were accidentally shot. One, remembers Shivers, was cleaning his .45 caliber automatic pistol. He had his middle finger over the muzzle and shot a hole in it. He was sent to Japan for three months. "He got an Article 15 for shooting himself," Shivers recalls the punishment.

In the second incident a rifle accidentally discharged, hitting a soldier nearby. Although it wasn't his fault, the owner of the rifle never got over the accident psychologically, claims Bernhardt.

The rest of the 11th Light Infantry Brigade arrived at Qui Nhon harbor on Dec. 19 and 22 and Charlie Company was permitted to rest. On Christmas day the company had a party at Gilligan's Island, complete with a Christmas tree that Medina had brought from Hawaii. Hobscheid, the company's first sergeant, scrounged up chairs and tables and all the other necessary niceties and the men had a pleasant interlude from the war. Actually it was more like a calm before the storm.

Christmas evening, Capt. Medina sat down and wrote a letter to his sister Erlinda and her family:

25 December, 1967

"Dear Linda, Don & family

"Just a few lines to let you know everything is alright.

"Received your packages, one on the 23rd and one today with your Christmas card, thank you very much for your nice medal, when I left Schofield I packed my gear in such a hurry that I forgot my Sunday missile (sic) and medal, I wasn't sure if it was blessed so I had it blessed today after Christmas mass.

"Cookies are very delicious and were really welcomed, they arrived in good shape.

"The rest of our brigade arrived on the 23rd of December, so my company moved into stand down status for a much needed rest, we held the base camp perimeter for 22 days. The company was spread pretty thin but they did a damn good job.

"Charlie probed our positions at night, tried to take a couple of my bunkers and got his a _ _ kicked trying it.

"Sure didn't seem like Christmas even tho we brought a Xmas tree with us and lights to decorate our mess tent. Had the usual Xmas day dinner with all the trimmings. They even flew in fresh milk (choc + white) and egg nog. Everyone gets plenty to eat.

"The men in the company will greatly appreciate the subscriptions you will send and I think it very nice of your group to do such a thing. If someone gets a book or magazine from home its passed from hand to hand. There's a total of 170 men in my company.

"Hon you don't have to get subscriptions to any particular magazine, anything would be appreciated, paper backs etc. and it don't have to be new issues, however I am sure that there would be no requirement for Ladies magazines (Ha-ha).

"You might stick labels on the things you send, such as:

IN APPRECIATION TO OUR

SOLDIERS FIGHTING IN VIET-NAM

DONATED BY

VFW POST _____

PICO-RIVERA CALIFORNIA

"Oh, by the way there is about 40 men in the company from California.

"Later on I'll write a letter of thanks to your post president. Something else that they sure need is stationary and envelopes (self-sealing type) the heat will stick the other kind together, maybe some of the business groups could help you out.

"Address whatever you send to

Commanding Officer

Company C, 1st Battalion, 20th Infantry

11th Infantry Brigade

Americal Division

APO San Francisco 96217

"You might also check into the possibility of free mail for this purpose.

"You and your lodge members can rest assured that the men will deeply appreciate it, they are a damn good group of men and your efforts will help their morale.

"Well I had better close for now. Hope you all had a Merry Christmas and a Happy New Year.

"God Bless you all

Love

ERNIE"

On January 1, 1968, New Year's Day, Charlie Company entered a new phase in its mission in Vietnam. Task Force Barker was activated and Charlie Company was one of three companies in the brigade picked to be part of this new unit. The new task force was named after

Barker, who would command it. Its mission would be to serve as a counter-guerrilla force in the Viet Cong-infested rice paddies and jungles of Quang Ngai province. The two other companies of the task force were Charlie's old rival in Hawaii, Bravo of the 4th Battalion, 3rd Infantry, and Alpha of the 3rd Battalion, 1st Infantry.

Naturally, the men of Charlie Company were filled with pride once more, this time to be among three companies of the 12 in the Brigade selected for a special mission. Each company was considered the best in its battalion. The reason, again, for the selection of these companies, was less the men in the ranks than their commanders. For their mission as a counter-guerrilla force would place them on almost perpetual patrol. Their commanders would have to be men who could draw blood from a stone.

The men didn't know this.

The men made one combat air assault in the mountains on January 3, remembers Medina, and on January 14 and 15 they conducted helicopter assaults from Gilligan's Island. But nothing ever happened.

"When we first went in the field we were real scared. But they put us where there wasn't too much VC activity for practice," Pendleton remembers.

"We played hide and seek. We'd go away and see their tracks from where we left," Medina recalls the battle of nerves with the VC, during those early days.

Van Leer remembers one of those air assaults in early January. As the men were rushing back to the helicopter, Van Leer tripped and fell on barbed wire. Medina was annoyed. "Get the hell up," the captain yelled at his RTO. Van Leer quickly rose and suddenly Medina was all concern.

"Are you alright, kid? Are you OK?" Medina asked.

"Yes sir," Van Leer said.

"Are you sure?" Medina asked again.

"Medina was a soft hearted person way inside," Van Leer remembers with a smile.

As a member of Task Force Barker, Charlie Company began going out on more and more patrols. Their only problem was they weren't exactly sure what they were supposed to do. They never quite understood what their mission was, except to search and destroy the enemy, kill VC and raise the body count. And as they plunged deeper into the alien surroundings to which their patrols took them, they became more dependent on each other for companionship, for information and for survival.

Even the rest of the Army seemed to be against Charlie Company. When they would return to their fire base from a lengthy patrol, the MPs, the artillerymen, the cooks and the other permanently assigned men there would put Charlie Company to work on dirty details. "The rear echelon treated us like dogs," remembers Bergthold. "They had it made just pulling bunker duty while we had to go out and fight all the time. I didn't like the way they treated us. Like we couldn't even go visit a village. But they could go any time they wanted to."

The infantry, which had long prided itself as the "Queen of Battle," had become a whore in Vietnam, to be used, abused and discarded. Charlie Company was being treated like the mud through which it dragged itself on patrols. Its fellow soldiers in the other branches of the Army were contemptuous of these kids. Bernhardt remembers the company was never issued PX ration cards. The conclusion he reached early was that the Army had no intention of letting Charlie Company out of the field and into the larger towns where PXs were located.

But Charlie Company did what it was told or what it thought had to be done. These were simple soldiers; they always followed orders, humping up and down mountains, sleeping in the rain and hacking through the jungles. Removed from civilization and even its own Army, Charlie Company was becoming America's pitiful answer to the Viet Cong. Except that these kids didn't know what they were doing. They were more a company of sad sacks than elite counter-guerrillas.

"The men came in touch with rice farmers only," observes Van Leer, "and you couldn't tell their feelings." Charlie Company was meeting the inscrutable Oriental —in person.

"Humping up north was hard. I got scars from punching trees," Van Leer says. But the men kept humping the fields and searching the villages because this was all so new and challenging and interesting.

Once, remembers Van Leer, he was climbing the side of a mountain straight up by rope and "Medina was so enthused he took a picture of me while I was coming up. Then he wanted me to take a picture of him."

Medina was the most enthusiastic of all. He was all over and everywhere. He knew what he was doing but apparently never shared his plans with his men. He set the pace, he pushed, cajoled, got angry, threatened and laughed the men into doing his bidding. And they did. And he was satisfied. But the men, who were never gung-ho soldiers to begin with, and certainly had no particular desire to be in Vietnam, gradually lost their enthusiasm as the intensity of their operations continued. And as they grew more tired, their bitterness increased. So did their fears. So did their hatred of the Vietnamese.

Pendleton, who weighed 125 pounds and carried equipment weighing at least half that, perhaps best expressed the feeling that was coming over the infantrymen. "Sometimes you're real scared and sometimes you're just used to it. Like when you're walking with all that heavy stuff, you just don't care any longer," he remembers.

On January 22, Widmer wrote a letter to his family after returning from 14 days in the field.

"Boy this place is really hell," Widmer wrote. "You ought to try living like an animal for a week or so because that's what you do in the field. I couldn't begin to tell you the shit we go through and put up with. I wish you could come along for just one operation and live it like we do. . . ."

Then Widmer added, "On the lighter side of things, I'm gaining weight."

Widmer said the company was going back into the field the following day. There was a rumor it would be headed north to the DMZ. The rumor was partly true. The company was headed north to LZ Dottie to begin field operations there. Dottie was 40 miles north of Duc Pho on Highway 1, a national road that begins in Cambodia and runs the length of both Vietnams.

From then on Charlie Company's troubles would only get worse.

The company's area of operation was about 150 square kilometers of rice paddies and marshlands that began on Highway 1 and swept eastward to the South China Sea. The territory for which they would be responsible was roughly shaped in the form of the United States. It ran north about ten kilometers from its southernmost boundary, which was two rather narrow rivers called the Song Ham Giang and the Song Diem Diem. Actually they were more like streams. The Song Diem Diem emptied into the sea through an inlet just north of a heavily populated area known as Pinkville because it was colored pink on Army maps. Pinkville was located about 2 ½ kilometers east of a hamlet called Mylai (4).

Mylai (4) was about one kilometer south of the Song Diem Diem. There are six Mylais on Army maps, each numbered in sequence. Collectively the six are known as Tu Cong, and all are in a region called Son My which encompasses about 16 square kilometers of little hills, lots of rice paddies and swamps as well as tree lines and clusters of other hamlets.

Pink on any army map indicates that an area is built up in population. All six Mylais were in the vicinity of Pinkville. It doesn't really matter what the names of these hamlets were. Armies don't go to war by taxi. They use field maps marked off horizontally and vertically by coordinates. Armies attack and defend coordinates that never change, even if place names do.

But Charlie Company, like GIs in every war, never really knew where they were and knew nothing about Pinkville or Mylai (4) until it was too late. Mylai (4) was outside their area of operation. Vaguely they referred to anything south of their river boundary as Pinkville. It was a good term because pink means communist and they knew that the 48th VC battalion was headquartered somewhere south of that river. It was a vague reference point. When they first got to LZ Dottie, they never even heard of Pinkville.

According to the plan of operations for Task Force Barker, one company would go on patrol in the rice fields, while one stayed at LZ Dottie and the third at LZ Uptight. LZ Uptight was well named because it was located in the middle of nowhere about ten kilometers directly east of LZ Dottie. It was very desolate and isolated. There were no showers available—or much of anything else. But there were artillery units here that provided direct support to the company in its field operations. LZ Dottie was a dreary outpost atop a slight knoll, but it did have showers and hot meals available. The men slept in subterranean bunkers with only the roofs and the entrances protruding above ground. The better bunkers had double- or triple-tiered wooden slabs, allowing for seven sleepers in a room. A barbed wire perimeter surrounded LZ Dottie.

But the infantry is expected to sleep outside the barbed wire in less comfortable and less protected bunkers, so it can be readily available to meet a sudden enemy attack on the outpost. The guards for the permanently assigned personnel of LZ Dottie were men like those in Charlie Company, infantrymen returned from long patrols in the field, ostensibly to rest, but who still had to maintain the constant vigilance of a combat soldier.

Terry, ever the devout Mormon, recalls there was a Christian church near Dottie. There were also lots of whore houses on nearby Highway 1 that led south to the city of Quang Ngai, less than 13 kilometers away. As infantrymen, members of Charlie Company weren't per-

mitted passes into Quang Ngai city as were permanent
personnel. But they sneaked in. As infantrymen, Charlie
Company was expected to use LZ Dottie only as a spring-
board for patrols into the rice paddies and primitive hamlets of their new area of operations. But the necessities of
life for a combat soldier were available. The church and
the whore houses were nearby. And if the troops couldn't
go on pass for their ass, the ever-obliging Vietnamese
women came to Dottie and for the right price would stay
all night. The enterprising South Vietnamese en-
trepeneurs were ever ready to provide Charlie Company
with women, American beer and liquor (which they got at
the PXs and sold to the infantry at black market prices)
—and pot.

Marijuana is a derivative of the Cannabis plant that
grows wild in South Vietnam, and the variety there is
more powerful than that found in the U. S.—and far
cheaper. A joint sold for ten cents. Depending on the
stress the GIs were under, Vietnamese pot could make
them angry, upset or paranoid. LZ Dottie became a place
to look forward to for relaxing pot parties after arduous
field duty.

If, in the unlikely event, a GI couldn't afford the ten
cents for a joint, he could get it for nothing. Carter claims
he used to find many caches of marijuana while searching the underground hideouts used by the VC in the villages. "I used to find whole buckets of weeds in the
tunnels," Carter recalls with a laugh.

Pot-smoking in the company became an accepted fact
of life in which many members indulged and which the
officers apparently ignored. "There was lots of pot-
smoking," says Terry, matter-of-factly. "Half the company did it. They'd unwind at the fire base with a pot
party." White says the men even smoked pot on patrols.
But Van Leer claims he refused offers twice to indulge
because "it's not good to be stoned in combat."

Carter insists everybody in Charlie Company tried it.

Indeed, one of the qualities that endeared Bobby Wilson to the company was his naïveté and his willingness to try pot. "In combat he got to smoking pot and he enjoyed it and I enjoyed giving it to him," Carter remembers nostalgically.

Patrolling the rice paddies and searching villages became a continuous preoccupation of Charlie Company after they set up their base of operations at LZ Dottie. Nobody can point a finger at the village or the point in time when Charlie Company really started getting rough with the Vietnamese. It happened, but it was a gradual development resulting from frustration, fear and mounting casualties that nibbled away at this company in a kind of war it was never taught to understand or trained to fight.

"In the beginning," remembers Widmer, "we'd go to the villages, have a beer or two, talk and never show much hate." But being friendly wouldn't pay off.

The men would bring C rations with them to be shared with the children, and at LZ Dottie Richard Pendleton even befriended a family where he'd go for dinner once in a while. The company had a Vietnamese child that it had adopted as a mascot at Dottie. It also had a dog called Charlie and a whiskey-drinking monkey that it kept at Dottie. Higher headquarters ordered the company to get rid of the dog.

The people in the villages they searched, however, were different from those found along Highway 1. The villages were backward and filthy by Western standards, the people dirty, impassive, uncommunicative. But along Highway 1, the GIs seemed to have more of an affinity with the Vietnamese they met because the people were in contact with cities and the American Army and civilization as it is known to Westerners.

The trouble, of course, was that the people along Highway 1 were highway robbers, whores, pimps, pot peddlers, thieves and black-market operators, a fact that would

grow more on the nerves of C Company as their tour in
Vietnam progressed.

"If only the guys had got a taste of actual Vietnamese
living," Van Leer lamented one time. "If the troops had
got a taste of Saigon or anywhere where people had goals
in life or wore suits, it would have been different. All we
saw were animals."

What Van Leer was saying in his own effective way was
that the backward villages of Vietnam provided a battle-
ground for a clash of cultures between two peasant
groups, one Western, the other Asian. The young Americans had no concept of the Asian way of life, which to
them seemed reprehensible. No one prepared them for
the shock of such an alien way of life. So they lost the
round in the battle for men's minds.

Indeed, the GIs sometimes seemed more ready to accept
the highway whores because these women were neatly
dressed in their ao dais, and they bathed and spoke some
English and displayed a higher degree of sophistication.

Saigon had paved streets and automobiles and air-con-
ditioned hotels and was a Westernized city in the Orient,
and people didn't urinate in the gutter. It wasn't at all that
way in the backward villages of Vietnam.

Van Leer, who was 18 when he was in Vietnam, still
hasn't gotten over the shock of one of his first experiences
with Vietnamese villagers. A crippled old woman with
blackened teeth dropped her pants to relieve herself right
in front of him. It happened when they had gone in to
search a village.

"We would order the people to stay in groups," Van Leer
remembers. "Then I saw this one old woman sneak back
into her house. I watched her to see what she would do.
She grabbed something and hid it. I thought it was a grenade."

Van Leer rushed into the house and confronted the
woman. She became so panicky she stepped outside,
dropped her pants and squatted as if to relieve herself.

What she was trying to do was to act nonchalant, to indicate to the American soldier that the only reason she left the group was because she had to go. In the villages in Vietnam, when you gotta go, you gotta go, and you do it right in the open. But the poor woman didn't realize that this is not the way it's done in the land of the flush toilet and privacy between the sexes.

"It freaked me out," Van Leer remembers. "I was shocked. She had no feelings. It was like a dog screwing another dog. It was the first time I've ever seen a woman using the bathroom in front of me, Vietnamese or American or Japanese or European."

Of course today Van Leer realizes that people have been relieving themselves long before flush toilets were invented. But no one bothered to warn him about those things then. And to this youngster that woman was nothing but an animal, "like a dog screwing another dog."

But this lack of understanding of one another's cultures only became more complicated as the situation in that village developed—a situation that would be humorous if it wasn't so tragic. Van Leer had seen the woman hide whatever she had grabbed in the house. She had placed it beneath her conical hat. He lifted the hat and found—candy, Vietnamese candy, crummy Vietnamese candy!

This only served to infuriate him further. Perhaps the Viet Cong stole candy from the villagers. Perhaps in Vietnam the candy she possessed was a real delicacy, an expensive item, a hard-to-get commodity. "I was so mad that she'd think I'd steal her candy, that I took it, gave her a handful and threw the rest in the rice paddies, so she would get the point that I didn't want it. Then I kicked two pots on the ground and broke them."

This immediately angered Capt. Medina, who was known to be quick-tempered. "Don't break the village up unless you have to," he reprimanded Van Leer. "Don't break her damned pots. They're of no value."

Van Leer was crestfallen. "I was hurt when he put me

down," he remembers. "But Medina was trying to tell us that these people's culture was different and for us to respect their customs. Like on the pots. He was trying to tell me that the people were so poor they couldn't afford a pot."

Van Leer talks in retrospect. And Medina may have tried in his own gruff manner to educate his troops. But they weren't Boy Scouts or members of the Peace Corps. And he wasn't a school teacher or a sociologist. His first concern had to be to maintain an effective fighting force constantly under enemy surveillance. He was an infantry officer in charge of a company of men who had been trained to fight and kill and who had not been trained to serve as diplomats.

Let the troops in civil action or psychological warfare or public relations units worry about images. Medina's primary concern was to worry about his combat missions and to bring his men safely home.

Combat in Vietnam means to kill or be killed; to destroy or die. The men should have been trained for other duties before they went to Vietnam, not on the job. This company had been taken from the plush and ultramodern environment of Hawaii and thrust centuries back in time into the backwash of Vietnam. It was a cultural shock from which these simple soldiers never recovered.

If Van Leer was shocked, then other members of the company must have been even more shaken by what they saw in the villages. For Van Leer, the son of a retired air force sergeant, had once spent a tour with his parents in the Philippines. And although he undoubtedly lived at a sanitized and Americanized air force base, he must have had some exposure to local conditions.

Recalling his tour in Vietnam, the young soldier observed of the villagers: "These people lived in mud, grass huts. Had I not been to the Philippines, I'd be really shocked."

★ ★ ★

CHAPTER VIII

PATROLS (2)

★ ★ ★ ★ ★ ★ ★ ★ ★ ★ ★ ★ ★ ★

". . . For the Christian riles and the Aryan smiles
And he weareth the Christian down . . ."

RUDYARD KIPLING

★ ★ ★ ★ ★ ★ ★ ★ ★ ★ ★ ★ ★ ★

As the men got down to the serious business of patrolling their area of operation (AO), to search for and hopefully to destroy an enemy both invisible and elusive, the novelty of their new life began to wear off—and their patience began to wear thin. As the patrols continued fruitlessly, pressures on the company began to mount. Not only were they never sure of what they were doing, but there never seemed to be a letup in the demands made on the men.

From the moment they had arrived in Vietnam, Charlie Company had been kept busy, 24 hours a day, performing physically exhausting chores—whether it was building a brigade base at Duc Pho or looking for an invisible enemy here in the rice paddies. There had been no rest for these men except for that brief Christmas respite, nor did it look as if there ever would be.

Added to their physical miseries was the psychological phenomenon of loneliness among this group of men. Charlie Company was becoming a world unto its own; it was a recluse company that lived by itself in the field. Its home, like that of a school of fish, was wherever the group was moving at the moment. Its walls were the perimeter it set up each night when it bedded down in the damp fields to sleep. News from the outside world, which meant anything beyond its perimeter, was rumor, gossip, a whispered word passed from mouth to ear, until, as in the game of telephone, the original meaning was lost somewhere in the ranks.

With unknown and unseen dangers lurking everywhere, anything that wasn't American was enemy to Charlie Company; indeed anything that wasn't Charlie Company was suspect. Men thus thrust into an alien environment and facing a common danger are drawn ever closer to each other. Charlie Company became as one man; or as Carter once put it, it became a company of brothers. It was tight.

"Any experience that happened to us was new, so we had to interpret it on the basis of our own ignorance," explains Van Leer. The company was like a group of children wandering, afraid, in the dark. There were no combat-wise veterans to tell these children not to be afraid. "The guys were always tired," Van Leer continues. "Their only rest was when they stopped for the day one-half hour before dark until they started again one-half hour before sunup. But they never got a complete night's rest. They never slept a whole night. They were freezing in the morning and they were soaking during the day."

A company in the field doesn't sleep. Some men rest. But the eyes and ears of a company must be ever vigilant. For there is no telling when a finger will have to squeeze a trigger. Thus the men slept fitfully at night. Often they slept in water. Van Leer would share makeshift quarters with Widmer, Medina, Doc White, John Paul and Sgt. Phu, the Vietnamese interpreter. At night the six would build a lean-to with three ponchos and use the other three to cover the wet ground. They would cover themselves with poncho liners.

During the night men had to take turns on radio watches and as perimeter guards. Always there was the fear of attack, an attack that would never come. Then they would wake before dawn and another miserable day would begin. This was combat—guerrilla style.

The field duty was rough, Terry remembers. "You'd get up about five in the morning and pull in your Claymore mines and put your grenades back. You'd pack your poncho and eat your rations. Your pack weighed about 80 pounds. And you'd begin to walk. I walked point a lot; me and Doherty."

Then the men would plod through the rice paddies, avoiding the causeways and the roads for fear of mines or ambushes, going instead into the slushy, muddy fields. And it wasn't only the tropical ants, the man-eating ants, and the blood-sucking leeches that bugged them, it was the heat and the filth and the horrible smell that no television camera could record.

"You're hot and sweaty and it would be just real miserable generally," Terry recalls. "You got two cold C rations a day and one hot meal. At dusk you'd eat and maybe write a quick letter and dig a fox hole for three guys. One guy would be on watch for an hour; that's how the night went. And that's bad enough. But we didn't get any direct action. The casualties we had was not from direct action. And that had a psychological effect.

"You didn't get a way to work out your frustrations. It builds up. Pressure built up and soon the whole morale was affected."

The men of Charlie Company were always so filthy that soon they became proud of being dirty. They wouldn't shave or bathe, and they liked it that way.

The hot meal came in the evening by helicopter. It was the only break of the day. Sometimes it didn't come and there would be another cold ration. Sometimes the men improvised. Van Leer's favorite delicacy was C ration pizza pie. You made it by taking the meat balls and spaghetti ration, putting it on a slice of bread and baking it over a hot ammo box. It was different.

Cut off from normal society, the men soon developed their own. Cut off from normal controls and rules of behavior, the men soon developed their own sets of customs and mores—and pecking system. Cliques, groups, friendships that had formed in Hawaii or developed since then were reaffirmed and cemented in the muddy rice paddies.

The men began to learn about each other and to distinguish the natural leaders from those simply ordained by the Army. In the third platoon, for example, S. Sgt. George Cox, a squad leader, easily became the most popular man, possibly in the entire company. Cox took an interest in his men even in Hawaii, where he would listen to their personal problems and try to resolve them so they would not turn into serious crises in Vietnam. In the field Cox still showed a willingness to talk and to listen to his men. But there were other little ways that made a true leader distinguishable.

Like when the C rations were distributed, or all the other little goodies that would arrive by helicopter with the hot evening meal.

Some men would eat anything in the C rations. Donnell (Joe) Bell was like that, remembers Carter. A pleasant-faced, happy kid, he would go around scrounging seconds or eating anything that somebody else didn't want. Others were picky and choosy. Tom Partsch, for example, couldn't stand the ham and lima beans. He did eat the chicken and the fruit. But his mother sent him canned meats regularly so he was taken care of. Garza would be stuck with the ham and lima beans; Calley got the good stuff. Bergthold had a weight problem so he was lucky. He was always trying to diet in the field, which is a better place than most to lose weight.

Leaders like Cox would let the men have first choice of their preference in rations and eat what was left. Cox would go out of his way to scrounge a few more cans of C ration than he was entitled to, so he could give his men what they liked. It was the sign of a good leader.

Medina, for example, had a firm policy that enlisted men ate first, then the sergeants, then the officers, and last himself. And he made sure his men were well clothed in the field. No torn or worn uniforms, sox, or boots for Charlie Company. Medina made sure his supply sergeant back at headquarters took care of the men in the field.

But the men agree it was different with Lt. Calley and S. Sgt. David Mitchell, one of his squad leaders. They took care of themselves first. When the sundry packs arrived with the cigarettes, candy bars and stationery, Calley grabbed for the good stuff first, remembers Carter. Calley went for the stationery and gave his troops the leavings.

Mitchell was the same way, recalls Hendrickson. "He wasn't looked too well upon. He was one-way." Mitchell was transferred to Calley's platoon from the third because of these habits, Hendrickson claims.

"He started taking our sundry packs. He hoarded the cigarettes and the Tootsie Rolls and the pipe tobacco. He wouldn't divide it. Word got to Medina and Mitchell was transferred." Carter, too, says he could never trust Mitchell, and others echoed similar sentiments. "He seemed sly," remembers Bob Shivers. "He would work when Medina went by, to impress him," claims Van Leer.

M. Sgt. Isaiah Cowan was popular with the troops of the first platoon. He was their platoon leader. He was an old-timer in the Army and the men liked him. "He would help anybody just as much as he could but still hold discipline," one soldier remembers.

The men of the second platoon liked Jay A. Buchanon. He was their platoon sergeant and one of the oldest men in the company.

"The company was not very intelligent," says Carter,

"but the first platoon was. It had most of the guys from the East Coast." Carter was talking of a clique which, for want of a better name, might be termed the Eastern Establishment, although they had nothing to do with the "effete corps of impudent snobs" that Spiro Agnew talks about.

Indeed, they were just the opposite. They were tough guys, New York dead-end-kid types, although they accepted in their ranks men they considered worthy who came from other parts of the country. In Charlie Company the highest standard of acceptance was being tough. The Eastern Establishment seemed to be the toughest group, although some men in the company think that was a put-on. But they did set the pace for toughness to which more timid members of the company aspired. To be accepted as a tough guy was to be accepted in the highest echelons of an infantryman's society.

Carter describes this group as "mostly from the ghetto." They were the hard-luck Negroes and hard-luck Italians. "The eastern bunch was a problem. They sure were a problem," Carter remembers with a laugh. They did what they wanted where they wanted, and how they wanted and when they wanted.

"Calley tried to get their friendship, but they resented authority," Carter says.

The eastern establishment came through when the going got rough, remembers Van Leer. "Everyone of these New York guys were the biggest troublemakers and the best soldiers. Everybody talked big, but when it came down to brass tacks the guys didn't come through. But the New York guys put their money where their mouths were.

"They were probably more crazy than brave. But that's the New York character," continues Van Leer. "When you're walking for a subway at two A.M. I guess you get like that."

One of Calley's problems was seeking favor with the

Eastern Establishment, whose members demanded more than a lieutenant's bar to gain their acceptance. Carter thinks Calley envied him because he was almost as short and slight as the lieutenant but much tougher.

Two guys apparently very popular in the company were Bill Weber and Bobby Wilson, both from Indiana. Weber was Calley's RTO and was close with Widmer, Shivers, Wood and Doc Robert Lee, another medic. Wilson was close with Carter and Billy Carney and Meadlo, also an Indiana boy.

Carter was particularly fond of Wilson, probably because the two were so different. Wilson had invited Carter to his farm after the war. Carter says Wilson was the only white guy who had ever done anything like that. Wilson had also offered to stake Carter to his own farm. Wilson was conscientious. He had a brother in Vietnam and knew he was entitled to leave the country. But he was having difficulty getting up the nerve to request the transfer. He didn't want the men to think he was running out on them.

Terry and Greg Olsen were very close, probably because both were Mormons. Terry also was quite friendly with Doherty and Bernhardt. All three of these men had been Lurps and considered themselves a little better than the ordinary infantrymen.

Two close friends in the second platoon were Vernado Simpson and Maurice Robinson, but one of the more unusual relationships was the friendship that had developed between Medina and Gustavo Rotger. Rotger, a New Yorker, was also close with Daniel Simone of Trenton, New Jersey, and he was apparently popular in the company.

Despite the trouble he had had in Hawaii, Rotger was proving to be an outstanding soldier in Vietnam. He always volunteered to be point man and risked his neck whenever he could. One reason he and Medina grew close was because the young private first class had been in so much trouble that he couldn't help but come to the attention of his commanding officer. Because of his own experiences in life, Medina went out of his way for kids like Rotger. One reason he let Rotger out of the stockade in Hawaii, to go with the company to Vietnam, was because he felt the kid had promise.

"Medina respected this man. That's why he let him out of the stockade. Rotger wanted to be significant," Van Leer says. Rotger was popular in the company, adds Van Leer, "because he was anti-Army. He showed the Army what the men felt deep down. If Rotger wanted off post, he just jumped the fence. If he didn't feel like it, he didn't show up for formation."

But Rotger also wanted to prove himself useful, worthy and needed. Medina must have sensed that in the kid and that's why the captain took such a liking to the private.

Doc White was close with Lee, and Mike Dunham, who joined the company with Pendleton, was described as a peacenik, but apparently was popular in the company. Dunham had a flower on his helmet. Terry says Dunham had a philosophical problem. "He couldn't adjust to the idea of having to shoot anybody." Terry thinks if that situation ever arose Dunham might have cracked.

As developments in the rice paddies grew steadily worse, men looked to each other for aid, comfort, and mutual boosting of morale. But because of their general ignorance of guerrilla warfare, it was becoming a case of the blind leading the blind.

Medina once proudly said that he had seen black and white members of his company, who had fought each other in Hawaii, smoke each other's cigarettes, eat together and even hold each other's hands in Vietnam. It is true that, with some minor exceptions, the racial problems of the United States were forgotten in Vietnam. But the reason probably had little to do with civil rights.

For the men, regardless of their origins, were faced

with a more immediate danger in Vietnam—instant
death. So the hazards of racial conflict at home would
have to wait. After all, how could the blacks and whites
live to fight each other in the streets of America if they
let the Oriental kill them off in the rice paddies of Vietnam.

The men of Charlie Company, regardless of race, were
united in their contempt for the Vietnamese, whom they
called gooks, dinks, slopes and slant-eyes. Even the South
Vietnamese intepreters, members of the company recall,
had no use for the Vietnamese they encountered in the
rice paddies. Some American writers, applying instant
psychoanalysis to the complicated problem of Vietnam,
seem to feel that racism was at the bottom of the hatred
that was part of Charlie Company's expression at Mylai
(4). Newsweek Magazine called it the "dink complex."
Bernhardt once said that the blacks in Charlie Company
didn't "relate" to the Vietnamese.

Carter recalls when he, Simone and Wilson were in a
village, going through a search and playing with the children.

"We wuz playing with the kids when I saw in one hootch
this lady. She was outside the hootch but I could sense
something was wrong. She kept looking at her house. So
I took out my .45 and went in. Wilson covered. Then me
and Wilson went in and there was this gook. We call them
all gooks. He said he was sick. But we found out later he
was a confirmed VC."

By referring to Vietnamese as gooks, Carter explained,
he didn't mean to suggest the company was racist. "We
just hated slant eyes. And that's not racist," Carter said
with finality. Then the black American ex-infantryman
went on:

"It's like this. If I went to Africa to fight, I'd probably
hate black Africans. They would be our enemies. When
you're fighting someone you're not supposed to like
him."

Actually, from the point of view of their mental health,
or at least to preserve their sanity, it was a good thing that
Charlie Company did look upon the Vietnamese with contempt. For it is unnatural for a man to kill his fellow man.
It is easier to kill a gook or a round-eye or a nigger or a
pig or a kraut or a kike or a wop—or an animal!

But these are simplistic conclusions, particularly since
Charlie Company represented so many races within its
ranks.

Konrad Lorenz, in his epic study "On Aggression," observes that ". . . personal acquaintance, indeed every kind
of brotherly feeling for the people to be attacked, consti-
tutes a strong obstacle to aggression. Every militant
ideology in history has propagated the belief that the
members of the other party are not quite human. . . ."
Perhaps Lorenz knows why Charlie Company's antipathy
to Vietnamese really has nothing to do with race.

It isn't easy for a reasonably normal man to kill his
fellow man. It is something he must learn, as in basic
training. He must be taught that the normal is abnormal
and the abnormal normal. As long as nations insist on
waging wars to settle their differences, such teachings
must continue.

There is a tendency in the United States, on the part of
its breast-beating, liberal intelligentsia, to feel that everything their country does is wrong and anything done
elsewhere is correct—and then to oversimplify the Mylai
affair by charging it off to American racism.

Robert Trumbell, the veteran Asian correspondent for
The New York Times, observed in his book "The Scrutable
East" that Americans are "unusually defensive" on the
racial question in the Orient, "forgetting that Asians pos-
sess strong color prejudices of their own."

This is not to deny there is racism in America—both
black racism and white racism. But there was no racism
involved in the attitude of Charlie Company. For if Lorenz is correct, then Charlie Company was just preparing

its collective conscience for what it would ultimately do
—what any infantry company of any army in the world
must do—kill, kill, kill.

If the charge of racism is true, then how can the policy
of Arab guerrillas be explained when they willfully and
with premeditation kill Israeli school children, when
both groups are members of the same Semitic stock? And
how can the deliberate murder of thousands upon thousands of Biafran children be explained, when the killers
were Nigerians who like their enemies were black Africans? And how can recurrent bitterness in North Ireland
be explained, where the same race of Irishmen kill each
other off because of religious differences?

And would Americans of World War II, then, be considered antiwhite racists because they referred to the Ger-
mans as krauts and to the Italians as wops—and looked
forward to killing them as much as to killing their gook
enemies in the Pacific, the Japanese?

Gooks and slant-eyes, of course, are terms that did not
result because of the horror of the Vietnam war, as many
critics of the conflict would like to believe. The Japanese
were called gooks, among other derogatory names, back
in World War II, a term that was used even before then,
in all probability, by the old "China hands," U. S. servicemen stationed in the Far East in the early decades of the
20th century.

The Vietnamese have their own terms of "racist" hate
for the Americans, who are called round-eyes and big-
noses, descriptive phrases as contemptuous to the Oriental as gook is to the black or white American.

Even Bernhardt notes that the hatred in Vietnam went
both ways, and that it stemmed from a mutual fear that
the Americans and the Vietnamese peasants had for each
other. It stemmed from a difference of cultures, a difference of religions, a difference of races, a difference of
economic standards, a difference of mores and customs
and styles, and a total lack of communication. These

were not gaps, they were bottomless chasms that could not be bridged.

In addition, the GIs were operating in what even today is known as "Indian country," an area whose inhabitants were known to bow before the likeness of Ho Chi Minh and who definitely were not friendly, helpless, innocent peasants.

Perhaps because of his better education and his military training both in high school and in college, Bernhardt made an extra effort to understand the Vietnamese. But he concedes that the barrier between Vietnamese and Americans was built on mutual hate. "They were afraid of us and I believe that they hated us too," Bernhardt says. "They had a sort of racial thing. Of course we presented a really repugnant appearance. You know, the beards and the blue eyes and all that; yeah and the blacks too."

The Americans were a totally alien people to the Vietnamese, who were a totally alien people to the Americans. It was a vicious circle. Each looked down on the other as subhuman. Lorenz must have been right.

They came, this company on patrol, big blacks and big whites, moving into lilliputian villages filled with tiny residents. The bodies of both races stank in the tropical heat, releasing odors that were even alien to the Oriental nose. They were unschooled, uncouth, undiplomatic and unshaven, these hirsute men, moving among a people who have no hair on their faces, arms or chests. Their khaki uniforms were gray with the mud of the rice paddies, their rifles were loaded and at the ready, their faces, showing fear and fatigue, were unfriendly. They were giant aliens, Westerners and invaders in a land that had witnessed for a thousand years foreign efforts to dominate it. And they moved among a people who for centuries had learned to fear all foreigners—regardless of their good intentions—and to resist them.

"Of course fear and hate kind of go together, don't they?" Bernhardt asks. "And this is what happens. People fear someone and they hate him. Or they hate someone and they fear him. In other words, basically, they didn't like us and they were afraid of us."

When Bernhardt observed: "You can't help knowing that they hate you," he was echoing a feeling that other members of the company also sensed and expressed. The Vietnamese peasants hated the American intruders and the simple GI felt it. As one white soldier pointed out, he felt the same hatred in a village as he would in a black neighborhood at home if he visited there during a period of anger in the land.

And the Americans of course were just as afraid of the Vietnamese. So a reaction developed on the part of the GIs.

The reaction of the GIs, relates Bernhardt, "to these people hating and fearing them was that they (the GIs) hated and feared them (the Vietnamese) in return. So that a lot of these guys just wanted to kill every one of them."

As the company became embittered, frightened, hateful, its ranks filled with "rumor, gossip, ignorance," Van Leer remembers. Charlie Company should have had its ranks filled with Bernhardts or, better still, with college graduates. For the war in Vietnam is psychological and political and sociological, and the infantry ranks need enlightened soldiers rather than the sword-and-spear type of warrior.

Charlie Company should have had its ranks filled with sociology majors and psychology majors and college students from the liberal arts.

Bernhardt could look at the situation with a certain objectivity because he was what Army psychiatrists would describe as the ideal fighting man. A study was made after World War II and a follow-up after the Korean War and the psychiatrists found that the ideal fighting man should not be a dead-end kid but a middle class youngster with at least a high-school education. Such kids have accepted the challenges and chores of growing up, like mowing the lawn and selling newspapers and continuing their education. They also will take on the responsibilities of being a combat soldier.

The more intellectual the combat soldier is, say the psychiatrists, the better he will react to the stress of battle. Such a kid finds himself subjectively removed from the action, looking at it with a detached point of view as an intellectual curiosity.

Bernhardt disapproves of what his company did but concedes he does not know how he would have reacted at Mylai (4) had he been in a position where he came across live inhabitants. When he arrived on the scene it was almost over. Still, Bernhardt, being bright and certain of himself, had the courage of his convictions that a kid with a lower mentality would not have.

His buddies in Charlie Company respect Bernhardt as a combat soldier but say he used to do a lot of complaining and writing of letters to his Congressman and to his Senator, Robert F. Kennedy of New York. He had a right to gripe, as every GI does, and, considering the caliber of the officer, he undoubtedly was superior to most. He would have taken a commission in the Army had they let him be a helicopter pilot.

The Army wanted him to extend his tour an extra year, but he didn't want to. Bright guys don't want to stay in the army any longer than they absolutely have to. Bernhardt was not an average GI and he was in a minority in the company. Although he griped and complained and criticized and told guys how he could do it better—and he probably could have—nevertheless he was a low-ranking enlisted man at the time.

Meanwhile, back in America were people who professed a compassion for their fellow man; they professed love. These were the people whom the ignorant, frightened, antagonistic peasants needed. These were the people who refused to serve.

Two months before Charlie Company left for Vietnam, 320 American intellectuals, professors, writers, clergymen vowed to raise funds to help young men avoid the draft. Dr. Benjamin Spock was among them and the Rev. William Sloane Coffin, the chaplain at Yale, and so was Allen Ginsberg, the hippie poet. They called on American youth to resist the draft. They said the war outraged the "deepest moral and religious sense" of an increasing number of the young.

It was a call for disobedience from a moral point of view. It was misplaced idealism. For it didn't serve to end the war but rather to prolong it, and to divide a nation, and to cause a Mylai.

Worse, those young men who refused to serve were not practicing a higher idealism, they were shirking their responsibility to their fellow man. If they didn't go, others had to. Thus many men not well endowed intellectually may well have died needlessly because others refused to serve.

The infantry, in this highly complicated, political-psychological war, should have been made up of American intellectuals, men who, like Bernhardt, could understand interpersonal relationships, could develop friendships instead of animosity—and possibly win the people's hearts and minds.

Doc White saw what was happening to Charlie Company, watched its moral disintegration disapprovingly, but he was in the minority.

"They were the kids next door who were trained to kill, programmed to kill," White said of his buddies.

"Everywhere you turned there was animosity over there," White said of the environment.

"Never could I remember anything in training other than we're fighting Communists; stopping the Communist aggression of Asia," White said of the army.

"They won all those awards in Hawaii. You put a company with that spirit in the field and they'll be just as aggressive," White said of the company.

"There was this animosity towards the Vietnamese. There was no respect for them. There was a rampant black market. The GIs sold to the black market and bought back from the black market," White said of the general situation.

"The company was psychologically conditioned to kill. When the opportunity presented itself, they were unable to distinguish the fine line between right and wrong."

When was it right to kill in combat and when was it wrong? Green, nervous troops are prone to itchy trigger fingers under the most ideal of war conditions. In Vietnam, where guerrillas, men, women and children all looked alike, conditions were atypical. The company was sniped at frequently as they were leaving villages and the men never knew who was firing at them.

What was obvious, however, was that, whenever they went, there was an absence of military-age males among the village populations. Even in the tragedy at Mylai (4) where much has been written of the deaths of women, children and old men, there were no reports of military-age males present at the hamlet.

Van Leer's observation on this point undoubtedly reflected the opinion of many men in the company. "The thing that got me, you'd go into a village and all you'd find is maybe 30 old women, and maybe 20, 70, 105 kids and 15 men. And the men had goatees so they were old papasans. And you'd think them old guys weren't producing 105 kids with the old women," Van Leer muses.

Bernhardt does not feel that such suspicions warranted the mistreatment of the villagers. He claims that while there was much in the conduct of the villagers to arouse suspicion, in his experience there he had never seen a villager do anything wrong to a GI. He concedes he heard many stories about villagers participating in hostilities but he never saw it.

Furthermore, Bernhardt had been a member of the

Lurps, therefore was elite among the infantry. He has said he never felt he could depend on the men in Charlie Company. He might have been right—they were ordinary infantrymen whereas his training had been far superior.

But the green kids of Charlie Company were slowly panicking in the field.

Once, recalls Terry, two Vietnamese were spotted trying to hide behind a rock. They were killed. A search of their bodies revealed they were members of the North Vietnamese Army. Was the killing justifiable? Probably.

Another time Charlie Company interrogated some Vietnamese males who claimed to be farmers. But an inspection of the hands of these Vietnamese revealed there were no callouses. They were ordered to strip down and their backs were inspected. Marks were found indicating they had carried heavy packs. Were they farmers or soldiers?

On one patrol, remembers Doc White, the company was moving down a hill. "The point man saw two people moving across a field. He opened up. It was a five year old boy and an old man. The guys were so jumpy they near tore the boy's arm off at the elbow." Was this shooting justifiable? Probably not. But the question that must be asked is what was the motivation? Did these kids kill with premeditation and in cold blood? Or were they a frightened bunch of untrained boys whose reaction was primarily one of fear.

Perhaps this growing fear for their own lives made this company of boys indifferent to the welfare of the Vietnamese around them.

The moral disintegration of the company began somewhere in the rice fields of Vietnam, where the value of life lost its meaning. "Almost every incident until March 16 had something to do with what happened at Mylai," Widmer once observed. Perhaps there weren't enough

Whites and Bernhardts in the company to help the men distinguish the fine line of difference between right and wrong.

The men weren't basically bad. They were, as Bernhardt once pointed out, not sure who they were against. "The company was nice guys, perfectly normal—if they had not been exposed to war," Bernhardt says.

There may have been, some people seem to think, potential criminal offenders within the ranks of Charlie Company, but that's natural if the selective service can only draft boys from the bottom of its manpower heap. However, under normal circumstances an inclination toward criminal acts might have been suppressed, even among the potential offenders.

Several of the men recall, for example, the time Charlie Company's patrolling took it to a village that was a monastery for Buddhist monks. As the company came into the clearing atop a hill and realized where they were, the normally noisy ranks suddenly fell silent. Wherever they looked they could see the monks with their shaven heads and saffron robes.

"The guys were awed at the Buddhist temple," remembers Van Leer. "They stepped around the graves and not on them. Even when nobody was looking they stepped around the graves." Though the religion was alien to them, Charlie Company fell silent in the presence of God.

The men noticed that this village had outhouses that were more sophisticated than those they had seen everywhere else they went. Charlie Company was impressed. The outhouses had no toilet seats; just holes in the ground over which one squatted. So the men placed ammo boxes over the holes as a gesture of friendship to the Buddhist priests.

It was the fact that this village was a holy place that changed the attitude of Charlie Company, which by that time had become rather rough. But it was also the "sophistication of the priests," Van Leer thinks. "They had houses with roofs, not thatched huts. And the roofs were made of shingle and brick. And they had outhouses." If the men were not sure who they were against, apparently they weren't against God, regardless of His religion.

If the Whites and the Bernhardts who were in the minority in Charlie Company were critical of Capt. Medina, their reasoning may well have stemmed more from an intellectual elitist snobbery toward a professional military man than from a genuine finding fault with his tactics. They didn't like Medina for his indifference to the Vietnamese around them, but they are agreed he ran a tight military organization. Bernhardt compares Medina with a Castro-type guerrilla leader in Cuba. The captain wasn't interested in whether the men shaved or bathed or shined their shoes or were civil to the population. His only concern was to carry out his mission and to make sure the men followed him. And they did.

It is in the nature of the infantryman to be rough. He is taught that right on up from basic training. His job is to kill and maim and destroy, or die. Let the guys in the rear echelon work out all the other problems.

In Vietnam, it had only become a secondary function of the infantryman to be friendly. These men weren't trained that way; Charlie Company just didn't know how.

Medina tried. Once in a village he saw a woman being physically pushed around by some of the men. He instantly reprimanded them. But the Vietnamese were unfriendly and the young GIs, reacting in typical American fashion, became unfriendly in return.

It seems to be an American characteristic to want to be loved. Americans seem to feel they are all entered in popularity contests. American tourists sometimes think they are loved all over the world. They cannot understand when their rude manners antagonize foreigners. They usually attribute the failings to the foreigners rather than to themselves.

Children want to be loved by their elders and by their peers. If they are rejected, they strike back. "If you're mad at me, I'll be mad at you," the child pouts. The GIs began to pout. If Charlie Company was hated, then its members began to hate back.

The army perhaps was asking too much of its GIs to expect an eighth-grade dropout to act as if he held a degree from Columbia University's two-year graduate school of international affairs. Then again, maybe the Army knew what it was doing. Bernhardt seems to think the company was being set up for the Mylai tragedy deliberately. He suspects the Army wanted the company to get so angry at the Vietnamese that they would do anything.

He says that the most miserable things imaginable always seemed to happen to Charlie Company. "Some units could avoid some things, but we seemed to catch it all. I was wondering what we were being set up for. I thought we were being conditioned for something, that they were priming us for something."

Certainly the Army, at its highest levels, should have known that combat troops haven't quite got the personality guaranteed to win friends and influence people for America. One young Army psychiatrist in Washington observed that the worst people in the world to send to Vietnam to win friends are combat soldiers. Recalling his own experiences in Vietnam, which were with airborne troops, the psychiatrist said:

"The airborne are high-school dropouts. You tell an airborne to win the hearts and minds of a people and he just can't do it. He'll screw the girls but that's as friendly as he'll get.

"They're the worst people for this kind of war. They make enemies," he said candidly. Then he asked: "But who's gonna run up Hamburger Hill? Not a college graduate. I couldn't have done it."

Still even college graduates are capable of hating the Vietnamese, added the psychiatrist. He recalled combat situations at field hospitals where wounded enemy Vietnamese would be taken. "Doctors would say 'Take those gooks out of here. I don't want to see them.' "

If airborne soldiers make enemies, then drafted infan-

trymen make sworn enemies. The lower a man is on the
social, economic and intelligence level of society, the
worse soldier he will make in Vietnam, even Army psychiatrists admit. "The college intellectual is more prone
to question orders," the psychiatrist said. "But the lower
echelon says it's his superior's job to think, not his. The
lower socio-economic level is used to more violence in
their lives. They do before they think. They are also more
suggestive."

The Army's chief psychiatrist, Col. Matthew Parrish,
who points out that everybody has hostility built into his
character, conceded that the "dumber" a person is the
more "impulsive" he is likely to be. "He is more action
conscious," Dr. Parrish said. "In civilian life such a man
won't write a letter of complaint, he'll hit you. The less
educated they are the more prone they are to physical
action."

Another psychologist who specializes in studying the
psyche of the army pointed out that "the less intelligent
a person is, the greater is his chance for misinterpreta-
tion." Dumb people are less likely to ask questions because they have been browbeaten all their lives. "They
have learned not to ask questions that would reveal they
are less bright," he said. "The lower the IQ a man has, the
more fear he will probably have and the more prone he
will be to react emotionally to a situation."

A less intelligent person also is less likely to question
authority, since all his life he has been told that those
over him, the "they" of society, were superior to him. If
a youngster has flunked out of school, failed to get a decent job, has come from a broken home and from the
lower socio-economic level of society, and has never succeeded in anything, it is difficult to see how he would
challenge the orders of his superiors in the Army. Should
he ever do such a thing, it would then be up to him to
prove in an Army court that he was right and his superior
wrong.

It was the failures of society who were dumped in the

Army infantry, sent to Vietnam and told to be soldier-diplomats. And a reasonably sophisticated nation has expressed shock because these kids couldn't do it.

Col. Parrish also points out another phenomenon apparently peculiar to Vietnam. The soldier in Vietnam, he says, doesn't fight for God and country. He fights for his company and his platoon. He fires his weapon for his team or squad or platoon or company too. The soldier fires his weapon because he feels his buddy expects him to fire his weapon. He cannot let his buddy down. He cannot let the team down.

An infantry company, or a platoon or a squad, therefore, become a team joined together out of mutual fear, explains still another psychologist. "Each man depends on the other; so a mutual security pact is formed because each needs the other to survive," he says.

Charlie Company signed a mutual security pact because of the fear and frustration its men shared in common as they continue to search for that invisible, elusive enemy who was growing increasingly more dangerous. Mixed with this fear and frustration was ignorance, the ignorance most prevalent among ordinary infantrymen.

Terry once tried to explain this. Terry had been to college and had been a Lurp, so that his military training was far more specialized. "The guys in the infantry were just not indoctrinated to know what they were doing. The average person drafted is a high-school dropout. He's not too bright. A lot over there was in the attitude in the guys' minds. I could read maps. I could talk on the radio. I could take care of myself. I was a Lurp. But in the infantry you didn't really know enough. Like if you caught a prisoner.

"It's better to rough a prisoner up, to scare him beforehand so he'll talk. These guys beat up prisoners, but for the wrong reasons. They hated."

Terry put his finger on one of the most tragic aspects of Charlie Company's confused role in Vietnam. The company has been charged with mistreating villagers, rape and murder before its tragic encounter at Mylai (4). But the motivation for its acts of violence have conveniently been ignored as interested parties pursue their goal of proving that Vietnam is more atrocious than other wars.

As their fears and frustrations increased, Charlie Company did become more prone to violence in Vietnam. For the fears gave birth to hate, and frustration turned to blind rage, and there was justification for what they did in the subtle Army policy of that period concerning the body count.

Killing Viet Cong was the name of the game in Vietnam. The body count became a contest among units of the U. S. Army in 1967 and 1968. Since the United States wasn't in Vietnam for conquest of territory or for military victory, it had to have some goal to which its troops could aspire.

The goal was to kill. If American troops could kill all the Viet Cong in South Vietnam, the war would end. The fact that nobody knew who the Viet Cong were didn't matter. All sorts of incentives were offered to men and units to raise the body count within their organizations. Two soldiers from Charlie Company had a private contest going between them. The one who killed the most Viet Cong by R-and-R time would get $50 from the other one. The two men were part of the group called McNamara's 100,000.

The reality of war to the infantryman is that one day he will be confronted by an enemy soldier and one or the other must die. The basic training and the advanced training given infantrymen leave an indelible mark on these young men. Just as sure as an aviation cadet would one day have to fly solo, an infantryman would one day have to kill.

"The company was obsessed with their training," remembers Widmer. "They would aim their weapons in the field and yell 'bang, bang.' Everybody wanted to kill. To kill a VC gave you a concrete reason for walking around. Everybody needs a reason for going on. You weren't fighting for a cause; you were fighting for your life. The only way was to kill or be killed," he concludes.

Thus the thought of killing possessed the mind of each member of Charlie Company. It was instilled in them through their training and it was encouraged by the brass until it became more than accepted. It was required. To have killed a VC was to have become the toughest guy in the company. The individual GI's thoughts progressed from the stage where he thought "I can't kill," to "Can I kill?" to "Will I kill?" to "Do I have the guts to kill?" to "I wonder what it's like to kill?" to "Kill, kill, kill!"

Killing then was becoming the ritual of acceptance into manhood. It was the confirmation; it was the Bar Mitzvah ceremony in which every member of Charlie Company would have to participate if he could look his buddy in the eye and say, "Today I am a man."

Abhorrent as this may seem to the uninitiated civilian mind, the society of the infantryman demands there be killers in its midst with the same insistence that the normal civilized society rejects killers. Killing soon became more than an obsession with Charlie Company. It was a compulsion, a sign of acceptance in a society where death is the way of life, where the only alternative to "to kill" is "to be killed."

But the question outstanding was who should be killed? With the assurances of headquarters that the company operated in a free-fire zone, and with the brass urging a higher and higher body count and with the villagers doing nothing to endear themselves to the Americans, that answer became simple. Anybody who wasn't for Charlie Company was against them. The company got so paranoiac about this that, at the time of the Mylai affair, an American helicopter pilot who tried to stop the shooting had to order his own gunners to cover him for fear he might be shot by Charlie Company.

It might have been wise if some of the higher-level

officers had visited more with the company in the field. But the company never was submitted to any outside influence from the higher-ranking officers, who seldom visited with the men.

The men resented this. The impression they had was that the brass wasn't out to get hurt; they just wanted medals and promotions. Why then should the troops endanger their lives? Their fight wasn't for victory, but for survival.

Bernhardt sometimes felt the colonels and the generals were as much the enemy as the Viet Cong. "Beers never landed on the fire base," Bernhardt said of his battalion commander, who was only in administrative control of the company while it was attached to the task force.

Widmer says Beers pushed the men too hard, and that is why they once put a price on his head. He said Beers was "out to win glory for himself." He says the same of Col. Oran K. Henderson who took command of the 11th the day of the Mylai affair, but had been with it since Hawaii. Henderson, charges Widmer, was "out to make a name for himself. Everything he did was for his benefit."

A recurrent complaint against the brass was that they inspired the troops to great deeds while flying overhead in a helicopter. Sometimes, say the soldiers, their leaders from higher headquarters flew at such high altitudes they couldn't even be seen.

One GI recalls a colonel who was always looking for Charlie Company from his helicopter by calling over the radio, "Pop smoke so I can see you." He wanted the company to send up a smoke grenade so he would know where his troops were.

Van Leer still laughs—sarcastically—as he recalls one of the rare visits made on the ground by a colonel. It was night and someone in the company sent up a flare. When a flare is released it emits a whistling sound. "When the colonel heard it he started running," Van Leer recalls.

Another soldier still talks bitterly of the pilot of a command helicopter, which is used to carry colonels around. The pilot was annoyed when he had to land in the field to pick up a wounded man. The blood dirtied the inside of his helicopter.

To put it mildly, Charlie Company was never inspired by the examples set by its leaders, particularly the brass from higher headquarters. In Vietnam nobody wants to die. In Vietnam nobody wants to take unnecessary risks either. In Vietnam the trick is to survive a year and go home. If you're a leader in Vietnam, and this may be your last war, the trick is to make the troops take the unnecessary risks so you can survive the year and go home and get a medal and a promotion and retire.

As the patrols continued, Charlie Company became more frightened, more tired, more frustrated, more embittered and angrier. And the angrier they became the more they thought of killing.

February 1968 was the month that destroyed Charlie Company. Actually, it started on January 29, when the company had its first booby-trap casualty. The injury was minor, therefore miraculous. But it served to remind the company of the most fearful form of combat in Vietnam: the hidden mine or booby trap.

Men would rather die or storm enemy divisions single-handedly than suffer the mutilations caused by these hidden weapons of war: mutilations that castrate and rip limbs from the body like an angry child playing with a doll; mutilations that get to the mind if they miss the body, because there is no defense against a booby trap or minefield. The booby trap and the minefield are the most frightening and the most frustrating weapons in the Viet Cong arsenal. For they can destroy the body and the mind at once—just as they finally destroyed Charlie Company.

On January 31 the Tet offensive began, sending South Vietnam and the United States into a panic. The following day, February 1, Charlie Company was introduced to a series of firsts: their first sight of the enemy, their first sight of a dead child and their first encounter with the bureaucratic red tape that has forced this war to bog down.

Quang Ngai was among the many cities of Vietnam that had been overrun by the enemy, and Charlie Company was on the top of a hill overlooking a valley leading from the provincial capital. The NVA had occupied Quang Ngai city for one day and now were leaving. When Medina put his binoculars to his eyes he could see a long column of the enemy moving down the valley. But seeing the enemy doesn't always mean you may kill them; in Vietnam that is. Such action call for authorization from higher headquarters, who in turn must seek political permission from the South Vietnamese.

Medina called for artillery fire but was told to wait while the request moved through channels. So the men of Charlie Company stood helplessly on their hilltop watching their enemy escape—an enemy that would live to kill Americans another day. That column in enemy troops may well have been the elusive 48th VC Battalion, target of the ill-fated assault on Mylai (4).

Van Leer remembers that first frustrating experience. "We were 100 meters up a hill overlooking this village. It was our first contact with the North Vietnamese and there were at least 200 of them. They were changing into civilian clothes as they fled." As Medina's RTO, Van Leer remembers making the call on the radio for artillery and helicopter gun ships.

But it took several hours before permission to fire was granted, and by then just a few stragglers could be seen. An enemy force of near battalion strength had escaped. "When the artillery and gun ships finally came," recalls Van Leer, "they killed civilians."

Carter remembers that incident too. "We called in the artillery and we had to wait for permission. But the time it came only two people were killed. We were playing by the rules.

"We wondered what in hell was going on. You're fighting a war and you have to get permission to kill. For crying out loud, we thought we had a license to kill when we went over there.

"The next morning we were coming off the hill and we found that some of them had been sleeping that night at the base of the hill. I don't know why they didn't attack us. Maybe old Ho Chi Minh was as slow as Washington. Medina was a little perturbed.

"We learned, when you wait for permission nothing happens," Carter recalls.

On the morning after the fiasco, Charlie Company was moving off the mountain and into the village that had come under attack. The company walked in single file on a muddy dike that served as a causeway across the rice paddies and as a path into the village. The sides of the dike were angled outward so that the shape of the path was like the letter A flattened at its top. There was a tree that grew right in the middle of the dike, and every man had to step gingerly around it by leaving the path momentarily, getting around the tree and then jumping back on the causeway.

Unknown to each man was the shocking sight that awaited him as he leaped back to the path on the other side of the tree. "You couldn't help but see it," Van Leer recalls, still with a grimace, two years later.

A body, that of a boy, was lying just on the other side of the tree, and every man in the company, as he stepped off onto the angle of the dike to bypass the tree, and then leaped back on the path, almost landed on the corpse. The kid couldn't have been older than Van Leer, although it is difficult to tell the age of a Vietnamese. The people are small and slight of build, and sometimes when you see a boy you think is four or five years old by American standards, he could turn out to be a teenager.

The kid was lying across the path of the dike, his open

eyes staring up into the blue and empty skies. Blood was still oozing from those eyes, and from his ears and out of his mouth and nose. And the blood had dried now in the heat of this tropical land, but its red streaks traced a path from the kid's nose and ears and eyes and mouth, down his cheeks and chin and neck to the black earth where it had formed in huge caked pools.

And off in the rice paddy was a dead carabao, also a victim of the artillery and gun ship assault, and the heat of the jungle had caused its body to start bloating sickeningly in the muddy rice field, and the flies had already gathered around it and the men saw that too.

But it was the dead kid with those staring eyes that grabbed these green young infantrymen, and suddenly there was silence in the normally wisecracking ranks. "It stunned you as you walked around the tree and there he was," Van Leer was recalling with difficulty. "And you could feel the shock because the guys didn't talk about it, because it was the first dead kid they ever saw."

Instead the troops talked about the dead carabao and how it was bloated, and nervously made cracks about the animal because they tried to get the dead kid out of their minds. "Capt. Medina never showed emotion, but he too was startled when he saw that kid," young Van Leer said.

And that was Charlie Company's first real encounter with the war and with the death of what appeared to be a young civilian, a death caused by bureaucracy and overly cautious rules of warfare. It was an unnecessary death, in the sense that if there had not been a breakdown in communications between the Americans and their South Vietnamese allies, the enemy could have been killed instead. But now the enemy was gone. Once more it had successfully hid behind the skirts of its women and the diapers of its babies while it continued its deadly game of sneak and snipe against the untested Americans.

Things progressed from bad to worse. The Company's efforts at friendship only brought icy reaction, or at best impassive stares, from the Vietnamese. "We tried to be

friendly with the people, but they don't tell you nothing,"
Widmer recalled of the frustrating patrols.

Once the company walked into a village and the men
were friendly to the inhabitants and handed out candy to
the kids. They smiled and the villagers smiled back. But
when they searched the village teacher's home, they
found documents indicating that he secretly taught Communism to his students. They looked for the teacher but
couldn't find him. So they burned his hut down. That was
their job. That was search and destroy. That's how a guerrilla war is fought.

"You walk into a village," Widmer remembers. "They
give you this 'no bic' stuff. They don't understand you,
they say. So we searched this village and we pulled out a
VC and a Red Chinese flag. What should we do? Should we
pat them on the back? We burned the village down. Those
people were our enemies."

But Widmer also understood the dilemma that the villagers faced. And many members of the company have
expressed their awareness of the bind in which the villagers were placed in this game of search and destroy and
seek and snipe.

"The people had two evils to fight. We were no better
than the VC. But I'll be damned if I'll pat a guy on the back
and say 'You helped the VC. Now you're a nice guy. So how
about giving me some information too.' That guy won't
talk," Widmer said.

"You had to counteract the fear the NVA and the VC
instilled in the people," Widmer explained. "If they
feared you more than the enemy, they'd be more help to
you. Even though some ways were not orthodox, like beating up prisoners, it wasn't on the scale of the VC who shot
people at the least resistance."

Widmer was thus pointing out a dilemma that has
plagued the American military conscience at least since
World War II. In the closing days of that war, many Nazis,
caught between advancing Russian and U. S. troops, went

out of their way to be captured by the Americans. For capture by the Russian Communists could mean a summary court martial in the field and instant execution. And in many cases this would have been justifiable. American captors, on the other hand, played the game strictly by the book and many a Nazi must be alive today because the Russians didn't get him first.

"The enemy didn't fight by the book, so why should we?" observed Carter of the attitude developing in Charlie Company towards the Viet Cong.

Thus, as the patrols and the searching and the endless field duty continued without letup, a new feeling developed in the company. "Tension, frustration and anger were building up," recalled Terry. And Charlie Company began to do what might be termed the wrong things, but for the right reasons—or maybe they did the right thing, but for the wrong reasons.

But whatever they did, it wasn't arbitrary.

Scaring a person to make him talk is a tactic of interrogation. Everybody in the business of interviewing people, from the police to district attorneys to newspaper reporters to intelligence agents, knows that the scare tactic sometimes is the best means of extracting information. But it has to be properly employed by a skilled interrogator. Sometimes a wiser tactic is to be gentle and friendly; it depends on the interviewer's skill and the situation.

The villagers were not reacting to American gestures of friendship. In the first place they didn't like the Americans. In the second place it was easier to fool the Americans than their own people. The VC tactic of terror in South Vietnam has been well documented, although rarely reported.

Somewhere between 50,000 to 100,000 North Vietnamese were ruthlessly killed to establish the ironclad rule of Ho Chi Minh. By the end of 1966 more than 26,000 South Vietnamese were deliberately killed and over 35,000 kidnapped by the Viet Cong. Nearly 3,000 civilians in Hue were murdered, many deliberately buried alive by North Vietnamese forces during the Tet offensive of 1968.

The murder is the message. The more brutal, the better it is read. To kill a village leader, a school teacher, the local mayor or clan chief, or to cut off the hands of his children, or to pull the entrails from his wife's vagina while she is alive, is a lesson the living won't easily forget. The South Vietnamese villagers were aware of what could happen to them if they didn't cooperate with the Viet Cong.

They knew that nothing would happen to them if they didn't cooperate with the Americans.

Perhaps there is a highly refined, cleverly designed, very sophisticated method of dealing with people facing such a dilemma. If anyone would know about it, psychiatrists might. But there were no psychiatrists in Charlie Company—just infantrymen, and very amateur infantrymen at that—just young GIs, and very unskilled young GIs at that—just boys, and very unschooled boys at that.

"To be a true infantryman, you have to be a savage, barbaric heathen." Carter once tried to explain the philosophy the Army taught him. "In advanced infantry training they teach you, 'Kill without mercy. I'm the infantry, queen of battle, blue is my color, follow me.'"

And so the blind led the blind; the members of Charlie Company held each other's hands and followed each other in doing things that they felt had to be done.

"We killed guys we knew were VC. We couldn't pin anything on them. But rather than send them back to the aid station we killed them. Otherwise, they'd come back again," Carter said. The philosophy of the company, he explained simply, was, "I'm gonna get you before you get me."

After all, the company operated in a free-fire zone. That assumes everybody is the enemy. It was the surest way to survive the year in Vietnam.

The change in the attitude of Charlie Company developed subtly, slowly. It evolved through ignorance as well as conscientiousness. But from all indications, nothing the company has been charged with doing was done through pure malice or premeditation.

The company knew who the VC suspects were. Capt. Medina carried a little black book with a list of Communist suspects and sympathizers. It had been given him by higher headquarters. The list was passed on to platoon leaders and platoon sergeants. When the men entered a village, they searched it and sought out the suspects on the list. All suspects were sent to Medina for questioning. If they were roughed up it was done with purpose. But gradually, as the men became more frustrated, they didn't bother sending suspects to Medina.

That was the danger. They were doing the wrong things for the right reasons. If they killed it wasn't for arbitrary reasons. They believed they were killing the enemy. If it wasn't the right thing to do, was it really wrong?

One soldier admitted that enemy suspects sometimes were killed. "In the pacification program you're supposed to send them back. But what good is it? Six months later they're out fighting us again." He was probably right.

If the men didn't know what they were doing, Medina did. To the average GI it seemed as if all he was doing was walking in one village and out the other. But each search-and-destroy operation was carefully planned, recalls Van Leer, who as Medina's RTO had more information available to him.

"Our mission was the search and seizure of men of military age and of documents and weapons that come into a village," he says. "We never hit a village cold. Medina would know where they were. We'd plan it the night before. We'd synchronize our watches. 'At zero six oh five there will be movement into the village' we'd be told."

Then the men would go to sleep, to awaken before sunup. "We'd come to a village before dawn and surround it to make sure there was no escape," Van Leer continues.

Each platoon had a code name: Diamond Charlie One,

Diamond Charlie Two or Diamond Charlie Three.
Medina was known as Diamond Head Charlie.

"Diamond Charlie One, this is Diamond Head Charlie,
over," Medina would whisper into the telephone as he
checked the position of his platoons in the predawn dark-
ness. "Diamond Head Charlie, this is Diamond Charlie
One," the response would come in.

"Diamond Charlie One proceed to position Alpha,"
Medina would order as his platoons and squads would
move to the prearranged points on their field maps that
had been designated during the planning the night
before.

"At first light we would jump the village," Van Leer
recalls. Then all the inhabitants would be ordered into the
village square and kept in groups under surveillance.
Each member of the company had his specific duties. The
men would quickly move into strategic positions in the
village; the centrally located village well, for example,
was one of these positions. Whatever their positions, the
men made sure that they could be seen by fellow members of the company and that they could observe every
inhabitant of the village.

"The people did what they were told. If we found tunnels we told everybody to get out of them. We'd make sure
there were no wires leading into the tunnels. Then Carter
would go in and search the tunnels. Carter wasn't afraid,"
Van Leer says, voicing the admiration that many members of Charlie Company had for Carter.

Carter was built small and light and strong. He would
wear sunglasses during patrols to keep his eyes accus-
tomed to the dark. Before entering a tunnel he would
close his eyes and keep them that way until he was inside,
so he could see better in the dark. Once inside the tunnel,
the only way out was to crawl backward. There was no
way of turning around, which was awkward particularly
if you bump into a Viet Cong.

Carter describes the intricate maze of tunnels he has

seen as "miracles" of construction and engineering.

Once he captured a VC in a tunnel. Once he almost tripped a booby trap in one. He always used his bayonet to probe the ground in front of him as he crawled forward. This was a precaution against hidden booby traps. Once, in an agonizing 40 minutes, Carter traced down a booby trap inside a tunnel and disconnected it. It was a Chinese Communist grenade, delicately hooked up to trip wires. Carter disconnected the wires, after finding them, by burning them off with a cigarette lighter.

He also uncovered caches of rice and other VC supplies in the many tunnels he searched. And there was talk of recommending Carter for the Silver Star for his exploits. But after the Mylai affair his country became ashamed of its heroes, and instead of applauding them, frantically set out to hang them.

While Carter searched the tunnels, the men searched the huts. "If we found mines or booby traps we exploded them in place," remembers Van Leer. "The men enjoyed confronting people instead of trees. The guys didn't have orgasms about it, but they liked what they were doing. It was why we were there; to seek and destroy the enemy.

"The way to destroy the enemy is to destroy his morale; the way to destroy his morale is to destroy his home." Thus from Van Leer, echoing a military maxim valid the world over in counter-guerrilla warfare.

On one occasion, the company went into a village and discovered an American-manufactured light antitank weapon. It is called a LAW and build of disposable plastic and aluminum. A LAW can launch a rocket grenade that can destroy a 60-ton tank. This LAW was set up in a tunnel and aimed for a person's head. The men also found papers and letters from Viet Cong addressed to their families.

"So what do you do? You burn the village down so they can't stay there, Van Leer said. "But you need higher permission. You call in. You need political clearance. You get it. You take everybody out and you burn the thing to the ground. You tell them not to be in the village or to rebuild it. They're in the middle. The VC and you force them there."

Sometimes the men would wait hours for the permission. But when it came, Medina would give the word and the men would burn the village. "If I knew it was a VC village it would give me a feeling of relief. It was a change from the routine," Van Leer says.

He remembers once when a woman tried to stop him from burning her hut. "I put one side on fire and she tried to put it out with a broom. Then I went to another side and she tried putting it out. Then I went to a third side."

But Charlie Company didn't burn wherever they went. "We went into more villages than we burned," Van Leer remembers.

One of the first casualties of the company, he recalls, was a man named Emerson who was shot just outside a village. "Right outside," said Van Leer. "The reaction was anger at a buddy getting killed. Excuse me—I say killed, because when they're hit they're sent away and they never come back."

Actually, Emerson was wounded. But to Charlie Company, as casualties increased, it didn't mean anything whether a man was killed or wounded. A helicopter came and took him away; the rest was rumor. The men were tired. They had to devote all their energies to just walking and surviving. A man was hit, a helicopter came to take him away and he might as well be dead. There were no replacements. It was one less body in the company and one additional chore for the living to assume.

The men kept trying the friendly approach but it wasn't working out. Once, remembers Medina, the company was walking down a trail, moving west, when they saw a woman and two young girls turn towards them from a deserted path. As the three approached the company, they were stopped and the woman's basket was searched.

"There was nothing in it," Medina related. "The inter-preter asked the woman if there were any booby traps or mines around. She said no. We patted the kids on the head, kept going, and then turned up the path from where they had come. Sgt. Mitchell saw a hole in the ground. There was a stick in it and a wire leading to a hollowed area."

It was a booby trap, and had it not been for Mitchell's vigilance some members of the company would have been taken away by the helicopter. "That woman had to know where it was. She came from that place," Medina recalled, his voice still sounding tense over the incident.

When it came to trying to be nice to civilians, the company got at least an "A" for effort if not for performance.

"We were sent into a couple of villages to check for bubonic plague. We found no evidence of it," Medina told. "We treated women and children, especially in the outlying areas. If we had supplies to spare I let the medics use it. But once in a village, just one-quarter mile off Highway 1, not far from LZ Dottie, we gave the people penicillin, gum, soap and candy. When we left we got sniper fire on the way out."

Even when the people were given medical aid, it had to be done with caution. Van Leer remembers one village where the children had developed a rash and he had two cans of foot powder for distribution. "I didn't give them the cans, because they'd use the cans to make booby traps. I spread the powder on each of the mothers' hands," he said.

Carter still laughs when he recalls an effort the company was ordered to make to befriend villagers. "You gotta understand, this company didn't know how to play. But one day Medina took us into this village to be friendly, to help the people, to play with the kids."

The company had by then developed a bitterness towards the Vietnamese, the result of their own long hours in the field and the experiences that indicated their friendship wasn't being reciprocated. Now this grimy, dirty company of infantrymen were trying to act like diplomats, under orders.

"Me and Simone," remembers Carter, "we had this poncho, so we were gonna play like fighting the bull. We turned our helmets sideways and we waved our ponchos and we said 'here toro, here toro,' and the kids liked it and we played all day.

"And we thought we made a hit. But the next time we went through that village we got sniped at," Carter recollects, still seeming surprised and hurt at this peculiarly requited gesture of love. "So we had a big discussion around the company. We would wonder. We come to help them. We give them medical supplies and they come and kick our ass. We wondered what the hell we were doing there in the first place.

The company couldn't understand what was happening to them, what they were supposed to do and why their gestures of friendship were not reciprocated. And they couldn't understand why they were so overworked, forced always to be in the field, never allowed to rest or relax. And they would discuss these things among themselves.

But who was to give them the answers? If the brightest minds in this country couldn't understand what was happening to America in Vietnam, it would not be easy for a company of eighth-grade dropouts to find easy solutions.

Pendleton used to correspond regularly with his sister Bonnie, a bright and attractive young woman married to a medical student in California. The year 1968, she recalled, "was some year." It was the year protest against the Vietnam war was at its height. It was the year Eugene McCarthy and Bobby Kennedy were fighting each other for the privilege of being the peace candidate for the presidency of the United States.

Bonnie recalled the weekly letters she would write her

brother. "I told him of McCarthy's following, and of the dissension at home. I told him people who followed McCarthy weren't against him (soldiers), but were trying to stop the war."

Pendleton remembers, "the company resented the war."

Worn out from his long tours in the field, Pendleton would come back to LZ Dottie and read his sister's letters. He would begin to wonder, as he was getting ready to go on guard duty or night patrol or maybe back into the field again, with little rest or break from the grinding routine.

"We knew that people back home was against the war and we thought it was kind of funny that people was against the war back home but we had to work so hard at it over there. We wondered why it was so important that we had to do all these things while people back home was against the war and it seemed funny that some people had to do so much and that some people was against the war. It seemed strange to me that there was so much of a difference," Pendleton recalled.

Even worse was that boys like Pendleton never quite knew what they were fighting for.

"They have people doing good things there, building bridges and giving medical help. We used to go down to the village and be nice to them. But they didn't tell us about them people, the farmers, I don't know what side they were on.

"I didn't hate the people who lived in the country. They had to worry about the Communists and the Americans. They probably don't go for any one of them.

"The GIs, they didn't know who to hate. They were kind of mixed up about what they had to do. Our allies, the Vietnamese, they didn't do anything. The people in the villages who acted like our friends, they were just trying to get our money. At least these people in the country, they weren't trying to get our money.

"C Company wasn't really mean guys. They raped and

all. But it was frustration and it was a little bit of thinking that it was OK to do it. Nobody told them it wasn't OK. Col. Beers left the people alone and nobody cared. I didn't care either and right there you lose the reason why you're there at all."

Pendleton could find no work long after he got out. He said he was "for and against the Vietnam War," as a result of his experiences. "I'm against some people having to do it all and some not having to do anything."

Pendleton, perhaps more than anyone else, put his finger on the mental attitude that permeated the company. No matter how hard they worked, they were pushed harder by ambitious superiors, by inept leaders. And they did as they were told.

And no matter how friendly they tried to be to a basically antagonistic population, they were rejected. Wherever they moved they were hated.

Even their allies, the South Vietnamese Army, took advantage of them. The ARVN would quit in the middle of an operation to break for tea or an afternoon rest or because they were afraid or they just didn't feel like fighting anymore.

The people in the backward areas acted like animals, at least by U. S. standards and so they were regarded as animals.

The Vietnamese kids near LZ Dottie would sell the GIs back their own PX wrist watches or cokes or American beer for exorbitant prices. The whores, even the high-class ones back at LZ Dottie, sold themselves for 500 piasters, which at black-market rates was little more than 2 bucks.

It seemed like every woman they met had a price. Or if she didn't have a price she'd be quiet for a price. It never went over 500 piasters. Anyone who sold herself that cheaply couldn't be any good, reasoned the GIs. The next logical step was that if they did it for two bucks they'd do it for nothing. And there were women who did it for nothing. Probably the women did it out of fear, but the GIs didn't know that. Or if the women raised a little fuss, the piaster notes would be thrown at them and the girls would quiet down.

The sexual incidents between members of Charlie Company and village women never took on the bad connotation of rape as understood at home. "Everytime we went to the villages, we took C rations and give it to the kids," remembers Terry." Then lots of times the guys raped. Sometimes there'd be a gang rape. Half the company raped. Even the guys who went to whore houses raped. But it wasn't in anger."

Richard Hendrickson, who kept away from village women because he had heard that venereal disease in Vietnam was incurable, remembers that an order had come down from Medina to leave the girls alone. "They did, until one time a gang tried. But somebody yelled that Medina was coming and everybody scattered," Hendrickson recalls.

"We felt sympathy for the kids. I never saw any kids beat," Hendrickson said, but apparently the company's compassion never went out to the adults, regardless of sex.

"If the men did bed down with the women," adds Hendrickson, "it wasn't forcible rape. Lots of times the women did it on their own." Once he remembers some screams coming from a hootch where two women were with some GIs. "The guys threw a handful of coins at the women. Some of the coins were French. The girls threw the French change on the ground and kept the rest."

Rape, which at home is reprehensible, had become, in Vietnam, a way for the company to react to the animosity shown towards the Americans. Sex, in the rice paddies of Quang Ngai province, then, became an expression of hate, not love.

Love turned to hate; friendship to animousity; right became wrong in the gradual deterioration of Charlie Company as it wallowed, lost and leaderless in the rice fields of an alien land. Not only was this the wrong war in the wrong place and the wrong time. But the wrong men were being sent to fight it.

If Charlie Company was turning wrong it was because something was wrong with the Army. If something was wrong with the Army it was because something was wrong with society.

By permitting bitter dissent in a time of war, and condoning draft dodging and desertion, America was not proving itself democratic. Instead the nation has succumbed to anarchy through the emergence of selfish groups of "elitist" individuals who could vociferously determine with impunity what they felt was best for themselves in the name of the country. For so long as qualified people are permitted to shirk their duty to society without penalty, by intellectualizing their opposition to a war that all decent human beings reject, then the Army had no alternative but to settle for mediocrity.

To be a leader one must be above average. Medina may have been. Calley by all accounts wasn't. When Medina gave an order in the field, his men followed. When Calley gave an order he had to remind them that "I'm the lieutenant; I'm the boss." Calley apparently wasn't a natural born leader and the company suffered.

"Calley was pretty much of a jerk," says Widmer quite candidly. "He had trouble finding where he was, even in Vietnam. It was simple mistakes he made, like reading off the wrong coordinates on a map. Medina would say 'Are you sure?' and Calley would say 'Yes' and then he'd read off the wrong coordinates again."

Widmer says the men paid no attention to Calley. "The guys just accepted Calley as being there. But as far as listening to him, it went in one ear and out the other. He was like a little boy trying to mimic his father—Medina. "Like a little boy will put a cigar in his mouth. He doesn't know why he does it. But he does it. Calley was just trying to put on something that he wasn't. He was more-or-less trying to be like Medina."

This may be cute for a little boy, but for Calley it resulted in tragic consequences. Unable to inspire or lead his men, Calley would try to act tougher than they, or copy Medina's mannerisms in the hopes that he could impress his troops. But it wasn't working.

So if Medina worked over a Vietnamese, it would be because the captive's name was listed in Medina's little black book of VC suspects. "Medina knew what he was looking for. Calley he'd do the same thing, but with no meaning or purpose behind it," Widmer says.

One day Bergthold spotted a Vietnamese farmer in the field. "We were going to set up a blocking force for another company and I spotted this guy out in the rice paddy. He was working with a hoe, so I brought him in," Bergthold remembers.

The young soldier turned the prisoner over to his platoon leader, Lt. Calley. Standing nearby were Carter and Billy Carney. "Lt. Calley started asking him questions," remembers Bergthold. "Then everybody was talking to him at one time."

"Calley called us over," remembers Carter, "and he didn't actually give us an order, but he said, 'Take care of him.' Calley was a person who you couldn't actually know what he was thinking. He was cold-blooded. Deep inside he may be worried, but he didn't show it."

When Carter was given the prisoner, he remembers, "We worked the hell out of him and threw him in the well. Somebody said, 'Let's see if you could swim,' and pushed him in the well."

The prisoner made no sound. "Vietnamese are very funny; they don't scream," Carter observes.

After the prisoner, described as a "young dude," was thrown in the well, relates Bergthold, "Lt. Calley just walked up and shot him. He took an M-16 in his right hand and pointed it down and shot him."

"After a while that company got so used to brutality, it enjoyed it," Carter says.

"The thing that got to me, you'd hump in one village and out the other and it seemed aimless. But every time you came into a village you had a good reason," recalls Van Leer. "One time we found a guy in a hidden wall of a hut. He got so scared he dropped his pants and crapped when we found it.

"All we saw were animals. Most people we ran into were VC sympathizers. John Paul went to school in Hawaii to speak Vietnamese. But they pretended they didn't understand him. Even Sgt. Phu was told by the people they couldn't understand him."

Phu was a South Vietnamese Army interpreter attached to the company. Paul and Ron Grzesik were American GIs who had studied Vietnamese in Hawaii to act as company interpreters.

"We were bitter," remembers Hendrickson. "We never had a real confrontation with the enemy. I didn't like Vietnam. Phu our interpreter was OK. We knew what he was doing. But the ARVNs were laying around doing nothing. Then you say to yourself, 'What am I doing here. Why should I fight for them.'

"When you go to a village you're supposed to be friends. But the first time you try something, they try to kill you. Besides they all look alike. You can't tell who's your friend and who's your foe.

"I didn't like the Vietnamese, but I don't know why. They're people and they're not dumb. They fix booby traps and it don't take no dummy to do that. We never underestimated them. The villagers, they were your friends when you were facing them. But when your back's to them, who knows. We were supposed to be protecting them, but they sniped at you when your back was turned."

Charlie Company was becoming totally frustrated, dog-tired and completely frightened. They were being pinged on their ears, slapped on the backs of their heads. They were the new kids on the block and they were really being worked over. But every time they turned around they'd stare into a sea of impassive faces.

If only they could really fight the enemy, Charlie Company would think. Then they'd show those VC bastards what soldiering was really like. This was becoming their one dream—to have a real good firefight with the enemy, and kill the dirty bastards.

Charlie Company had carried out every order the authorities had given them. Killing was about the only thing most of the men had not yet done. If they ever had that dream battle with the enemy, Charlie Company asked itself, would they kill? Did they have the guts to kill, Charlie Company wondered, as it wandered relentlessly across the rice fields. Charlie Company kept thinking. Charlie Company indulged itself in wishful thinking.

Time had begun to work on the men. The freshness of being in Vietnam was over. The curiosity had worn off. The men were settling into a routine—a grinding, grueling routine that showed no evidence of ever letting up.

Nor would anything pleasant ever happen to these men. It would be one miserable patrol after another; in one stinking village and out another, with never a friend in sight and meeting only people who hate you. With leaders who are afraid to visit with you, but who spur you on to elusive victories from their helicopters; with folks back home who tell you not to do what you don't want to do anyhow. With the drill instructor's last admonishment still ringing in your ears to "kill, kill, kill"; with the higher headquarters call for "body count, body count, body count." With the warning from combat veterans not to trust anybody, and with the brass assuring you that there are no civilians where you are because it's all a free-fire zone. Therefore, anything that moves may be killed, killed, killed.

"We felt crapped on," Van Leer remembers. "Booby traps were a constant threat. The Vietnamese were filthy,

cruddy people. That's why I never got sexually aroused
with their women. The women's teeth were black from
betel nuts. I hated their teeth.

"Their food disgusted me. The smell in the villages disgusted me. They were unclean. They used dirty fingers to
pick up their food. Human waste was all over the village.
So were the flies. The flies would go from the human
waste to the people's faces and they didn't even try to
brush them off.

"I couldn't comprehend a dead Vietnamese as being
dead. Once I saw four dead Vietnamese. Ants were crawl-
ing straight up the chest of one guy into his mouth and
eyes. If I saw a dead kid in the United States it would
effect me more than a dead Vietnamese kid.

"And the people in the villages were so damned fakey.
We went through a village and there was this woman and
a few kids. The woman slapped the kids on the arm and
they started chanting, 'GI number one, GI number one.'
Medina told Phu to tell them to shut up. They did."

The men grew more tired and frustrated and filled with
hate. And as they did they became more unpleasant to the
outside world—in this case the Vietnamese. Terry tried to
explain it once. "These guys were draftees and most
draftees don't want to be in the Army or in Vietnam. They
took it out on the Vietnamese people."

Medina must have been aware of what was happening.
He tried to get R and R for the men. Rest and relaxation
is a leave most soldiers get after they have been in Vietnam for six months. Medina was trying to get it sooner for
his men.

For he must have known what they didn't. The Viet
Cong don't fight conventional battles. Their tactic is to
hit and run and live to fight another day. Their tactic is
to fire and fade—to be where the enemy isn't and to disappear where the enemy is, to jab as in a boxing
ring, to jab, jab, jab, keep jabbing, but never to swing that
right. They were too small and weak to have power in

their right hand. But if they could keep jabbing their op-
ponent he might get bloodied enough to quit—or to make
a mistake and do something foolish. The tactic works
well.

In guerrilla warfare the village is the sea, said Mao Tse
Tung, the leader and master theoretician of Chinese
Communism. The guerrillas are the fish. The fish must
live in the sea. The sea must support the fish.

Lin Piao, Communist China's defense minister, carries
the anology one step forward. The people of under-
developed nations are like the peasants in the countryside, he says. The people of the modern nations are like
city dwellers. And one day the people of the under-
developed nations will overwhelm the people of the modern nations and Communism will triumph around the
world.

Charlie Company didn't like the Vietnamese people.
The men didn't like the shit on the road and the smell of
fish and sauce in the villages. They didn't like the arrogance of the peasant, and his reticence, indifference and
antagonism. For kids who had never held jobs or performed the most menial of tasks, these youngsters made
good infantrymen. They could put up a tent or build you
a bunker or hump the fields all day for you. But, Uncle
Samuel, you picked the wrong guys if you were looking
for soldier-diplomats. You took kids who came from the
lowest strata of American society and you asked them to
go win friends for you among the peasants of another
culture.

You know what Carter said about that, once? Carter
said these kids were poor, hard-luck ghetto types who had
been pushed around all their lives. Now they found somebody else even lower than they were. You hired them to
be diplomats when you wouldn't even hire them to be
ditch diggers at home. Uncle Sam, you must be kidding.
You got what you asked for.

Charlie Company did what the Army bid them do. They

performed all the menial tasks of the infantry. They even heeded the bidding of their superiors to try to keep the body count up. But they just were not capable of being diplomatic. They were what you trained them to be, Uncle Sam.

Charlie Company didn't realize they were witnessing a political philosophy in practice and that it was their role to prove it unworkable. All they knew is that they didn't like Vietnam and the villagers in it. And their patience was being put to the test. Charlie Company didn't know they were being defeated in the villages of Vietnam. Soon they would be given their chance to be defeated on the battlefield.

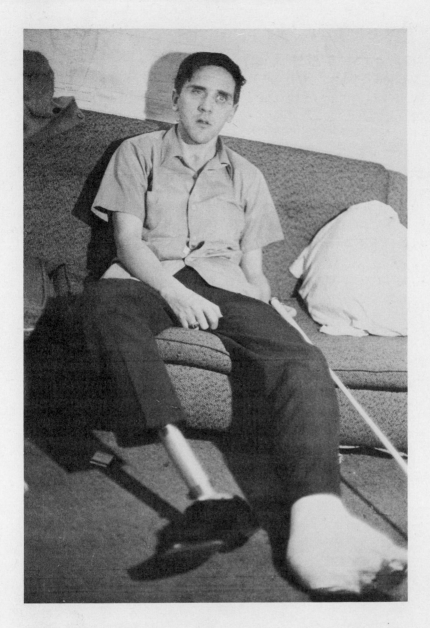

Richard Hendrickson sits in living room of home, blind, deaf, his right leg gone, his left going, his left arm useless. His survival of a booby trap explosion that killed Sgt. Cox is miraculous. He was one of the men Charlie Company sought to avenge at Mylai. Van Leer was another.

James R. Bergthold *(left)* stands with friend outside rooming house in Niagara Falls, N. Y., where he lives and works as a $60-a-week truck driver's helper. He is a member of a group of youths who got the flag idea from the movie *Easy Rider.* He describes his group as a motorcycle club without motorcycles because none can afford them.

The author, Martin Gershen, on patrol with an infantry company in Vietnam on one of his several trips to the battle-ridden country. Gershen is preparing to cross a small stream known as the Ia Kral River near the Cambodian border in the central highlands of South Vietnam. He is with a company from the Fourth Infantry Division, commanded at the time by Gen. Peers who later would be charged with investigating the Mylai affair. Charlie Company was part of the 11th Light Infantry Brigade which relieved the Third Brigade of the Fourth Infantry Division in Vietnam.

Herbert Louis Carter is treated by medic at Mylai after being shot in left leg. That cigarette in his right hand is pot. Carter says he was high on pot that morning as were many members of the company. Widmer corroborates this noting he (Widmer) gave Carter a marijuana cigarette before the wounded GI was taken to a medivac helicopter. Former Sgt. West has testified before Dodd committee that perhaps 60 percent of C Company smoked pot and many the night before Mylai. When Haeberle said Carter smiling as he was being carried in a litter to the medivac. Carter says the wound was accidental and he was smiling because he was high on pot.

ROW 1, L—R: Janet Seiler, Jerri Palecino, Barbara Mese, Sally McCune, Ray Martin, Judy Combs, Betty Masculine, Betty Jean Proctor, Susan Van Atta, Margie Albright, Teddy Neuweiler, Mike Sissine, ROW 2: Gordon Nitto, Richard Green, Joan Orsello, Cheryl Claiborne, Sharon Mills, Jolene Mitchell, Bonnie Dywer, Alice Adeeb, Marcia Bethea, Judy Dentamaro, Ann Diehl, Ann Wiborg, Suzanne Ogden, Madelyn Rohlfs, Larry Valle, Ken Woods, Billy Mickleberry. ROW 3: Dick Tracy, Al Smith, Eddie DuBois, Jim Lester, Alan Edwards, Jim Bennett, Larry Beckman, Ronnie Reese, Linda Grant, Pat Mathewson, Beth Webb, Donnie Morton, Bruce Snider, Ken Mashburn. ROW 4: Tom Saunders, Neil Valliev, Ed Todd, Dick Whitaker, Eddie Albert, Gary Livingston, Alfie Newton, Jim Marks, Pat Haley, Richard Urbano, Chris Scrapper, Tony Francis, Butch Renaldo, Rusty Calley.

Calley with classmates in high school yearbook photo. Calley is second from right in last row. Only his forehead shows. His whole life seemed to be marked by these bad breaks. A little, perhaps tragic figure of a man who always sought recognition but never achieved it. Everything about Calley has been described as average by high school friends, neighbors, enlisted men, and teachers. A better word perhaps would have been mediocre. He is more to be pitied than hated.

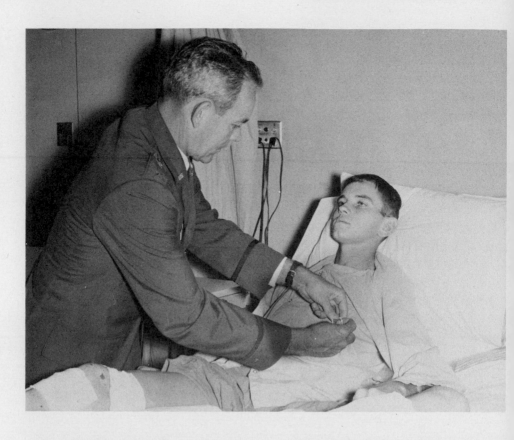

Robert Joel Van Leer who lost part of a foot in the minefield disaster February 25 looks gaunt, proud and frightened as a purple heart is pinned to his pajama top after he was brought to a stateside hospital.

Herbert Louis Carter became an itinerant laborer in Texas after his discharge, haunted by the war and the horror he had seen and taunted by antiwar types for being a member of Charlie Company and by prowar types for allegedly shooting himself in the foot. Carter was an innocent victim of the Vietnam war, as innocent as many of the Vietnamese of Mylai.

Author Martin Gershen at a forward fire-support base in Vietnam stands before a helicopter preparing to bring troops and supplies out to an infantry company on a search and destroy operation.

★ ★ ★

CHAPTER IX

WEBER

★ ★ ★ ★ ★ ★ ★ ★ ★ ★ ★ ★ ★ ★

"We always got our ass tore trying to get to Pinkville."

FRED WIDMER
A member of Charlie Company

★ ★ ★ ★ ★ ★ ★ ★ ★ ★ ★ ★ ★ ★

Charlie Company never really heard of Pinkville until it was too late. That was on February 12, 1968, when Bill Weber, Calley's RTO, was killed. He was the company's first man killed in action. The men never got over it. But until a few days before February 12, Charlie Company was dreaming of a situation like the one that developed at Pinkville. Their search and destroy operations, which they had been on constantly since early January, were proving fruitless, futile and frustrating.

The villagers the company was encountering were hostile and uncooperative. There were increasing incidents of sniper fire that left more scars on the men's minds than on their bodies, because there was no way to strike back at a hidden guerrilla rifleman. Hidden mines and booby traps also were working on the men's minds. For there is nothing more damaging psychologically in warfare than to be struck by a hidden mine or a command-detonated bobby trap.

Command-detonated means that somewhere someone

is watching a GI approach a booby trap. And when the young soldier is close enough, it is manually detonated. It means that somewhere an enemy is watching you, waiting for the right moment to kill you.

Contact with the invisible enemy was becoming more frequent after the month of February began, but the men never saw the guerrillas trying to kill them. All they saw were the families of the enemy; the old papa-sans and mama-sans and children, who saw nothing, heard nothing and spoke nothing.

What Charlie Company needed badly, for its own peace of mind, was a good firefight with the enemy; an eyeball-to-eyeball confrontation where they could see the people trying to kill them, and shoot back.

About one week before February 12, remembers Doc White, the company had begun to make more serious contact with the enemy. It was sometime during that week that Ron Zeigler tripped a mine, severely wounding himself and slightly injuring Allen Boyce who was behind him. Zeigler was the first serious casualty in the company. He wasn't killed, but he was taken away, which in the minds of lots of the men was the same as being dead.

To the members of Charlie Company, the difference between being wounded or killed was sometimes indistinguishable, just as they were having some difficulty recalling the chronology of events leading to Weber's death.

Van Leer tried to explain why being wounded sometimes assumed the same significance in the minds of the men as being dead. "A man dies, he gets sent out by helicopter, the same as if he's hurt. The atmosphere was the same whether you were killed or wounded. You missed him as much in either case. In our minds they were gone, dead.

"The only thing they brought back of Zeigler was a sweater full of shrapnel," remembers Van Leer.

Boyce's wounds were slight. He was too embarrassed

even to put in for a Purple Heart. But they were of a sufficiently serious nature to get him out of the field for a few days. So he missed the gun fight in which Weber was killed.

Nobody who has been in combat sees the entire battle. A battle is a highly individualized, very subjective action seen through the eyes and felt through the emotions of the participating soldier. It is left for the historians and the television scenario writers and the Monday-morning quarterbacks to draw the big picture, and to explain through hindsight why it should or should not have happened the way it did, and what went right and what went wrong.

Charlie Company was operating out of LZ Uptight, and on February 12 they were flown down to Giem Dien (1), five kilometers south of their fire base and one kilometer north of Mylai (4). The company was maneuvering into position for what was expected to be its first chance actually to engage the enemy in a real knockdown-drag-out battle, just like in the World War II movies that some of these kids might have watched on the Late Late Show while being raised on television.

Indeed, some of the members recall the ensuing three-day action, which officially began on February 13, as something out of Hollywood. Many were eagerly looking forward to it.

"It was just like TV, with bullets pinging around," remembers Terry.

"It reminded me of a war movie," adds Doc White. "The platoon was in a country farm house and suddenly there was sniper fire coming from the river."

"We enjoyed gun fights," Bernhardt recalls. "I liked the idea of action. I did enjoy it when we did have some shooting."

The significance of the situation developing on February 12 was that all three companies of Task Force Barker were being given their first introduction to Pinkville, a place name they had never heard before but would never forget.

Charlie Company, of course, would also suffer its first death in action, an event for which the men weren't quite prepared; because, while Vietnam until now was a miserable place in which to be, at least nobody was getting killed. And Charlie Company would be introduced to still another place name on February 12, a name it had never heard before, but which would forever be linked to it— Mylai (4).

The plan for February 13, 1968, was to attempt to flush out the 48th Local Force battalion, an enemy Viet Cong unit numbering between 250 and 300 persons, ages and sexes unknown. The 48th had suffered heavy losses during the Tet offensive and now, perhaps, the U.S. Army was hoping to wipe them out forever. To do this, Charlie Company was ordered to act as a blocking force north and northwest of Mylai (4), near Giem Dien (1) and Van Thien (1), two neighboring hamlets.

Giem Dien (1) sat on a site marking the confluence of two small rivers, the Song Ham Giang and the Song Diem Diem, which zigzagged roughly in a west-east direction from Highway 1 to the South China Sea. Mylai (4), about one kilometer south of Giem Dien (1), was just outside Charlie Company's area of operation, whose southern-most boundary was the two zigzagging rivers.

With Charlie Company in the blocking position, the other two companies of Task Force Barker, Bravo 4/3 and Alpha 3/1, were to sweep north and east through Mylai (4) and towards Pinkville on the coast, 2½ kilometers away.

Running in a northeast-southwest direction, several hundred meters below Mylai (4), was a loose-surface road called Route 521. South Vietnam's 2nd Division (2d ARVN Div) would also participate in the operation as allies of the Americans, but would remain south of Route 521.

Starting from just north of Route 521, B company was to push north towards Mylai (4) while A company was to

attack east through Mylai (4) to Mylai (1), which was the
official name for Pinkville. As B Company approached
Mylai (4) on February 13, it received heavy enemy small-
arms fire from the Vietcong, well entrenched in prepared
positions in the hedgerows and treelines. One platoon of
B Company became pinned down, and was extracted only
after a platoon of armored personnel carriers (APCs)
were sent to the rescue with guns blazing.

Sometime during the night the ARVN forces withdrew,
for reasons unknown, so B Company had to withdraw
also. It lost one man killed and five wounded in the action.
The next day A Company continued its attack eastward
but encountered heavy resistance from Pinkville. On the
third day B Company was flown into Mylai (1) to help A
Company but the Vietcong had slipped away.

A search of the area uncovered 3 tons of enemy equipment in a tunnel complex that was between 12 to 20 feet
underground. The American forces lost 3 men killed and
15 wounded in the frustrating operation.

On February 12, after being airlifted from LZ Uptight,
which was on a 300-foot mountain called Nui A Linh,
Charlie Company set up its headquarters section in a hut
at Giem Dien (1). Van Leer was left behind to monitor the
radios at Uptight. He remembers that the speaker on Weber's radio wasn't working that morning. "I told him I'd
fix it when he got back," Van Leer says.

The 15-hut hamlet where the company set up its headquarters was just on the confluence of the two rivers. The
third platoon went out to patrol the area and immediately
got pinned down by enemy fire. Hearing the third was in
trouble, remembers Carter, the rest of the company left
Giem Dien (1) to rescue its buddies.

"There aren't too many men who would run towards
death," remembers Carter. "But when they heard of the
firefight and they heard the third needed help, that company ran." Actually, the second platoon stayed behind
because February 12 was its day to rest. Every day one

platoon was supposed to rest while the other two went out on patrol. Bernhardt stayed behind with the second, but he manned the radio telephone for Capt. Medina.

Weber was a short, chubby, popular kid. He had his radio set on his back and stayed right behind Calley, who led the first platoon down to the stream.

When the third ran into the heavy small-arms fire, Pendleton remembers seeing dirt kick up just ten feet in front of him where an enemy bullet landed. He and his squad were dashing over some rolling fields when the firing began. When he saw that bullet bite the dust, Pendleton dived into a gully and did the same. "I was scared," he says quite candidly.

But he didn't stay long. He hugged the earth, he estimates, for about 15 seconds, then cautiously picked up his head to look around. He saw the other members of the squad still huddled down into the ground.

Pendleton leaped up and dashed for a mound overlooking the river, and began firing in the direction of the enemy positions to the south. The platoon was being held up at the northern bank of the river by entrenched guerrillas dug in on the southern side, their backs facing Mylai (4).

Then, says Pendleton, Charles (Butch) Gruver, one of the platoon's machine gunners, set up his weapon and began firing across the river. Pendleton dashed over to a small bridge, as some members of his platoon tried to cross it in the face of the withering enemy fire. He remembers watching as Gerald A. Smith and Joe Grimes attempted to cross the river.

Grimes, a squad leader, was one of the men who kept the third platoon together, says Terry. He was a big man, a Texan and a Mexican-American who had the respect of most members of the platoon. The platoon leader, recalls Terry, "put quite a bit of weight on Grimes."

Grimes crouched real low and attempted to dash across the bridge. Smith jumped into the river to try to get across by wading it. Gruver provided machine-gun fire to cover both men. But the two men had to withdraw. The enemy fire was too heavy.

Hendrickson remembers the effort of the third platoon to cross the bridge. "We saw shells hit the water. Then machine guns opened up. Rifle grenades were going off. Then we started getting mortar fire." But the third platoon just couldn't do it. So it requested artillery fire to cover its advance, but the request was denied.

"They wouldn't put artillery in. It was an ARVN area," Pendleton says dryly. The area from where the fire was coming was supposed to be under control of the South Vietnamese Army. The third platoon was ordered to withdraw.

"It was all we could do getting out of there," Pendleton recalls.

While the third platoon was having its hands full, the first platoon also ran into intense enemy fire as it attempted to cross a stream. Back at Giem Dien (1), Bernhardt was listening to reports of the firefight shaping up, while at Uptight, Van Leer monitored his radios.

It was difficult making out the reports from the first platoon because Weber's radio hadn't been working well. "Medina was taking it like a cat on a hot tin roof. He didn't know what was happening," recalled Doc White. White remembers Medina appeared "anxious for his people," as he listened to the incoming reports.

Also concerned was Doc Lee, a close friend of Weber's.

The company was eager and excited, but also understandably nervous, since this was their first big firefight. The two platoons were under fire for a good part of the day. Later, veterans of Charlie Company who would be in far more serious battles long after Mylai (4), would recall the incident of February 12 as of minor importance. "When I say firefight," Pendleton once explained. "It wasn't a big battle; just some sniping."

But that didn't ease Medina's concern. He had always

cautioned his men to stay off dikes and walk in the rice paddies instead, or to cut through the woods and never take the same route twice.

As the first platoon attempted to cross the river—walking on a dike—Bergthold recalls he was ten feet in front of Weber who, as Calley's RTO, presumably was following in the footsteps of his platoon leader. Carter, his M-16 grasped firmly in front of him, was to Weber's right. Close by was Weber's buddy, John Wood, along with Billy Carney and Robert Maples, a machine gunner with the first platoon.

The men were advancing into sporadic small-arms fire. "Suddenly there were explosions. I had a full pack on with a lot of explosives in it," Carter recalls. "So I had to get into the river even though I couldn't swim." As the company's tunnel rat, Carter carried explosives to stick in the underground hideouts of Viet Cong in the villages that were searched.

When Carter jumped into the river, Bergthold was already there. Weber never made it. "I seen him fall," said Bergthold. "He screamed for the medic."

"I'm gonna die, I'm gonna die," Bergthold remembers Weber saying in fear. Then Weber began to cry. He turned to his buddy, Wood, who was kneeling beside him and said, helplessly, "I'm doomed."

"The guy was moaning like an animal," remembers Terry, sadly.

"I was scared; I mean really scared," Bergthold says.

Hendrickson said an armor-piercing shell went through the middle of Weber's body and came out the radio pack on his back.

Weber wasn't dead yet and word got back to the command section. Doc Lee dashed out immediately and, despite intense enemy fire, raced to the aid of his fallen buddy.

The men were terribly shaken, remembers Carter. It was obvious that Weber was dying. Charlie Company, the tight family of brothers, was about to lose one of its own. No matter how much death is anticipated, when it strikes it is unbelievable. A helicopter came down and Weber was gently placed aboard. He was dead.

Hurt mingled with panic in the ranks. Weber was dead. This war was really getting serious. Nobody seemed to know what to do. Carter remembers the immediate reaction was a hesitancy over reporting Weber's death for fear it would hurt the morale of the company. Calley has been unfairly criticized for this initial hesitancy. But Calley obviously was terribly shaken by the sudden tragedy. Death is hard to accept under the best of circumstances. For the first fleeting moments the platoon didn't want to accept the inevitable.

Carter picked up the radio transmitter from the dead man. Then Calley called the message in. At Uptight, Van Leer listened to the dreaded report.

"We have an elephant," Calley called in, using the code word for killed in action. Medina, listening on his radio, repeated the message. "We have a KIA," he said, using the military abbreviation for killed in action.

"We didn't know who got it," Van Leer remembers. "We don't use names. We had roster numbers. We knew it was an RTO."

And way back at Duc Pho, where the company's rear was located—the cooks, and the clerks and the mortar platoon—Shivers heard conflicting reports. First the word came that Weber was wounded. Shivers and Lt. Jensen immediately prepared to drive the 55 miles to Chu Lai to visit Weber in the hospital. Then, just before they left, they received the second message; Weber was dead.

"I think everybody liked Bill. I didn't know anybody who didn't," Shivers remembered two years later, still saddened over the death.

Meanwhile the enemy small-arms fire wouldn't cease. A shocked platoon stood helplessly on the north bank of the river, unable to cross it, unable to advance, unable to meet the enemy as the GIs thought they would.

Then over the rifle fire a voice was heard. It cried in anger and shock and fear and hurt. It was a mournful voice, yet it tried to hurl out its challenge bravely.

"You killed Bill Weber, mother-fucker," the voice cried. "Come down to my turf and I'll tell you to your face, after I spit in it with disgust."

The pathetic challenge had been tossed across the river. The kid on the new block couldn't take the tormenting any longer. "Come out and fight like a man," is what he would have screamed back home. But there was no answer. Just a sea of impassive faces. This wasn't the streets back home. This was Vietnam. This was Pinkville. This was Viet Cong territory. This was war. You don't fight like a man in war. You only fight like a man in the movies. You fight to win in war. You fight to live in war. The Viet Cong was a clever enemy. He fought well. He had just taken his toll, physically and psychologically: one man dead, more than 100 wounded, mentally.

And if a Viet Cong could speak English he would have shouted back: "You're on our turf, GI, and this is the way we fight. You want to fight us? You play the game by our rules." But the Viet Cong couldn't speak English. Instead he opened up with all the small-arms and mortar fire he could muster.

The first and the third platoons were ordered to withdraw back to Giem Dien (1). The company had had its first firefight. The company had had it. The men were willing but they weren't able. They suffered their first man killed. And they were forced to retreat. This was their first real live confrontation. And it was a defeat.

There has been some criticism over how this particular operation was handled. But Carter dismisses such talk contemptuously. "You can't blame Weber's death on anyone. The only good guys are in the movies. We didn't do nothing wrong that day. We fought our way out of everything we got into that day."

The company was less mad than confused when they returned to Giem Dien (1).

"We got shot at from the bushes and we didn't know who was shooting at us," Bergthold remembers. "They might be VC sympathizers or civilians. But if you can't catch them with a weapon then they're not enemy."

After returning to the hamlet, Bergthold was ordered to set up his machine gun in the cellar of a hut overlooking a causeway. One side of the causeway was all swamps and the other side all water. "Calley said if anybody tries to get in or out of the village to shoot and shoot to kill," Bergthold remembers the orders he received.

As he stared down the causeway over the rice paddies, Bergthold saw a figure moving towards him. "I saw a guy come out of nowhere." He remembers squeezing the trigger on his machine gun, but it jammed. "I shot him with my rifle. I never had any thoughts about it. I felt I did my job," he says simply.

Back at Giem Dien the men were in a bad mood. They were demoralized. "They were pretty shocked when Weber was killed," Medina remembers. "He was the first one killed. They realized that not all would be coming back."

"That company was a pretty rugged bunch of dudes," Carter recalls with pride. "So when they get in the dumps it's for a good reason. I liked Bill Weber . . . good old crazy Bill." Carter lowered his voice sadly as he recalled the incident that still upset him 20 months later.

"Everybody was super upset," recollects Van Leer. "They demanded a Bronze Star for Weber. It was a shock. This war was getting dangerous. I never pictured I'd die. I was always concerned for other people.

"I remember Wood took it hard. He was right beside Weber when the guy got killed. Can you just imagine your friend, your close buddy, just lying there dead?" Van Leer asks, also apparently upset over an incident that occurred nearly two years before.

"The only thing going through my mind after Weber

died was 'there's a life that's gone.' He was gonna be a veterinarian. And now he's gone. He's dead."

The company was airlifted back to Uptight and they sat in the dirt talking about their disastrous encounter. "I remember Medina was upset," Van Leer says. "He was talking and I wasn't even listening, I was so upset. Then Lt. Calley brought a paper to Medina, citing Weber for bravery above and beyond the call of duty, and Medina signed it."

In the roster of infantrymen killed in action in Vietnam, which is kept at Ft. Benning, Georgia, the home of the queen of battle, Weber is listed as being the recipient of the Bronze Star medal and the Purple Heart.

Medina talked to the men that evening, recalls Carter. "Medina said tomorrow it might be me or it might be you."

"He said these things happen," recalls Doc White. "He said, 'It's too bad it was Bill, but let's not forget him.' "

"After Weber was killed, it wasn't so much that we were scared as that we hadn't accomplished the mission," Van Leer remembers. "We had to pull back. It was the first time we had to pull out under fire."

Apparently Weber's death affected Lt. Calley, although the young officer never revealed his feelings much. Carter says Calley was too demanding of the men. He was a GI-type officer and the men resented him.

"Calley tried to change everybody—till Weber died," Carter recalls, observing that the lieutenant wanted his men to be clean-shaven and neat and respectful of all regulations, even in the field. "We didn't dig shaving and all that. One guy complained about going back to base camp because you had to shower and shave and all that shit. All that matters is being a good field soldier. A clean-shaven man doesn't make a good infantryman."

But then Calley changed, said Carter. "Weber's shooting was the turning point. Suddenly we realized a guy could get killed out here. So let's get our revenge before we go. Calley changed. He was no longer GI. He got to be a savage too. He had his savage membership card," remembers Carter.

The war had become a very personal thing for Charlie Company. They had suffered their first death and it was a traumatic experience. In war, no man thinks he will be killed; it's always the other guy that might get it. That feeling might permeate a group of men too. Charlie Company had been pretty lucky so far. Now they suffered their first real casualty.

"Our feeling was we all knew it might happen sometime," remembers Richard Hendrickson. "But the sudden realization that you can get kille . . . well, when he got it I'm afraid that if we saw a gook running across the field that day we'd fire on him."

A new mood swept over Charlie Company. The men would never forget the day Weber was killed—or the place he died. It was on a little river, south of which was a place called Pinkville. The men didn't know exactly where Pinkville was, except that it was south of a little river where Bill Weber got it and from where the company was forced to withdraw.

But if the men were having trouble with their memories, the Viet Cong would help refresh them. For the next three days, each time Charlie Company tried to cross the river it was turned back by the VC entrenched north of Mylai (4).

Two days after Weber's death the second and third platoons got clobbered.

"The second platoon got its ass tore in the rice paddies north of Pinkville," remembers Widmer. "It was over by the Song Diem Diem. The second platoon was in a causeway. They walked into an ambush. It was just north of Mylai. It was the second time we got tore up in the same spot."

Two men from the second were wounded and evacuated.

"Every time we went down to Pinkville," said Medina, "before we crossed the river we took a whacking."

"That operation kept rubbing the guys," Van Leer remembers. "Mylai was Pinkville to them and they couldn't go in. They tried three times and they couldn't get in.

"I remember we were sitting around at Uptight, waiting for a funeral service for Weber. But no chaplain came. So the guys got around and somebody said something nice about Weber, and then a few guys said a few prayers."

The war had taken a new turn for Charlie Company. It had become very personal. For once, they knew what they were fighting for. It was Bill Weber. Charlie Company declared personal war against Vietnam. It had suffered a bitter lesson at Pinkville. But the men were alone in their misery. Not even a chaplain came to console them. Nobody had time for Charlie Company. Not even God.

★ ★ ★

CHAPTER X

PREMINEFIELD

★ ★ ★ ★ ★ ★ ★ ★ ★ ★ ★ ★ ★ ★

"Most of us just wanted to get home."

JAMES BERGTHOLD
A member of Charlie Company

★ ★ ★ ★ ★ ★ ★ ★ ★ ★ ★ ★ ★ ★

The death of Bill Weber on February 12 marked the beginning of a series of tragedies that was to end 13 days later with the annihilation of Charlie Company as an effective fighting force. It is one of the tragedies of this company cursed with misfortune that even when it died, for all practical purposes, the Army and the nation would not permit it to rest in peace.

One might understand why the Army refused to recognize what happened to Charlie Company.

A blow to a man's mind can be as psychologically devastating as a bullet to his heart. However, when George Washington conceived the Purple Heart Sigmund Freud wasn't born yet, so psychology was unknown. The Army apparently prefers still to keep it that way, because it gives no Purple Hearts to soldiers psychologically shattered as a result of enemy action.

The Army has recognized, at least since World War I, that soldiers can suffer nervous breakdowns on the battlefield. It was called shell shock then. In World War II the

term was battle fatigue. But General George S. Patton, a
hero of the second war, pretty much typified the official
Army attitude towards men who suffer mental breakdowns in combat when he slapped a soldier at a forward
medical-aid station because the poor man showed no
physical signs of battlefield injuries.

The Army refuses to accept mental illness. So did the
public in the case of Charlie Company. In all the reports of
Charlie Company's tour in Vietnam, the nation's press
emphasized the deeds of these men at Mylai. The enlightened press corps, a profession that prides itself on compassion and the championship of the underdog, was more
concerned with what happened at Mylai than why it happened. Indeed except for passing references to some combat incidents, there was no mention of Charlie Company's
agonizing experiences on the Vietnam battlefield.

Even if the company had seen no action, its grueling
chores in the field, from the moment of its arrival in
Vietnam, were enough to bring its men near the breaking
point from sheer fatigue alone. But the death of Weber
and the subsequent tragedies of the company in the 13
jinx-filled days to follow were enough to guarantee its
destruction.

When Weber was killed, he wasn't just a casualty; he
wasn't some vague reference, or a kid from the first platoon who got it, or Calley's RTO who was zapped. He was
Bill Weber. Bill Weber, good old Bill Weber was killed, and
the guys in the third platoon were as hurt as the guys in
the first platoon—and even the cooks and the company
clerks back in the rear.

Charlie Company was too well organized, too closely
knit, to become as callous as an infantry unit should be.
It was truly a company of brothers, a family that would
mourn the passing of any of its members.

"If you hurt one of us, you hurt us all," Carter was to
recall, and if one man died something was wrenched out
of the hearts of every man.

"The company was formed and trained in Hawaii. We were more than a company. We shouldn't have been kept together," laments Van Leer.

Men in war should not be permitted to become too friendly.

When Charlie Company left the field after the three-day battle over Mylai (4), they were in poor spirits. Calley apparently was very much shaken. It was he who wanted to recommend Weber for the Bronze Star with V clasp for valor. The men, too, demanded that Medina get some medal for Weber. "We wanted his family to have something nice to remember," explains Van Leer.

The men returned to LZ Uptight, crestfallen. They had lost the action and lost a buddy. "It could very well have been Weber's death that touched these guys off," Doc White, an intelligent and astute young man, was to reflect long after he returned home.

When the men got back to LZ Uptight there were some packages of books and magazines and cookies waiting for them. They were sent by the VFW in Pico Rivera, California, where Medina's brother-in-law was a member. They were nice to have, but the men were more shaken over Weber's death. This war was becoming dangerous. A man could actually get killed out here.

The company stayed at Uptight for a few days, going out on platoon- or squad-size patrols, licking their wounds, probably smoking pot, since there was nothing else to do at this remote outpost. Being at Uptight was hardly any different than being in the field.

On February 18, 1968, Medina sat down to write another letter to his sister. Medina, who had vowed to bring his company back alive, had also once confided to his sister that some of these men might never return. At that time he might have been overly dramatic, as soldiers who are about to go off to the wars sometimes are likely to be.

Now, however he had one casualty. Bill Weber was dead.

What should he tell his sister, Medina might have wondered. About Weber's death? Or the three-day battle near
Mylai from which the company had had to withdraw? Or
should he write about the windmill-tilting patrols that
had kept the company occupied every moment so far of
their tour in Vietnam?

As Medina sat and pondered the message to the folks
back home, Americans were biting their fingernails as a
national debate raged over the battle for Khe Sanh, then
shaping up just south of the demilitarized zone. Here
5,000 Marines were holding out against an enemy force
estimated at anywhere between 2 to 5 North Vietnamese
divisions, numbering anywhere between 20,000 to 50,000
men.

The big question that filled the front pages of American
newspapers and monopolized the television screens was:
Are the Americans surrounded and about to be annihilated, or are five North Vietnamese divisions being
kept from moving south?

The answer to both parts of the question was "yes." The
Marines were surrounded in an old-fashioned sense. They
could have gotten out by air at any time. But five enemy
divisions were being kept from participating in the Tet
offensive, which, even without these extra men, had
proved a psychological victory for the communist forces.
That psychological victory might also have turned into a
military triumph had those five divisions been allowed to
continue their move south.

Instead, of course, the enemy forces would suffer a devastating blow militarily. But even the North Vietnamese
setback in the Tet offensive would go largely unnoticed,
because, from a publicity point of view, it was being her-
alded as a success. The North Vietnamese again would
prove their brilliance on the battlefield by using the
enemy press to its own advantage.

For the big argument at home was not over the tactics being employed by the U. S. forces at Khe Sanh. Panicked newsmen and television stars were asking was Khe Sanh necessary. And their argument against the Khe Sanh stand had nothing to do with military tactics.

The 14th anniversary of the French defeat at Dienbienphu was approaching at this same time, and newsmen with little background in history or military strategy were comparing the two battles just because of a coincidence of dates. Naturally, ran the logic, if the French were defeated 14 years ago today at Dienbienphu, then the Americans must be defeated at Khe Sanh.

So heated was this furor that the press found little room to report the massacre at Hue that had been going on during this same period. While Hue was being occupied by North Vietnamese troops, its civilian population was being systematically executed. Squads of Communist soldiers, armed with the names and addresses of civilians considered unfriendly to the Hanoi regime, were knocking at doors and taking entire families—men, women, children and babies—away to the slaughterhouse. Innocent civilians of both sexes and all ages were being deliberately executed by firing squads or buried alive and left to die by suffocation.

The story of the Hue massacre, in which at least 3,000 innocent civilians were murdered by the Communists, never really got good play in the U. S. press until the story of the Mylai tragedy broke some 20 months later. Instead the press was busy in February 1968, playing up a story about a village in South Vietnam, Ben Tre, which, it was claimed, was being destroyed by U. S. forces to save it.

Employing a tactic as old as military history, suicide units of North Vietnamese troops imbedded themselves in the village, forcing U. S. soldiers to shell it in order to dislodge the enemy. The alternative would be for American soldiers to die attempting to retake the village in hand to hand combat.

This tactic was used by the North Vietnamese in Hue, too, and two years later in Angkor Wat, Cambodia's famous ancient and historical city.

German Nazis employed this same tactic at Monte Casino in Italy, when they retreated into the monastery, forcing U. S. troops to destroy this shrine to save it—and themselves.

Cities have been destroyed in warfare, and their populations wiped out, at least since 1200 B.C. when Joshua fought the battle of Jericho and made the walls come tumbling down. Also in Biblical times, Roman soldiers sacked the temple of Jerusalem in 70 A.D., leaving only one wall standing. In medieval times, cities were walled to protect their civilian populations from marauding armies that gave no quarter once they gained entry.

Walls, of course, became useless with the development of aerial warfare. But that didn't stop Allied and Nazi forces from destroying cities like London, Berlin, Leningrad, Coventry, Darmstadt, Le Havre and Rotterdam, among others, and slaughtering thousands upon thousands of civilians.

In other wars other armies had the support of their civilian populations. A nation cannot go off to war without the support of its people. Even among primitive people, Indian and African tribesmen worked their warriors up to a fighting pitch with the use of drums, while Scottish clansmen marched into battle listening to the stirring martial music of the bagpipe. But Vietnam has been different. The Vietnam war has been fought by reluctant American warriors serving a divided and dubious nation.

In October 1967, when Charlie Company learned it would leave for Vietnam the following month instead of after Christmas, thousands of its American countrymen were marching on the Pentagon to protest the war. In November 1967, Noam Chomsky and other well-known domestic critics of the war called for civil disobedience. Bobby Kennedy admitted that he and his brother John had had something to do with starting the war, but now he had changed his mind completely. For, despite the deaths of so many young men, Bobby Kennedy was a politician so he had to go the way the wind blows. That same month, members of the government were arguing publicly over the merits of a war that Charlie Company was marching off to fight.

In December 1967, too late for Charlie Company, it had been discovered that Columbia University's selective service counseling program had been under the direction of an antiwar demonstrator. In New York, kids at City College were burning their draft cards. Four sailors jumped ship and deserted to Sweden via Russia; the ACLU defended six war critics; and a week of antiwar riots led by Dr. Benjamin Spock disrupted New York. Sen. J. William Fulbright called the war immoral; Cathleen Fitt, the daughter of an assistant secretary of defense, was taken into custody as a war protester; and President Johnson had to fly to Cardinal Spellman's funeral in New York by helicopter, because his safety in the city could not be guaranteed.

That month, Pvt. Richard G. Perrin, a GI deserter in Europe, said there was a growing antiwar movement within the Army.

Medina sat and wondered what to write to his sister in California. He knew his company was tired and distraught over Weber's death. He could use replacements but he knew he wouldn't get any.

The U. S. Army was stretched thin in Vietnam. President Johnson, afraid of U. S. public opinion, had reluctantly agreed to send 10,500 more troops to Vietnam. At least 20,000 U. S. soldiers were on alert in Vietnam to rush to the rescue of the besieged Marines in Khe Sanh. There were no troops to spare for a simple infantry company patrolling the rice fields of Vietnam.

Medina knew his men were worn out. Army policy permitted soldiers to go on a rest leave after six months in Vietnam, but Medina tried to push that time period up. Although his company had only been in Vietnam two and a half months, they needed some rest if they were to continue.

The best he could do was to give some men three-day passes. So Calley and two enlisted men left for a three-day rest inside Vietnam, and didn't return for ten days. Calley thus missed the date with death and destruction on February 25.

On December 18, just before leaving for his ill-fated patrol, Medina dashed off a letter to Erlinda. He spelled Quang Ngai wrong, calling it Quang Nahi, but that was excusable since most soldiers have no idea where they are, let alone how to spell the strange place names in which they are sent to die.

"Dear Linda, Don & Family," wrote Medina.

"Just a very few short lines to let you know that everything is alright. We have been busy as hell and there is lots going on as you can tell by the news.

"We are leaving for the field again to continue more sustained combat ground operations in the morning and it's very late right now but I did want to answer your letter and let you know that I'm alright.

"Linda thank you a million for your packages that the VFW sent, they were received greatly by the troops and you people did a lot for the men's morale.

"My X. O. (executive officer) typed up a short thank you note which I signed in the middle of a rice paddie while we were moving against the V. C. Again, thanks loads, it was just great.

"Please write when ever you can, mail is greatly appreciated.

"Please let me know where Dad is, I don't know where

to write to him—let me know soonest.

"Regards to all and don't worry everything will be alright.

Love
Ernie

Mrs. Erlinda Lovato, ten years older than her brother and almost like a mother to him, breathed another sigh of relief as she refolded the latest letter from Ernie. She replaced it in the flimsy air mail envelope and lovingly put it away to read another time.

Ernie was still alive and apparently doing OK. She would tell their father, an old ranch hand who had never been able to get the restlessness out of his blood. She was in touch with him.

And their grandfather who had raised them would be proud too, she thought. Everybody in the family was proud of her brother, Ernie, the Army officer. He had really gotten ahead in life.

But Mrs. Lovato's face looked worn beyond her years. Ernie was doing alright, she thought. He kept saying it over and over in his letter. But that didn't stop Erlinda Lovato from worrying. She worried about her brother in Vietnam. She had every right to.

★ ★ ★

CHAPTER XI

BAD WEEK

★ ★ ★ ★ ★ ★ ★ ★ ★ ★ ★ ★ ★ ★

"The way to destroy the enemy is to destroy his morale."
ROBERT JOEL VAN LEER
A member of Charlie Company

★ ★ ★ ★ ★ ★ ★ ★ ★ ★ ★ ★ ★ ★

Charlie Company stayed at LZ Uptight a day longer than Medina had expected, but early on February 20 the men packed to go into the field again. For many it would be their last patrol.

The company was on a sweep of particularly hostile Viet Cong-controlled villages just five miles north of Mylai (4). This area had once been under the control of the South Korean Marines, who had a reputation of being exceptionally harsh on the Vietnamese villagers suspected of guerrilla activities.

The objective that night was to reach Hill 128, called Nui Phuong Hoang by the Vietnamese, and they did it with little incident. But the company sensed they were being tailed by one or two Viet Cong snipers. Because that's the way the war went. No battle, just nagging attacks, like a mosquito that won't quit. The company also could see that the natives were decidedly unfriendly in this area.

"You could feel the hostility in the villages," remembers Medina. "We'd see a kid standing and smiling at us, but we knew damn well he was counting the men and the machine guns as we passed by."

The next day, February 21, the company ran into the first of its string of casualties that would end with the disaster on Sunday, February 25.

By then they had progressed four kilometers more in a northeasterly direction and were preparing to bivouac on Hill 74. A night defensive perimeter was being set up. Two men, both shorttimers who had volunteered to go to Vietnam although they only had six months to serve, were clearing some underbrush, when they set off a booby trap and were badly wounded.

In some respects booby traps are worse than mines, because they don't always come up from the ground to get you. Booby traps have been known to be placed in bushes or in branches of trees at face level. They can be mortar rounds or 105 mm. shells or 155 mm. shells, or hand grenades with the safety pin removed, placed into tin cans so an accidental kick will knock them out and blow you up.

Booby traps are horrible when they hit you face on, almost guaranteed to blind or disfigure or take an arm, just as a mine is guaranteed to take a leg or a testicle if it doesn't split you open completely. But the most frightening thing about booby traps and mines is that you never know where they are; thus every motion involved in the act of walking or moving forward becomes a cautious, concentrated effort.

Men begin to walk with their eyes fixed on the ground, looking for some telltale sign they should avoid. Is that little thing ahead the three prongs of a Bouncing Betty or just three blades of grass? As your right foot moves in front of your left foot, should you place it down on that rock just ahead, or behind the rock, or in front of the rock, or to the side of the rock . . . which side of the rock . . . the left side or the right side?

Those gooks are uncanny and very clever. They must

reason that you will want to place your foot on hard ground, so maybe they put the mine beneath the rock. So maybe you shouldn't place your right foot anywhere near that rock. Maybe you should move over to the left a little or to the right. Then again, why not place your foot in the step of the man ahead of you? But he's already too far ahead of you. And if you walk too close to him, he'll get angry because if you trip a mine he'll get it too. And if you walk too close to him, he might trip a mine and you'll get it too.

What do you do with your right foot? You can't stand on your left foot forever. And after you finally put your right foot down and nothing happens, your next decision is what to do with your left foot, which, in the act of walking, comes up when the right foot goes down.

A man can go crazy if he lets the thought of mines and booby traps obsess him, which is one of the purposes of mines and booby traps. Even if they're not tripped they can drive a man crazy.

With the wounding of two men by booby traps, the company knew they were in bad territory. Psychologically, they had been hit again.

On February 22 the company moved farther north, and in one village they uncovered an unusually large cache of rice and other supplies. They also took two prisoners, two males of military age found without identification. One had been badly burned, so badly burned that when a soldier put his hand on the captive's arm, the skin crackled and peeled away. The company called for a helicopter to remove the prisoners.

February 23 was the day the second battle of Mylai (4) began, just about in the same place that Weber had been killed 11 days earlier. This time Charlie Company was about ten kilometers north of the action. But Alpha and Bravo companies, together with a platoon of armored personnel carriers, were right in the thick of things and were having a bad time.

Medina remembers hearing mortar and small-arms fire throughout the night, and got word that a company was in trouble down there.

In this firefight, Bravo Company took a blocking position north and northeast of Mylai (4), while Alpha Company swept east from Mylai (4) to Mylai (1), which is Pinkville, and the sea. The platoon of APCs moved on Highway 521, the loose-surface road on Alpha's right flank.

U. S. artillery and air strikes were called in because of the heavy enemy fire the two companies were encountering from around Mylai (4), enemy fire that included mortars, recoilless rifles, rockets and automatic weapons. Considering that Mylai (4) was a hamlet of innocent civilians, it must have come as a surprise to the American forces when two of the APCs were hit and the platoon leader seriously wounded.

Then Alpha company lost its commanding officer, who was wounded, and its forward momentum broke. By late afternoon the enemy broke off contact and escaped by mingling with the civilians or hiding in the maze of tunnels that connected the Son My complex.

Bravo company lost one man killed and ten wounded from enemy grenades and booby traps. Alpha company lost two killed and 13 wounded. Both companies lost the enemy, so the battle was indecisive.

One of the participants in this battle was Ronald Lee Ridenhour, the young GI who was not in the infantry but who blew the whistle on Charlie Company at Mylai (4) when he wrote a letter to his congressman and numerous others complaining of the happening on March 16.

Ridenhour was a helicopter door gunner and remembers flying air support in that battle. "I flew air support and neutralized ground fire," he recalls. Neutralizing ground fire means killing people down around Mylai (4) who might be firing weapons.

Meanwhile Charlie Company was having problems up

where they were. The VC who had been tailing the company since it left LZ Uptight had a field day on February
23.

The company had arrived at a spot where they would
bivouac for the night on the side of a hill. There had
evidently been an earlier action in the area for a burned
out APC could be seen in the field, another casualty of the
war. It was still light enough and Van Leer decided it
would make a good picture if he climbed into the APC and
had someone photograph him.

Mark Pate of the first platoon came up to watch Van
Leer and to make some kind of wise crack, when suddenly
a shot rang out of the bushes. Pate screamed. It was a
frightening scream, the scream of a man who realized
that what he feared the most had just happened to him.
Van Leer was shocked, shaken with fright. Then everybody started firing into the direction from where the shot
had come. It was a useless gesture.

Pate had only been hit in the shoulder and Medina was
instantly at his side. When the young soldier realized he
wasn't killed or seriously wounded, his sense of relief was
shared by the men watching him.

"Boy, I'm going home. I won't be coming back," Pate
said to Medina, almost joyfully. It looked like he had received that million-dollar wound—the one that gets you
out of combat but never seriously disables you. A dustoff
(medical evacuation helicopter) was sent to get Pate. He
was back in the company within 30 days and was to be
wounded twice more before his year in Vietnam would
end.

The men were shaken. Three casualties in as many
days. Medina called his sergeants together to tell them
his plans for the evening and to outline the perimeter he
was setting up for the night. Then Medina told the sergeants to come with him as he inspected the perimeter.

As the men were moving away from the center of the
company area, Medina, who always walked with his gaze

to the ground for fear of mines, saw what appeared to be a tiny piece of plastic sticking up from the earth. At the last moment, as he was almost on it, he managed to leap over it, at the same time warning the other men near him to freeze. Then he got down on his hands and knees and probed the foreign object in the earth with his bayonet. Beneath the tiny bit of plastic was a 175 mm. shell, a booby trap.

A disaster was narrowly averted. Medina ordered the booby trap to be detonated in place, and it went off with a fearful explosion. Smoke and dirt rose into the air, settling into the gaping hole left in the ground. The men gingerly came up to look at the hole, deep enough to serve as a grave for the dead. Although nobody had been hurt, the sound of the explosion and the sight of the hole it made had a further psychological effect on the men.

An exploding mine or booby trap can serve its purpose even when it kills or injures no one.

Among the men with Medina was Mike Dunham of the third platoon. Dunham was the soldier who wore a flower in his helmet.

Suddenly the ground rumbled in anger and smoke rose from the earth. Dunham leaped aside. He had stepped on a Bouncing Betty, but it proved to be a dud. It smoked and rumbled but didn't explode.

The sweat glistened on the faces of the men who saw this second narrow escape. The sweat had nothing to do with the evening's heat. Medina's heart beat faster. There were booby traps and mines and snipers all around them —in the trees, in the underbrush, under the ground— everywhere.

The smoke continued to seep out of the ground as many of the men hit the dirt, burying their faces in the earth. Others froze. "You ought to see some of those guys eat dirt." Widmer could smile now as he recalls the episode.

But nothing happened. The Bouncing Betty was a dud. So Medina ordered it exploded in place.

A Bouncing Betty is a delayed-action mine. Usually the man who detonates it has time to take between one and two more steps before it explodes, tearing his backside off. The man behind him gets wounded on the front of his body. If the man behind is too close, he gets his groin and legs ripped to shreds.

"It's very frightening," Medina says. "A mine, perhaps, has the most demoralizing effect on an individual or a unit. You don't know where it is. You can't fight back. Sniper fire at least you can hear, and take cover and fire back. Mines you can't see or hear until it's too late.

Once, said Medina, his men saw the remains of a sergeant from another company who had been blown up by a mine. "They put what was left in an ammo box," Medina recalls.

Charlie Company had had enough scares that evening to keep its collective heart beating in fear for a month. But the evening was young.

A helicopter came down with hot chow for the evening meal. Dunham and Ron Harris were waiting on the chow line together. Dunham had removed his helmet, which he didn't like to wear, and put on a soft hat. It was a bone of contention between him and Medina; Medina was always reprimanding Dunham for not wearing his helmet. Doc White was eating chow with the other medics and with his buddy Tom Turner. They had gone to the opposite side of the company area from where the helicopter had come in, to avoid the dust and the dirt the blades were kicking up. Now the helicopter had left and the men were quietly enjoying their hot food. But White and Turner were a little nervous sitting in what they considered an exposed position.

A soldier got up to go into the bushes to relieve himself. White and Turner suggested to the others eating with them that they all go into the bushes to continue their supper. Just as they were about to go, remembers White, "a gook jumped up and let loose." It was the sniper who had been trailing the company. Dunham and Harris, waiting on the chow line, dropped to the ground hit. The sniper disappeared.

All of the medics were together and none had their aid bags with them. They hadn't expected anything to happen. Perhaps they thought enough had happened to the company that day.

Dunham had been hit in his legs. White rushed up to Dunham and Harris; Dunham lay quietly on the ground, singing a war protest song, remembers White. "Come you masters of war," Dunham sang the words made famous by Bob Dylan. Then he sang "Age of Destruction."

Medina was by Dunham's side. Medina was always where the action was—or where the trouble was. He pulled out a needle to give Dunham a shot of morphine. He also wanted to thank Dunham for serving with him, war protest songs or not.

"You're hard on people because you're trying to make them do what's right. And suddenly, snap, they're gone, shot," Medina thought. "You'll be alright," Medina assured Dunham.

Dunham looked up at the captain. "I'm sorry for the hard time I gave you with my soft hat," he said. The two soldiers had made peace with each other.

Dunham's wounds were not serious, but bad enough to end the war for him. Terry thinks Dunham was lucky getting shot in the legs before he had to face a situation where he might have had to shoot at a Vietnamese. "He would have cracked eventually," Terry says.

That night one man did. It was after Dunham and Harris were given first aid and made comfortable. It would be unfair to mention the name of the man who cracked, because there was a question as to whether he was shamming or suffering a psychological breakdown.

Most of the men seem to feel he was a coward. "He done

that another time to us. He was a fake. He was the only guy without any reason who ever chickened out on us," remembers Hendrickson.

After Dunham and Harris got hit, this soldier became hysterical. He fell to the ground and began shaking and sobbing. He didn't want to go on any longer. He couldn't take it, he indicated. The soldier was the same one whose rifle, through no fault of his own, had accidentally discharged, wounding another GI, when the company had first arrived in Vietnam.

"It was my own personal opinion there wasn't anything wrong except a little yellowitis," Medina recalls. Others in the company have expressed the same opinion. But Medina did not want to make a final decision on a situation such as this. It would be unfair to the other men in the company to allow one to shirk his duty when all were equally scared of the situation that they were facing.

At the same time, some men are just not as strong psychologically as others. Medina sent for White, his senior medic, for an expert opinion. White wasn't too sure either. But the medic was aware of the gun accident. "There was something going on in this guy," White recalls. "He couldn't take it any more. He was useless to us." White recommended to Medina he be evacuated with the physically wounded; Medina concurred.

A medical evacuation helicopter was called in. The GIs lay on the ground flashing red lights into the night to guide the helicopter pilot in. When the helicopter landed, some of the soldiers grabbed the litters in which Dunham and Harris had been placed. But the man who broke down wouldn't wait. He tried to get into the chopper before the wounded. Medina grabbed him and held him until the two litters were placed in the helicopter.

The soldier who broke down was sent to a hospital. He was released the following day and ordered to return to the company. Shivers remembers that he and the supply sergeant drove the soldier back to the helicopter pad in Duc Pho to place him on a chopper returning to the company. The soldier jumped out and refused to go. Medina pressed charges against him and he was court-martialed. He was fined $25 and ordered returned to the United States. The last word was that he had been made a recruiting sergeant.

It was about this time that Gus Rotger had come to talk to Medina. Rotger had had more than his share of trouble with the captain but there seemed to be an affinity between them. Medina understood kids from low-income minority groups who were in trouble.

Medina had had lots of trouble with Rotger in Hawaii. But in Vietnam he was proving to be a valiant soldier. He would always volunteer to be point man, leading his platoon or squad as they moved forward on their endless patrols.

"Sir," Rotger said to Medina. "You remember in Hawaii you made us fill out those SLGI forms for insurance?" He was talking about the government life insurance applications that give every soldier's family a guarantee of $10,000 if he is killed. A soldier has to request this insurance and pay for it through allotment.

Medina said he remembered urging the troops to apply for the insurance.

"Well, sir, I have a mother and a sister. And I want to know would they get the money if anything happened to me," Rotger said.

"Yes, Rotger," Medina said. "They'd get $10,000 and six months pay."

"Thank you, sir," Rotger said. "I just wondered because," and the young soldier hesitated, "because I'm not going to make it."

Medina quickly stopped the soldier.

"A lot of us are scared," Medina said. "We have these thoughts and feelings. But we'll make it. Just stay alert and be careful."

"Yes, sir," Rotger said and walked away.

Charlie Company had a rough day that February 23. They had suffered four casualties. Since leaving Uptight on February 20, they had lost six men. It was more than one a day. Charlie Company bedded down for the night, and if they slept well it was only because they were worn out.

On the morning of February 24, Medina was ordered to sweep south to serve as a blocking force because of the battle that had been going on at Mylai (4). The company was in an area where VC snipers shot at 707 commercial jets flying troops into Vietnam. The company was told to break into squad size patrols and clover-leaf the area seeking out the snipers.

The battle for Mylai (4) had fizzled out, but the search for snipers proved useless too. The company was tired and their job wasn't made any easier by the fact that they carried the equipment of the six men who had been wounded since they started on this operation.

The company was moving through some hedgerows when suddenly they walked into sniper fire. The men fired back and whoever was in the bushes faded away. There were no physical casualties. There was one light moment, however, when one of the GIs, a tobacco chewer, thought he had been hit in the stomach. It turned out he had become so nervous when the enemy gunners opened up, he swallowed his plug of tobacco. He thought the burning sensation he felt in his stomach was a bullet that had found its mark.

Sometime in the afternoon the company was ordered to turn north and move to Tan Hoi and secure the area. Then a helicopter arrived with the brigade S-3, the planning officer. He told Medina that Charlie Company had been selected to help the 198th Infantry Brigade, an entirely different unit, operating north of Task Force Barker and the 11th Brigade's area of operations. Charlie Company was picked to serve as a blocking force for units of the

198th that would be sweeping the hamlets of Nam Yen
(4), (5) and (6).

Medina was ordered to proceed before sunup the following morning to coordinates BS 683908 and BS 699909.
The attack by the 198th was to begin at first light. The
area was up near the Batanga Cape, known as particularly rough country because the VC operated there in
strength. It was a new territory for Charlie Company,
outside its normal area.

When Carter heard the company was going to be a
blocking force again, he didn't like the idea at all. The
company had been operating for nearly a month now between LZ Uptight and the field with maybe a day or two
at LZ Dottie and the field.

"It seemed like only a week ago we wuz in another
blocking force and we caught hell. That's when Weber got
it," Carter remembers. "Everybody was kinda leery of
these blocking forces. Evertime you go you get it."

After he received his orders, Medina decided to bivouac
for the night on a little hill. It is always safer to bivouac on
high ground than in the valley. That way the enemy can't
shoot down at you. As the men were walking up the hill
they saw movement in the woodline. Nobody was supposed to be there; the area was a free-fire zone. That
means anything that moves could be shot. "We took a shot
at the gook but we couldn't hit him," Carter remembers.

Before evening the chopper came in with the hot meal
for the day. It was roast beef with mashed potatoes and
gravy. The liquid refreshment was soda pop, distributed
in individual cans.

"The troops were happy because that's always a treat.
Joe Bell came around." Carter was smiling as he recalled
a former buddy known for his pleasant disposition. "He
was scrounging food as usual. Tell him you didn't like
something and he'd be around to eat it."

It would be Donnell Bell's last supper.

The gook the men had missed earlier that day may have

been the same sniper who caused trouble after the men had eaten and just before they bedded down for the night. The company needed all the sleep it could get, because it would be starting long before sunup the next morning in order to reach its destination.

After eating, one of the soldiers placed his can of soda pop in the side pocket of his fatigue pants and went into the bushes to relieve himself. He was saving the soda for later. As he was squatting, with his pants down around his lower thighs and over his knees, a sniper's bullet rang out and found its mark. The soldier heard the snap of the bullet as it hit and felt his leg grow wet from the spilled blood.

Frightened into near hysteria, he leaped from his awkward position and raced back to the company area, desperately trying to pull up his pants as he ran, screaming "I'm hit, I'm hit." Other members of the company looked up in concern. But their grim faces turned to broad grins as they realized what had happened. The bullet had gone through the can of soda pop, releasing its contents over the soldier's legs. The "blood" the soldier felt pouring over him was nothing but the liquid from a punctured can.

As the men busied themselves setting up their encampment for the night, Medina was busy supervising the departure of the last of the helicopters that had brought in food and supplies for the company. He noticed that Bobby Wilson was standing hesitantly nearby. Allen Boyce also remembers the scene that took place next.

"I saw him hanging around and he looked like he wanted to tell me something," Medina remembers. "But I wasn't going to say to him, 'What's wrong, son?' "

Wilson had a brother in the Marines Corps who had just arrived in Vietnam, and he was aware of the Defense Department regulation that no two members of the same family need serve in Vietnam at the same time. Where brothers, or even fathers and sons, have served in Vietnam together, it has been through a matter of choice. For it is up to the soldier to inform his commanding officer of the situation and to request a transfer out of the country.

That's what Bobby Wilson wanted to do. After discussing it by mail with his brother, it was decided that Bobby would seek a reassignment home. There was nothing wrong with getting a transfer under such conditions. Indeed most members of Charlie Company would have grabbed at the opportunity and none would look down on a fellow soldier lucky enough to get out. Nevertheless, young Wilson was embarrassed about the idea of leaving the company. There was a loyalty that the men had for each other and, especially in the last few days with all the enemy activity that the company was encountering, it seemed a bit awkward to ask out.

Most specifically, the incident of the soldier who had broken down didn't help Wilson's plans too much. The men grumbled about the soldier's cowardice in leaving the company and Wilson didn't want to be placed in the same category. Still he was entitled to go and things were getting pretty hazardous and he wanted to talk to Medina about it. So he hung around as Medina supervised the departure of the last helicopter, and then he hesitantly approached the captain.

"Sir, I'd like to talk to you," Wilson told the captain.

"What is it, Wilson?" Medina asked.

"Sir, I don't want you to think I'm doing this because I'm afraid or because I'm running out on the company." Wilson began hesitatingly as Medina listened patiently.

"I'd like to say, sir, I got a lot of friends here," Wilson continued. "But I got a brother here in the Marines and we talked it over and we decided I should be out. So I'd like to apply for a transfer out."

The night had fallen now on the humid, tropical countryside, and the sweat glistened on the faces of the two men talking. The engine noise of the departing helicopter slowly faded in the distance, leaving the company again alone in this hostile field.

Medina's face reflected concern over tomorrow's operation, and Wilson's showed the fatigue of all of yesterday's operations and the fear of the future and the embarrassment of that moment. Medina, ever the professional soldier, looked at the kid before him. There had been shammers in his company and goldbricks, legitimate and otherwise, and at least one coward, but Wilson was none of these.

The kid felt guilty for wanting to leave the company, Medina knew, but he had a perfect right to leave. Was there a man in Charlie Company who would stay in this rotten country, fighting this miserable thankless war if he didn't have to? If the kid hadn't felt so guilty he could have been on his way right now, Medina thought. The regulations were clear on this point. But the last chopper had gone for the night and tomorrow there was the operation scheduled.

"Why didn't you tell me about this earlier?" Medina asked, partly in annoyance, partly in despair, partly in sorrow for the kid who missed his chance.

"You should have told me earlier and we'd have got you out on that last helicopter. Now we'll have to wait until tomorrow."

Nearby, Boyce heard the conversation and so did Bergthold, and soon the word was spread to the company. Wilson was going home. That lucky bastard. Less than three months out in the Nam and he was going home.

The men were worn out and they prepared to bed down early, for tomorrow would be a long day. They dug their trenches in the sandy ground, and cut down trees for protection which they set up on the parapets alongside them. This hadn't been a good patrol. They had lost six men in five days and tomorrow it would probably get worse, the men thought. But probably not a single one of them could have imagined that night how much worse the next day would be.

This whole goddamned war had been going from bad to

worse. It had been pretty easy for Charlie Company those first seven weeks when they were operating out of Duc Pho and just climbing up and down the mountains. In a way, it had even been easier than Hawaii, physically, and the men had begun to think they had this Vietnam thing really beat. But ever since they had come down to LZ Dottie and had begun operating around this place called Pinkville, things had become increasingly unpleasant.

Not only were the natives unfriendly; they were downright hateful. They smiled at you in the daytime and took potshots at you at night, just as that gook sniper who had been following the company was doing. The women and the children would grin at you as you walked through their hamlets, but where the hell were the men? Where were all the young men? Where had all the young men gone, like that song the peaceniks sing back home? They'd gone out to ambush the round-eyes, that's where they'd gone.

You go through a village and hand out chewing gum and the kids stare at you like it's the last time they'll see you alive. Or sometimes they look at you and you wonder how come they don't stick their finger in their ears because you're going to step on one of their well-concealed mines before the day is over.

How the hell are you going to win their hearts and minds when they're out to get your ass?

This was getting to be one hell of a lousy war. First Weber, and lately one guy a day. Who would it be tomorrow? At this rate we'll all die before the year is over. How do you stop it? Who do you hit back? The sniper? The booby trap? Can you shoot a mine?

The company started going to sleep about seven in the evening. It was a wet night, remembers Carter, although there was no rain. It was a dark night too, and warm, although there had been hotter nights. Carter, Sledge, Stanley, Doines and Wilson were in the same squad. Mitchell was the squad leader. David Reed was another squad leader in the 1st platoon. He had Allen Boyce in his squad and Grzesik and Mauro. That night both squads slept near each other. Just before dozing off Carter remembers one of the men wisecracking about how many VC he hoped to find in the morning. Charlie Company always dreamed of meeting the VC.

During the night Medina, who only slept fitfully, was awakened by the chirping of crickets and what he thought was another sound. Suddenly a Claymore mine went off and Medina leaped up and dashed to the sound of the explosion. Somebody had been probing the company perimeter and had tripped the mine. There was blood near where it had detonated, but whoever had set it off was gone—probably the same gook the men had tried to kill earlier in the day.

They were like rats, these VC. You could hear them and feel them and sometimes they even sprang your traps. But you couldn't catch them. Just like rats. Animals. They were animals, these VC. These Vietnamese were nothing but animals.

About four in the morning Mitchell woke Carter. It was reveille, time to go. The operation was scheduled to begin at first light and Charlie Company was expected to be in place before then. Wearily the men crawled from under their wet ponchos to prepare for another miserable day.

Wilson told the guys in his squad he wasn't feeling well, remembers Carter, and everybody kidded the Indiana farm boy, because before this day was over Wilson would be going home and there was no reason to feel bad about that. Later, however, the guys felt that Wilson's remark should have been taken as an omen.

Carter took point for his squad as the company started out for its blocking position. Boyce was the rear security for his squad. In Calley's absence, M. Sgt. Isaiah Cowan was acting as the first platoon's leader. Medina stayed near Cowan, while his headquarters section trailed the captain. The second platoon, with Lt. Karl S. Brooks, took the right flank, while the new 2d lieutenant, Robert Blemings, took the center block as leader of the third platoon.

Blemings, a short bespectacled man, was not too experienced. He had joined the company two weeks earlier, replacing Lt. Houk who had become the company's executive officer and thus removed from field duty. Blemings came from a rear-echelon job as a finance officer. He wanted action and he sure was going to get it. Brooks too was comparatively new, having replaced Lt. Jensen who had gone to battalion. Medina had trouble getting good officers in the field. Anytime one showed promise he was moved up to battalion and out of the field.

Carter was being directed by Mitchell, who had a field map. The young tunnel rat stayed inside the woodline, hacking away at the underbrush as he led his squad to the company's rendezvous with catastrophe. Mitchell stayed behind Carter, directing him, while Wilson was about 50 feet to the young GI's left. Reed was a little further back and Boyce behind him. Also to Carter's left and somewhere behind him were Cowan, Medina, and the headquarters section, which included Widmer, Van Leer and Doc White. Over to Carter's right was the third platoon, and to their right, but separated by a hedgerow, was the second platoon.

Gus Rotger, as usual, was point man with the lead squad of the second platoon. The platoon was deployed by squads in three lines abreast. Tom Partsch was end man in the center squad. The second platoon was to the right and behind the first and third platoons. At the end of a rank in the second was Vernado Simpson, and behind him his best buddy, Maurice Robinson. Master Sergeant Jay A. Buchanon, the platoon sergeant of the second, was behind Partsch and was followed by Bernhardt.

Partsch was a quiet kid, a little on the religious side and scholarly looking with his glasses, but tough. He kept a meticulous diary all the time he was with Charlie Company.

Bernhardt noted the area in which the company was walking was a big plain with lots of wild undergrowth and overgrown hedges and lots of scrub and low grass. In some places there were many trees. The ground was brown, gravelly and sandy. The area looked as if it might have been inhabited at one time. But it had been deserted for so long that it looked uncultivated, unpopulated and currently unoccupied.

It was a long, grueling walk in the sun as the men continued their trek toward the two coordinates, just south of the hamlets of Lac Son (4) and Lac Son (6). Bernhardt kept walking and not thinking. "I didn't run the company; I just went along with them," he remembers laconically.

"I guess I must have hacked away for a couple of hours," Carter remembers the march. The point man does all the work and takes all the risks. He must clear the path for the men who follow. He also is likely to take the first mine or booby trap in the company's path. Sometimes he is fair game for the sniper's attack. But sometimes the sniper let's the point man through, to trap those who follow.

Thinking back to those last moments in the life of Charlie Company, Carter observes: "I've often wondered that if I'd known where I was headed to, would I have went on anyway."

But despite their losses in the last few days and despite the hardships of field duty, Charlie Company, at that moment in time, had a feeling deep down that they had Vietnam licked. The men were dirty, they hadn't bathed for days, they stunk and they were tired, but they were doing everything they had been told to do. Physically they could keep up any pace, even the rapid one they now were on as they rushed to their rendezvous.

They were even proud of their slovenly appearance, their unshaven faces and the gray color of their khaki fatigues, reflecting the very color of the earth in which they slept, ate and lived. The men felt they were doing a good job. They were proud.

Weren't they always on call by the brass? That's because they were the best damned infantry company in the United States Army. That's why they were on this very operation which didn't even have anything to do with Task Force Barker. They were going to be a blocking force for units of an entirely different brigade. That's because they were good. They could do anything.

As the men kept moving onward, Bernhardt saw a red clay road ahead. Carter heard a sudden crack that he recalls sounded "like a cannon." Somewhere in the ranks someone got scared. But it was only the underbrush crackling beneath the weight of a GI and a soldier, sensing the fear that had momentarily run through the squad, called out: "What's the matter? You scared of dying?"

And somewhere some guys laughed, and one soldier said "Yeh."

Then Carter saw that the direction in which he was moving was taking the squad out of the woodline and towards a hill. There was a little knoll to the right of the hill. Carter, with Wilson to his left, still kept heading towards the hill. "Go right, go right," Mitchell suddenly ordered, directing his squad towards the knoll.

"I veered to the knoll on my right when Mitchell told me to," Carter remembers. Wilson kept walking straight ahead.

Suddenly there was an explosion that tore through the early morning stillness and a man screamed. Then there was another explosion, coming almost on top of the first, and another man screamed. Then there was another explosion, and another, and another and another.

Wilson hadn't made that turn to the right in time. He went down screaming "Medic."

Rotger was on his back, both his legs amputated, begging to know what happened to him. Joe Bell was burning to death, and Sgt. David Reid looked like he was bleeding to death.

At the sound of the first explosion Carter dropped down, as did the surviving members of his squad. Squatting tensely, he held his rifle tightly, pointing it towards the direction of the explosion that had sent a vibration through the ground, literally making him shake.

Then he heard a whole series of explosions go off in the direction of the third platoon.

Charlie Company was being annihilated. Its men screamed as they died, because they wanted to live.

★ ★ ★

CHAPTER XII

MINEFIELD

★ ★ ★ ★ ★ ★ ★ ★ ★ ★ ★ ★ ★ ★

"The attitude of the company has changed considerable since that unforgettable day in the minefield."
Letter to Doc White from a buddy still with Charlie Company

★ ★ ★ ★ ★ ★ ★ ★ ★ ★ ★ ★ ★ ★

That early Sunday morning, the 25th of February, 1968, was the beginning of the end for Charlie Company as an effective fighting unit of infantrymen in Vietnam. The disaster near those two tiny hamlets called Lac Son (4) and Lac Son (6) ended with the physical, mental, spiritual and moral destruction of Charlie Company.

The tragedy that struck the company, for some reason still never explained, has seldom been mentioned in any of the reports on the Mylai affair that monopolized the front pages of the world's newspapers.

There are times in combat, notes Bernhardt, when the wisest thing to do is to do nothing—freeze. That's what Captain Medina ordered his men to do when he heard those first explosions.

The first two explosions seemed to come almost simultaneously, one close enough to Carter that he felt the ground tremble, the other way off to the right and behind him. Boyce remembers being stunned into immobility, as were some others nearby, when he saw a cloud of smoke rising where Wilson had been moments before.

"Oh no, oh no," Boyce kept repeating as he heard the explosions continue. Then he began to weep. Others wept too.

"It happened up front and I was in the rear," Boyce almost apologizes for the position he held in his squad. "I froze. That's what you're supposed to do," he adds defensively. "I figured there was no need for me to help. The medics and stuff, they were outstanding. That's the hardest job in the company, medics. I surely wouldn't want to be one."

All around him Boyce remembers men rushing to help the fallen. "You heard a boom and you just kept hearing them. It stunned everybody." And as the explosions continued Boyce remembers whispering, "Oh God, oh God."

As his squad squatted tensely on the ground, Mitchell shouted above the roar of the explosions, "What happened? What happened?" There was no answer. Only the screams of the dying could be heard—and the explosions of the mines going off. And with each explosion more men dropped, screaming, cursing, praying, dying.

Then a voice in Mitchell's squad cried out, "One dead and two wounded."

"Who?" someone called out.

"It's —ilson." The name was drowned out by another explosion.

"Olsen?" someone repeated. There was a Greg Olsen, a Mormon and close friend of Terry, in the company.

"No, not Olsen. Wilson," the voice said.

Carter was heartbroken. "Wilson?" he cried out. "Not Bobby Wilson. No, not Bobby Wilson. Oh, please, not Bobby Wilson," Carter cried.

The destruction of Charlie Company was only just beginning.

Charlie Company wasn't freezing. It is to their credit that most men didn't panic either when those mines went off. But the trouble with the company was that the men, emotionally, were too close to each other—and they were green.

So they did the next worse thing to panicking. They tried to race to each other's aid. And every time someone got up to help a fallen buddy, he stepped on a mine and blew himself up and maimed the people directly in front and behind him.

"It was all pretty much mass hysteria," remembers Hendrickson.

"I was just a Pfc. team leader. Our chain of command wasn't too good. Even our squad leaders didn't know what we were going to do," Terry recalls.

Terry had been walking point at the head of his squad. He had just crossed onto a trail when he met Lt. Blemings. At that very moment there was another explosion: Blemings' RTO, Joe Bell, had stepped on a mine.

"As soon as it happened six guys were lying on the ground," remembers Terry. One of the soldiers was screaming "I'm hit, I'm hit." His back was peppered with shrapnel that ripped through his fatigue jacket, leaving holes that were now turning red. Terry was about to rush to his aid when someone behind him pushed him aside and went instead, only to step on still another mine and go down screaming in pain and panic.

Terry thinks he heard sniper fire. But what he remembers most was the smell of burning powder and metal. Van Leer still recalls that odor also. Neither man remembers the smell of burning flesh, although Bell was being burned to death.

Bell, the cheerful GI chowhound, had been carrying six purple smoke grenades, used as markers when calling in helicopters or identifying the position of a unit in the field. The grenades had been hooked to Bell's web belt and were located behind him and beneath his heavy pack and radio transmitter. When he stepped on the mine both of his legs were blown off, sending red blood gushing into the brown mud, now turning dark. At the same time all his grenades were ignited as he fell backward on top of them. They were searing holes into the screaming boy's back and sending up an eerie purple glow.

"He lost his legs and his will to live. The guy behind him got hit in the front and died. Bleming was laying right in front of me. Oh, there was a lot of screaming and crying and moaning," Terry still remembers.

"I'm dying, I'm dying," Terry heard Bell sob feebly as he and Doc Bruce Foreman, the platoon medic, and other members of the squad worked feverishly and fruitlessly to save the RTO's life.

"We bandaged who we could. We tried to help. It seems like there was one or two sniper shots while we were doing it," recalls Terry.

Sgt. David Reed and Pfc. Andrew C. Rodgers fell with Bell and Blemings, remembers Hendrickson. Hendrickson had been in the squad behind Terry's.

"They were a hundred feet ahead of me. We didn't know what to do and we got down. It seems only seconds later that our squad got it," Hendrickson said.

Reed, who had been in front of Bell when the mine blew up, was lying on his stomach. He had shrapnel in his back, and the right side of his head was bleeding. Each time he breathed, blood oozed slowly from his back wounds. Blemings, who had also been in front of Bell, was hit in the back of his legs and his toes. He was lying in the mud in pain, begging for morphine.

It seemed as if they were dropping all around Hendrickson. First a man in front of Henrickson fell with shrapnel in his chest. Then Sgt. Kenneth Carlson went down.

Foreman was overwhelmed by the wounded, each of whom was in need of major surgery. Foreman was trying to do singlehandedly for several men what a staff of surgeons, attending physicians and nurses would not have been able to do for each of these wounded under ideal conditions—save their lives or their limbs.

There are rarely minor injuries when mines are detonated. Men lose arms, legs, testicles, or they suffer serious internal injuries or bad head wounds—that is, if they don't die immediately. Many would prefer death to the mutilation that a mine can cause.

Foreman tried to give most of his attention to Bell, who was dying. More first aid pouches were needed; bandages were needed. Hendrickson collected what he could and passed them on to Foreman and another soldier trying to take care of Rodgers.

"Rodgers was pretty badly torn up," remembers Hendrickson. "There was a big red mass of flesh oozing out of the back of his right shoe. He had a hole in his right thigh and a hole in his chest. And his weapon was just ripped apart. His M-16 was torn to hell. The barrel was twisted and the safeguards were knocked off.

"His wrist watch was ripped off and there were holes in his hands starting from the back and coming through his palms. His face was all bloody, but not too bad, I guess, because it wasn't distorted. But his eyes were glassy."

Blood from a head wound was pouring down Rodgers' forehead, into his eyes and down his face. This panicked the young soldier, who thought he had gone blind. "I can't see, I can't see," he screamed.

Reed, lying quietly on the ground, called out reassuringly, "Don't worry, it's only blood in your eyes."

Then Hendrickson leaned down and whispered to the badly wounded man: "Don't worry; we're getting you out of here." And Rodgers, reassured, tried to smile.

Foreman was fighting a losing battle for Bell's life. But the medic was determined to save the young RTO. He was on his hands and knees, cutting the clothes from Bell's burned and battered body. The RTO lay on his back, screaming, the front of his black body exposed, naked and bloody. He mumbled incoherently.

The men worked on their hands and knees afraid to move. Just behind Rodgers, on a bush, was a little white plastic cup. It was another mine. A soldier pulled out his bayonet and frantically, yet carefully began probing the ground near the wounded and dying in search of more of the deadly traps.

And the explosions still kept going off. Each time one did, remembers Van Leer, he winced. It wasn't the noise that hurt him but the realization that every time a cloud of black dirt rose into the air, another member of Charlie Company was being blown up.

Doc James White, the company's senior medic was behind Medina when the first mine went off. As soon as he heard it, White pushed past the captain and raced in the direction of the explosion. It had come from where Bobby Wilson had been.

The first wounded man White saw had been hit in the face, chest, legs and feet and was bleeding from all the gaping holes made in his body. He had been directly behind Wilson. "Why is this happening to me?" the soldier was crying in disbelief. "Oh, it hurts, it hurts," he wept in pain.

Two soldiers rushed to help the wounded man. At the same moment White heard Reed shouting for a medic. White wheeled about and instantly raced in the direction of the call for help. As he was skidding down a little embankment near a hedgerow he saw Wilson.

"He was cleaved down the middle," White remembers with a shudder 20 months later, as he tries to describe a human body cut open from the neck to the crotch. "The chest cavity was open. I could see the intestines and the stomach, and his lungs were moving."

Wilson's body shook spasmodically as his veins and arteries pulsated, oozing blood onto the ground. Wilson's organs still functioned because they hadn't been told by his brain that his body was dead. Today was the day the war was supposed to be over for Wilson. It was.

There was nothing White could do, so he kept running to where Reed was lying on his stomach. As White finished treating the wounded sergeant, two other soldiers rushed up to help. At the same moment there was another explosion. It came from the direction of where Medina and his command section had been. White leaped up to go there. He took five steps and was almost on top of the dead Wilson, when he felt himself being hurled into the air.

Doc White had stepped on a mine. It blew his right boot off, as well as his big toe. As he was flying through the air, White muttered, "Oh shit, here it is." Then he felt his body being slammed hard on the ground. But he never lost his presence of mind.

Quickly the medic began examining himself, even as he lay on the ground. First he felt for his groin and his testicles and his crotch. They were all right. He moved his hands upward to check his chest, then down to his buttocks. No wounds. Then White sat up to examine his feet and his legs. He looked at his right foot. The boot was gone and the foot was opened wide and bleeding. Some toes were missing.

Doc White looked up to the sky as desperately he tried to assimilate the different thoughts rushing through his mind. The wounds weren't fatal. They were bad enough for him to be evacuated. But the company was being blown apart here. The men needed him. He was happy to be going and ridden with feelings of guilt that he would be leaving.

Doc White began to scream, to scream for everything that had happened, was happening and would be happening to him. "Goddamn mother-fucker, Goddamn mother-fucker, Goddamn mother-fucker," he screamed over and over and over again in despair and frustration, and in anger and fear and in pain.

Reed heard it and looked up, shocked not at the language but at the fact the medic had been wounded. Medics are like mothers to an infantry company. Everybody depends on them but nothing is supposed to happen to them. "Oh my God, Doc White's hit," Reed shouted.

And somewhere in the distance White heard the usually gruff voice of Daniel Simone saying gently over and over again: "Hey, don't worry Doc White, you're gonna be OK, Doc White; hey, don't worry Doc White, you're gonna be OK, Doc White." It was more like a prayer or a plea than words of assurance.

Some soldiers gathered around the medic and eager hands reached into his first aid kit to get morphine to give him. But then the men didn't know how to administer it. They forgot to pull the plunger. White gave himself a shot of morphine. With the aid of some others, White cut away the remains of the boot on his wounded foot and set it in a wire splint. His leg was burning.

While the men tried to console him, White started screaming again: "Mother-fuuuckerrrr, goddamn mother-fuuuckerrrr . . ." The war for him was over, but the disaster had just begun and he knew it and he felt guilty and he wanted to leave and he didn't want to leave and he screamed the only prayer an infantry man understands "Goddamn, mother-fuuuuckerrrrrr . . ." Doc White's prayers and curses echoed over the minefield.

Medina, says Terry, was the coolest man in the minefield that day. When he heard the first mine explode off to the right of where he was, Medina looked up and shouted for everybody to freeze as he saw the cloud of black dirt rise in the air.

His RTO, Van Leer, looking up at the same moment thought, "Oh God, some poor guy got it."

Medina ordered Van Leer to call in for a dustoff, a medical evacuation helicopter. Then he yelled out for a report. "Wilson, Reed and Rodgers," the word came back through the ranks.

As the explosions continued and Medina realized the men weren't freezing, he quickly rushed to clear a landing zone for the helicopter and to set off a smoke grenade

so the pilot could find the company. Van Leer and Widmer, Medina's other RTO, followed close behind the captain.

Suddenly, Van Leer remembers: "I heard another explosion and I smelled smoke and I found myself on the
ground and I tried to get up, but the radio seemed too
heavy."

Van Leer didn't realize, in those first moments, that he
had stepped on a mine. Then he looked down and thought
he saw a foot lying by itself on the ground. He thought his
varicose veins were acting up on him as they had done in
Hawaii.

"Oh God, mother-fucker," Van Leer remembers thinking to himself. "I said the first half out loud but thought
the second half," Van Leer recalls two years later.

Medina was quickly by his RTO's side.

"Oh, God, I blew my foot off." Van Leer looked up at the
captain, shouting and cursing.

"No you didn't, no you didn't," Medina said quietly.

But Van Leer could feel nothing from his left knee
down. Then he looked and saw that the bottom of his left
foot "was blown open like an exploding cigar." He could
see beefy red meat at his heel, mixed thick with the black
of his dirty feet. White bone fragments were sticking out
in stark contrast against the red and the black.

Widmer stooped down to try to pick up Van Leer's left
leg.

"Don't touch it," Van Leer screamed in pain. "It's hot.
It's burning. It's on fire."

Medina had always felt close to the 18-year-old radio
operator who candidly says he looked to the captain as to
his own father. In the company the men would jokingly
refer to Van Leer as "Medina's son." Now Van Leer felt
bad about being wounded, as if it was his fault, as if
he was letting Medina down. He wanted to tell Medina he
was sorry to be a disappointment to the company. He
wanted to assure Medina that he wasn't afraid.

But the captain was already on his hands and knees treating Van Leer's mangled foot. Then he picked up Van Leer and, with Widmer's help, rushed the boy to a waiting helicopter.

"Don't worry," Medina shouted above the roar of the rotor blades and the explosions still going off.

"Be careful, captain. Please be careful. Take care of yourself," Van Leer yelled back.

But Medina was already gone, tending to his dying company. And as the helicopter rose, Van Leer felt glad to be leaving the company and guilty to be leaving the company. He felt he hadn't accomplished as much as he had wanted to do. Then above the roar of the helicopter engine, he heard two more explosions.

As the helicopter began to move away from the minefield, Van Leer suddenly realized he wouldn't see the company again. He waved to them. Then he realized it was a ridiculous gesture. Charlie Company was being blown to bits and Van Leer was waving goodbye as if he was just leaving his family to go on a little trip.

Meanwhile, down on the ground, Hendrickson and some of the others picked Rodgers up in a poncho and brought him to a helicopter. Some other men got to White and carried him past Medina to another helicopter.

Medina reached out and shook White's hand and told the medic he would be all right and thanked him for all his help.

White was seated in the open doorway of the helicopter with his burning, wounded foot hanging out.

When it landed they rushed him to a hospital. And while he was lying in a litter, another helicopter arrived with six more wounded. White looked at the men and realized he knew them all. They were another load from Charlie Company. He became hysterical. He began screaming and cursing and demanding to know what was happening to his company.

"They need me there, they need me there," White

screamed, as he tried to get off the litter and return to the minefield. "They need my help," he screamed. A chaplain came to console the medic and to tell him there was nothing that could be done. Then they took White to the operating room and removed his big toe.

White was right. Charlie Company needed him. The slaughter was still going on.

While the first and third platoons were together, and in places even mixed, the second platoon was off to the right and a little distance from the other two. But they were closing the gap, because the second was supposed to marry up with the first and the third platoons, Partsch remembers.

The second was moving through some underbrush and there was a hedgerow to its left. There was an opening in the hedgerow and some of the men had already passed through on their way to meet the first and the third platoons when the first explosion tore the early morning stillness.

Something was happening over by the first and third. They must be getting hit, Partsch remembers thinking.

As the men stopped and stared, realizing they were a little distance from the explosions, Partsch remembers hearing somebody in the ranks say, "Boy, we're lucky."

Suddenly there was another explosion. This one was "real close. It was a big explosion," Bernhardt recalls. A mine had been tripped just on the other side of the hedgerow.

Gus Rotger who had been walking point, his favorite position, went down screaming, along with three other men.

"I didn't even know anybody was over there because of the hedgerow between us," Bernhardt remembers. "That's probably why we didn't get any of it." Bernhardt, who had been walking behind Buchanon, saw the platoon sergeant fall to the ground face down and lie still. Bernhardt also dropped to the ground where he was. But noticing the sergeant lying motionless, Bernhardt crawled up to him.

"Hey, are you all right?" Bernhardt shouted above the exploding mines.

Slowly Buchanon turned around. He appeared dazed and shaken. "What happened?" he asked.

"A mine went off so you'd better lie still," Bernhardt said.

Buchanon was instantly on his feet taking charge.

"Everybody stand still," the platoon sergeant roared in that deep booming voice that no one could mistake. Then he started to go towards where the explosion had occurred.

Bernhardt tried to stop Buchanon, but the sergeant shook him off.

"No," muttered Buchanon, apparently still a little dazed. "I gotta go over there. I'm the platoon sergeant. My men need me."

"No, wait a minute," Bernhardt pleaded. "The medics are already over there. You don't have to go over there."

But Buchanon was already gone, rushing to Rotger's side.

Another member of the second platoon panicked when he saw what was happening. Realizing that he couldn't move, he began to shout hysterically: "Get me out of here; hey, get me out of here." There was a road just a little ahead of where the platoon was trapped and the hysterical soldier wanted to make a dash for it. He rose to start running for the road, when others grabbed him and forced him down again, urging him to try to calm himself.

Buchanon, meanwhile, was beside Rotger, whose legs had been severed from his body. "My legs hurt," Rotger was screaming. "They hurt." His screams could be heard by the men in the second platoon.

"His legs blew apart," Partsch remembers. It was a mess. They were just shattered.

Then Rotger begged to know if his legs were all right.

Instantly, Buchanon placed himself in front of the boy so he would be unable to see one of his legs that was lying by itself on the ground.

"Don't tell my parents I got hit," Rotger cried. Then apparently sensing or realizing what had happened to him, Rotger screamed out: "I want to die. If I lost both legs I want to die."

Nobody said anything.

Then Captain Medina was beside the dying boy. Rotger recognized him.

"I'm dying; I'm dying," he cried. Medina stared helplessly.

"Please write to my mother. Tell my mother I was a good soldier, captain. I was a good soldier, wasn't I captain?" Rotger asked. Medina nodded.

Someone heard Rotger say, "I'm going home." Then God granted the final wish to the boy who didn't want to live without his legs. And that was how Gustavo Rotger died for the country that didn't do too much for him.

Medina was heartbroken, Widmer remembers. "It really hurt Captain Medina. He became depressed. He just wasn't his normal self."

Two kids to whom Medina had grown attached were torn from him in two quick strokes. The bond between Medina and Van Leer was almost like father and son. So was the bond between Rotger and Medina, except that Rotger had given the captain trouble at times. Ironically that was what brought the two together.

"In Hawaii, one of Medina's leading troublemakers was Gus Rotger." Widmer was explaining the relationship between the two. "But the guys who were troublemakers in Hawaii were better soldiers in Vietnam. Gus may have had trouble in Hawaii and at home. But in the field he couldn't be a better point man."

Medina himself had come from a background that equipped him to understand boys like Rotger. And Medina, the professional, had seen in Rotger the qualities of a good soldier. And Medina had tried to develop those qualities, only to see them blown up in the minefield.

"All Gus ever wanted was a medal so his parents could be proud of him," Widmer remembers sadly.

When Rotger went, Medina was shaken. He issued orders immediately to those around him, that the news of Rotger's death was not to be relayed to Simone. Simone, who was in the first platoon, was Rotger's best buddy. Medina wanted to tell Simone personally—if he ever got out of the minefield.

Medina had vowed that he would bring his company back home safely. Now he was watching it being destroyed. It didn't look as if anyone would get out of there alive. The explosions continued and so did the screams of the dying and the badly wounded and the frightened men.

Partsch found a way to sit still and stay cool. Since he was keeping a meticulous diary of the company in Vietnam, Partsch just sat and pulled the tiny notebook out of one of his pockets. Then he recorded the tragic events as they were unfolding.

When Col. Barker, the task force commander, heard of what was happening to Charlie Company, he flew to the scene of the disaster. He landed his helicopter near where Rotger died. The young GI's body was placed in Barker's helicopter. It may have been at this time that the helicopter pilot protested. Widmer remembers that once the pilot of a command helicopter protested putting a bloody body in his aircraft. It was dirtying up the interior.

When the explosions seemed to subside, the second platoon decided to try to get out of their trap.

Maurice Robinson was a close buddy of Vernado Simpson, who would later tell publicly how he fired at Vietnamese in Mylai (4) only to discover he had killed a woman and child. Simpson was walking in front of Robinson as the platoon tried to get to the road nearby. Suddenly there was another explosion. Robinson had stepped on a mine over which Simpson had apparently passed.

When he turned around and saw what happened to his buddy, Simpson broke down. "He got scared because he realized he could have gotten it," recalls Partsch. Simpson fell to the ground and wept.

"He was laying there whimpering," Bernhardt remembers. Then Simpson wanted to break and run, and had to be forcibly restrained by the other men around him. The second platoon was ordered to freeze.

Meanwhile, Doc Foreman was trying to treat the mortally wounded Bell, for whom there was no longer any hope.

Carlson, who had triggered a mine himself when he tried to help Bell, was sitting on the ground in a daze. A boot had been ripped off one of his feet, revealing another glob of beefy, red, bloody flesh. Carlson kept staring at the ground as if searching for something. Hendrickson watched in amazement as Carlson found what he was looking for. It was Carlson's toe, his right big toe, lying in the mud by itself. Carlson picked up the severed toe, looked at it and laughed hysterically. Then Carlson waved the toe three times around his head and threw it over his right shoulder, laughing, laughing, laughing.

"He was laughing with tears in his eyes. We couldn't understand it," Hendrickson remembers.

Then Bell died and, when Foreman realized it, the young medic took it as a personal affront. Bell never had a chance, but Foreman blamed himself for a situation even God couldn't avert. After they placed Bell in a helicopter, Foreman broke completely. He got down on his hands and knees and raised his head to the sky and the angry gods. Then he wept.

Tears ran from his eyes and spittle dripped from the corners of his mouth as the medic blamed himself for Bell's death. "I didn't do my best," Foreman kept repeating over and over. "I didn't do my job."

The worn-out, frightened men around him tried to console the heroic medic. "You did all you could," Hendrickson said softly. But Foreman wouldn't listen. "No I didn't; no I didn't," he cried.

So Hendrickson took the limp medic and forced him to lie on the ground, and placed a blanket over him. Another soldier placed a poncho over the blanket. A third gave him water to drink. Then Hendrickson lifted Foreman by his feet and another soldier grasped him under the arms and they tried to carry the shocked medic to the helicopter in which Bell had already been placed.

But Foreman fought back. "I don't want to go. Damn it, I'm not going. They need me." The medic struggled with the two GIs. Forcefully, the two soldiers threw the medic into the helicopter, where the door gunner left his post to sit on Foreman as the chopper lifted off with another load of the dead and dying.

"They took him away screaming," remembers Hendrickson. "He did his job and as far as I'm concerned he did it damned well. He was working on Bell and that took all the knowhow a man could have."

Now Robert J. Lee of Wisconsin was the only medic left in the company. Along with Medina, Widmer and Cowan, Lee struggled to get Wilson's body into a helicopter.

Wilson's face was peaceful, like a little boy sleeping, Medina recalls. He was going home. But the rest of his body told of the horror of the minefield. His legs were bent grotesquely in unnatural positions. His body, from his testicles to his throat, was split open like a pig in a butcher shop.

Blood oozed from his liver and out of his lungs and heart, staining the men as they struggled to place Wilson in a poncho. Then they began to drag the poncho into a waiting helicopter. It tripped another mine and Wilson's body blew up in Lee's face.

The medic's face and the entire front of his body looked as if someone had placed a sieve in front of it and tossed a bucket of red paint through the holes, remembered one soldier. There was a religious medallion around Lee's neck. He looked down and saw a huge, red glob of Wilson's liver hanging on it.

It was too much. Doc Lee broke.

First he mumbled incoherently. Then he started to scream. Medina rushed up and grabbed his one surviving medic, but Lee was completely hysterical and sobbed uncontrollably. Then Medina started to slap Lee.

"Doc, doc," Medina was almost in tears. "I need you, doc, I need you. You're the only medic I got left. Don't go, doc. Please, I need you. You're all we have," Medina pleaded.

Slowly the words sank in as Lee began to comprehend what Medina was saying. And slowly, slowly he reacted. It was a superhuman effort, but Lee came out of it and returned to what was left of the company.

Medina was all over and everywhere. Now he had to get his company out of the minefield. It was impossible for the second platoon to move, so helicopters were sent in for them. Even so, the men had to move 30 yards to get to the landing zone where the helicopter was. Each man followed in the footsteps of the man in front of him, remembers Partsch.

"Somehow we cried our way out of it," Bernhardt remembers. Bernhardt was extracautious. He didn't even trust the footsteps of the man ahead of him. "Nobody, no matter how good he is at setting mines, can stamp the ground down on top of it," Bernhardt says. So he looked for hard ground to step on.

Slowly, ever so slowly, the men eased their way to the helicopters 30 yards away, which took them out in relays.

The second platoon was rewarded for their harrowing experience. The men were told they didn't have to go to the field for awhile. "They said they would take us to guard bridges, and that's where we went," remembers Partsch. "But a week later we had to go back to that same area and search it," he adds dryly.

The first and third platoons weren't so lucky. Using

bayonets to probe the ground for mines, and under Medina's leadership, the two platoons painstakingly retraced their steps for some 90 minutes until they were out of the minefield. Although they were no longer expected to serve as a blocking force, they were told they would have to walk back to LZ Dottie.

Charlie Company had lost about 20 percent of its men in that minefield and had undergone a psychological nightmare that had destroyed the rest of them, but still they could not be spared from the war.

Nevertheless, for all practical purposes, Charlie Company was dead.

The minefield didn't only kill and maim 32 young men. It wiped out the company psychologically. Nor could it be dismissed as a simple incident, as was done when the tragedy of Mylai (4) broke around the world.

"That minefield destroyed a lot of things the guys thought they had," said Carter. "The guys thought they had guts and stamina and that they were good infantrymen and that they could do anything.

"But the minefield told them it takes a hell of a lot more than what you think you have to put up with what's over here. There's more and worse to come, the minefield told them.

"After the minefield, the guys felt they had to start all over again to build theirselves up. The minefield took a lot of them and a lot out of them," Carter concluded.

"What hurt most was after it was done and you're sitting loading bodies on the choppers and all the brass came down. Big deal," remembers Fred Widmer bitterly. "It didn't really bother the colonels," he adds. "There was a hatred between the higher-ranking officers and the enlisted men."

"Losing all those guys like that made everybody feel bad," remembers Bergthold. "We just weren't prepared to lose so many guys at one time."

Psychologically, the company was shattered. Maybe

someday the company might forget the sound of those explosions. Maybe someday the company might forget the machine-gunlike staccato of the helicopter engines. Maybe someday the company might forget the terror of sniper fire.

But never would the company be able to shut out the screams of the men who didn't want to die but realized that they were about to.

"The way guerrilla warfare is set up," Terry was explaining, "if a guy sets up a booby trap, it'll kill you the same as a guy shooting. It's a demoralizing type of conflict —which is what they intended it to be."

Charlie Company was defeated by the Viet Cong on February 25, 1968.

★ ★ ★

CHAPTER XIII

POSTMINEFIELD

★ ★ ★ ★ ★ ★ ★ ★ ★ ★ ★ ★ ★ ★

"The psychological effect of the minefield was more devastating than
the physical effect."

MICHAEL BERNHARDT
A member of Charlie Company

★ ★ ★ ★ ★ ★ ★ ★ ★ ★ ★ ★ ★ ★

The annihilation of Charlie Company that Sunday morning in February went unheralded largely because the
press didn't know what happened, the Army didn't want
to know what happened, the company didn't understand
what happened and the folks back home didn't care what
happened.

The valor of the company, as it died, thus proved as
futile and thankless as its service to the nation in the 12
short weeks it had been in Vietnam.

Medina and White received Silver Stars for their heroism in the minefield; Terry and Charles West were
recommended for Silver Stars; Rotger, Wilson and Bell
each got the Bronze Star medal, which was useless since
they were dead, and at least 25 Purple Hearts were distributed.

The Eastern Establishment, that gang of tough guys
who set the prerequisites of manhood in the company,
distinguished themselves for their bravery in the mine-

field, ignoring their own personal safety to aid their fallen comrades.

"I used to think they were all talk until the minefield," Van Leer remembers the Eastern Establishment. "But they went out of the way to help people. They were running around helping the wounded. They were carrying men to the helicopter. They were heroic."

However, the company's heroism was in vain. Nobody mentioned it, since the press apparently wasn't interested in stories of American valor in Vietnam. And the heroism was bought at the terrible price of the company's psychological destruction. The men had needed a rest even before then. Afterwards, they should have been sent to a hospital, not back to LZ Dottie, whence they were reassigned.

The failure here must rest with the Army, which apparently still is governed by a Patton-type mentality that dictates slapping a soldier with combat fatigue. If you don't bleed, you're not wounded and you'll get no Purple Heart. That is Army policy.

The second platoon of the company was airlifted out of the minefield to LZ Dottie. A week later the platoon was ordered back into the minefield area on a search mission but nobody was hurt.

The first and third platoons were ordered to walk back, a horrible form of torture after the men had just learned that putting one foot in front of the other could kill you.

The men were terribly shaken walking back. They had lost so many members of their "family" and it had all happened so fast. Those who went were popular men, sergeants who were liked and enlisted men who got along with most members of the company. In the minds of Charlie Company, as they were walking, only one fact stood out. All these men were dead. When a helicopter comes down to take a body away, it's dead.

Carter refused to accept Bobby Wilson's death when the word was passed at the minefield that the Indiana farm boy had been the first casualty. "That old redhead was a good kid. He liked to drink Miller High Life. He was just a country farm boy but he turned out to be a regular man. And he was always worried about his brother in the Marines," Carter kept thinking.

As he walked Carter wanted to cry but he was ashamed. He didn't know what the other guys would think if he cried. He didn't think it was manly to cry.

A lot of the men, he remembers, refused to believe Wilson was dead.

"In the minefield I didn't believe it. I didn't believe it 'till they packed him in that damn poncho and threw him in the helicopter. And even after that I couldn't believe Bobby was dead."

Carter kept thinking of Bobby Wilson as the company walked. "I wuz gonna make a fighter out of him. I used to punch him around when I'd see him. That guy had potentiality. Anything he wanted to be Bobby could have been. I really liked the cat," Carter remembers.

And two years later, he adds. "I still like Bobby Wilson; I still think of him."

The attitude of the company changed drastically after the minefield. If they didn't like Vietnamese before, now they hated them. Truly the company had become a danger to the Army and to U. S. policy in Vietnam.

For all intents and purposes Charlie Company was dead, but the Army didn't have the decency to bury it. Instead the survivors were placed on defensive patrol that day. In the evening they were still in the field. Medina remembers when the men lined up for the hot meal there was silence in the ranks. Each man had his head bowed. Medina stood at the head of the line to shake each man's hand. But it was no use. The company had had it.

The next day they headed for LZ Dottie, coming under sniper fire all the way back. As they approached their fire base, the members of the company were besieged by Viet-

namese kids offering to sell them beer and soft drinks—
American beer and soft drinks at exhorbitant prices. A
ten-cent American beer, probably stolen from the PX, sold
for $1.50 in the field.

At other times the men would play along with this
ridiculous situation. As one of them explained, "In the
field you get thirsty." But now they were angry. They took
the beer and they beat up the kids.

"They send missionaries to win hearts and minds. We
were sent as an advance party to fight. If they wanted us
to win their hearts and minds they should have given us
candy bars instead of ammo. Fuck their hearts and
minds. These people were after our ass," Carter remembers the attitude of the company.

Shivers remembers watching as the men arrived. They
were in a dejected state. "They hadn't shaved in a week
and a half or maybe two weeks. They hadn't bathed in a
month. The morale was pretty low," Shivers said of the
filthy, tired, beaten men arriving. Once there, the men
went bathing in a river.

The reward for their tragic loss was to be stationed at
LZ Dottie, which had whore houses, a Christian church
and showers, instead of Uptight, which had nothing.

There have been charges made that Charlie Company
walked into a Korean minefield, the implication being
that what happened to them was their own fault.

Even if this were true, and it is not, accidental deaths
in time of war are even more tragic than combat deaths.
And a company as green as these men were would be
entitled to make a fatal error as charged—particularly
since the men had never been in the area of Lac Son (4)
and (6) before. But members of the company who had
access to field maps at that time insist there was no indication of mines marked in the area in which the tragedy
occurred.

This writer is in possession of the field maps used by
that company on February 25 and at a subsequent period

when they went back to that area. There were minefields
in the vicinity of where the company had been, but everybody knew that the Batanga Cape was minefield territory,
just as every VC area is. There was no indication of minefields where the company had walked.

Thus one of several things went wrong, none of which
could be blamed on Charlie Company.

If indeed the South Korean marines had laid a minefield, it was their responsibility to inform a higher headquarters, which in turn would inform the Americal
division, which in turn would inform the 11th LIB, which
in turn would inform Task Force Barker, which in turn
would inform Medina of the danger. Since Medina had no
information of the danger, then the failure must rest
with a higher headquarters.

Actually, the South Korean marines weren't relieved by
the 11th. The 11th relieved the Third Brigade of the
Fourth Infantry Division, at one time under command of
then Maj. Gen. William Peers who later would be charged
with investigating Charlie Company. Therefore if there
were mines in that area, the Third Brigade should have
known about them and relayed that information on down
to Charlie Company.

It appears unlikely, however, that the South Koreans
did lay minefields.

The use of minefields at that period in Vietnam was
popular only with the Viet Cong. U. S. infantrymen on
search-and-destroy operations against the North Vietnamese army never had much of a worry about minefields.

The North Vietnamese didn't use mines for the same
reason the Americans didn't use mines. This horrible
weapon, like poison gas, can backfire and kill friends instead of enemies. Since both the North Vietnamese and
the Americans are foreigners in South Vietnam, neither
side is too familiar with the terrain. Therefore they don't
use mines for fear of stepping on their own deadly weap-

ons during the far-ranging patrols in which each side engages.

The Viet Cong on the other hand are indigenous to the area in which they operate. Like a small town boy at home, every VC knows his hamlet and the countryside around it as well as he knows the wrinkles on his mother's face.

Since foreign armies in South Vietnam avoid the use of mines where possible, it seems unlikely that the South Koreans would employ them.

When the survivors of Charlie Company returned to LZ Dottie, they found mail and cookies and gifts waiting for them from home and from the VFW post to which Medina's brother-in-law belonged.

And from Hawaii where she was still living, Mrs. Brigitta Cox sent her husband, Sgt. George Cox, a brand-new dress uniform.

Medina had been trying to get his worn-out company R-and-R leaves, although technically the men weren't entitled to such a rest until they had been in Vietnam six months. But Cox was due to go to Hawaii on an R-and-R leave about the third week in March. His men were happy for him, and he too was eagerly looking forward to it.

Apparently, after hearing what happened to the company in the minefield, Mrs. Cox became worried about her husband. Once she approached Mrs. Medina and said she had a premonition that something bad would happen. But Mrs. Medina kidded her out of her concern.

Although the company was back at Dottie, they still were expected to carry out their duties as infantrymen. They were sent on squad- and platoon-size operations to nearby villages and hamlets, or they guarded the bridges of the fire-base perimeter, or performed the other menial tasks considered inappropriate for an artilleryman or an MP or any of the other rear-echelon types.

The men's hatred towards the Vietnamese was not

unanimous, but did manifest itself in some rather bizarre acts.

Somewhere they had heard that in the Buddhist faith, a body could not go to heaven if it is dismembered. So when they would see a dead Vietnamese they would cut off a finger or an ear—a practice, sad to say, in which American troops engaged as far back as World War II.

The men also would cut off the pigtails of Vietnamese girls and decorate the barrels of their rifles with these trophies.

Not all of the men were hate-filled, and even those who were probably understood the dilemma of the Vietnamese. Pendleton, for example, befriended a Vietnamese family near Dottie, and says he tried to understand the problems confronting both sides.

It wasn't easy to be understanding. Charlie Company had really been beaten by the Viet Cong and these kids were staggering. On March 4 the VC dealt the company still another blow when it mortared LZ Dottie. Nobody was hurt, but all of the men's personal possessions were destroyed.

A portion of the meticulous diary that Partsch had been keeping was totally destroyed. He had decided to leave his notes at the base for fear of losing them in the field. He was away on a patrol when the mortar attack came. Widmer lost many of the pictures that he had been taking of company life. Everybody lost pictures and letters from home. "Everybody lost everything they had," remembers Shivers.

The company that had felt alienated and ignored now had its last link to home destroyed. It was another miserable blow in a chain of events that never seemed to get any better.

It is amazing, therefore, that the men still tried to understand their enemies. On March 12 Pendleton sat down and wrote a letter to his sister Bonnie, who had been keeping him informed of the dissension and political battles at home. He wrote:

"March 12

"Dear Bonnie

"I got your package yesterday with the cookies and socks and things. These packages you send are really good for out here. I can use all the things that you send. Right now I'm about 10 miles from Quang Lai (sic). Last week I went there with some friends. It was a lot of fun. We've been at Landing Zone Dotty for the last 10 days. We've been going on patrols about every other day so it's been pretty good here. But tomorrow I think we're going out to the field again. I've been going to a village close to here every chance I get and I've made friends with a Vietnamese family. Actually I have several friends in the village. Yesterday I was invited to have lunch with them. We had rice and fish. This is pretty good because most of the people here don't like Americans and are afraid of us. This is because most Americans treat Vietnamese badly because of the war. This is especially true in the infantry because when friends are killed and people are always out looking for VC in the field, they start hating all Vietnamese people. Also because Vietnamese don't have much to do with the war and let us fight it. Then build different kinds of stores with fantastic prices and make lots of money. I guess you can figure out just about how its like here with what I just wrote. I'm sure this is whats happening in most of Vietnam but I've only seen just the part I'm in. There are mainly two kinds of people here. The people that live in big cities or villages near high way where people are protected by U. S. and Vietnamese troops. They are pretty much on our side and dont want communism. The other people are people who live out in the hill sides and grow rice and have cattle. These people are usually more poor than city people but they don't need money out there. In the little villages they have there is usually no military aged men in them. VC come and they are forced to join. When they are found they are taken in and interigated (sic). They are usually VC symphasizers (sic) when VC are there and American symphasizers (sic) when we are there. Well I guess thats about all for now. What have you been doin (sic) lately? How is David and Dana doing?

"Love Rick"

Pendleton hadn't been in the minefield. He had twisted his ankle just before the company left on that operation and was left behind. He was sent out to rejoin the company as it was returning from the minefield.

He tried to understand the Vietnamese but admitted he couldn't. "They didn't like, they didn't trust Americans. And they say one thing but you didn't know what they're thinking all the time," he says.

Many of the men felt the Vietnamese were in a bind. But many of the men felt they were also in a bind. And if someone had to be killed they preferred that it be from the other side.

On March 14 the Viet Cong delivered the coup de grace to Charlie Company. It began when the understrength third platoon, now down to some 20 of its original 40 men, was sent out on a routine patrol about one mile down Highway 1.

The company had never received any replacements since it came to Vietnam and certainly none since the minefield disaster. Sgt. Cox of the third platoon was one of the last remaining NCOs respected by the younger enlisted men. Cox was the kind of guy who scrounged extra rations for his men in the field. They could talk to him about personal problems. He had patience with the men and took time to concern himself with them. He was like a father or big brother.

Now, two days before the Mylai affair, Cox, with this oversized squad that called itself a platoon, was moving down Highway 1 to search hamlets along the route.

What happened next has been very badly reported. It is almost as if the newsmen who tell and repeat this story are determined to prove that Charlie Company was made up of cold-blooded killers, even if certain facts are deliberately left out to establish this point. Perhaps it is best to tell this story in the words of the men who were actually there and who suffered the most.

Hendrickson was actually there and saw and heard what happened next. The reason he remembers it so vividly is because it was the last thing he ever saw.

"I was on a platoon search-and-clear mission at Landing Zone Dottie," he relates. "We didn't know what we were looking for. We had walked through this village the day before and searched it and there was nothing there. No people, nothing.

"This time we found a package of TNT powder in a glass jar with a Claymore wire and a detonator. Then we uncovered a 105 mm. round. The nose cone was off. There was a wire looped around two pins.

"George—we always called each other by our first names—George (Sgt. Cox) was looking at it. The next thing I remember somebody was calling me. I think it was Dyson. I reached for my weapon which was leaning against a tree. I don't know what happened after that. I was in a helicopter and I was cold and I asked for a blanket and someone said he couldn't put one on me because it might contaminate me.

"I remember one thing. The middle finger on my left hand felt completely disjointed. Then I woke up and I couldn't see. There was just a greyness. I didn't know until I woke up that I was blind. I asked the doctor would I see and he said no, it's permanent, and I broke up and cried. Losing the leg didn't bother me as much as the eyes."

When the platoon, being led by Lt. Jeffery La Cross, arrived at the hamlet, Sgt. Cox led his squad inside while the rest of the men sat around and waited. Pendleton, Terry and West were among those who waited.

As Cox was examining the 105 mm. shell, holding it in his hand, it blew up. There wasn't much left of Cox. It fell to William Doherty to scoop up the remains.

Pendleton also remembers what happened. He had been seated outside the hamlet in the rice paddy about 200 feet away, with the rest of the platoon, waiting for Cox and his squad to return. Suddenly the men heard the explosion. It was so powerful that shrapnel fell at their feet. Some pieces hit the jacket worn by Lt. La Cross.

Sitting back at LZ Dottie, Carter heard the explosion and looking up saw a huge cloud of black smoke rise into the sky. He didn't know it yet, but a squad of the third platoon had just been wiped out.

Then Pendleton relates: "We ran real fast to the explosion. We found them all laying around, Cox, Hendrickson, Dyson and another guy. Hendrickson was all black from powder burns. His legs were messed up and his arms were bloody. Muscles and stuff were hanging out from his arms and legs."

The finger that Hendrickson thought was disjointed actually had been blown off. He was badly hit in his testicles and his penis. His chest was punctured and one of his lungs destroyed. His face was a mess of red blood and black powder burns and blood ran from where his eyes had been. But he was still alive.

"Hendrickson kept mumbling about home," Pendleton continues. "He said 'I guess I'm going home now to see my mom and dad. I'm not gonna die. I'm gonna live.' But he looked like he was gonna die."

Hendrickson didn't have a mother. She had died of a heart attack when he was 12. She died in front of his eyes, lying on a couch in the living room.

"Dyson, he was in better shape," Pendleton remembers. "One leg was bent and the bones were kind of splintered. The other leg was hanging by the muscles. We knew he was gonna lose both legs.

"But Cox, he was the worst one. Somebody went to pick him up from the bottom. They lifted his legs but there was nothing there at all. The whole middle was gone. He was curled up. His hands were under his head like when you're born.

"Everybody felt bad. When the medevac came, they stacked them two and two. Garfolo and Grimes helped pick them up. We had all this extra equipment. So we picked it up and started walking back. Everybody didn't feel too good.

"We saw a guy on a bike. We kicked over his bike. We started to beat up the guy. But he backed off, talking real fast. Then he ran off."

Dyson had also been wounded in his groin. If there are fears worse than death in a man, it is losing his testicles or penis. After that is the fear of losing limbs. Death is more welcome than injuries such as these.

If there is anything more horrible than being blown to bits by a mine or booby trap, it is being alive to pick up the pieces. Van Leer remembers, after he was evacuated from the minefield, that he was glad for one thing: he wasn't around to pick up the pieces.

"The only way to really know what it's like is to experience it," Widmer advises anyone who wants to understand the feeling of Charlie Company by March 14.

"And that's where a lot of Americans are lacking in their understanding of the Vietnam situation. The only thing they get is what they hear on the radio. And this they can accept or reject.

"If I tell you we lost 28 men wounded and 4 killed in that minefield, that's not the same as you being there and watching us lose those people.

"Hendrickson lost his arm, his legs, his sight and he's going deaf. I'd rather be dead than to come home de-capped."

The booby trap had been hand-detonated, the men remember. That meant that somebody had been watching and waiting for the squad to come near the 105 and then pushed a button setting it off. That meant that the people in this area knew what was happening. This infuriated the men even more. But at that moment they weren't as mad as they were heartbroken. First Weber and then the minefield and now this. Forty-two men gone in 32 days and the company had never even seen the enemy.

Forty-two men gone from a company that operated in the field at a strength of 90 to 100 men. That's at least 40 percent casualties in about one month. And they never saw the enemy. And it was all happening right in this area. Somebody had to be doing this. Something would have to be done about this. At this rate the company would be wiped out in another month. The men had to destroy that enemy or die. It was kill or be killed. That's what they taught in the infantry. And it was true.

"It was frustrating and frightening," Widmer remem-bers. The guys began to think what kind of a war is this anyway? What the hell am I here for? "We've taken so many losses and we've never run into the enemy. I'd rather go out and walk into a whole platoon of NVA by myself than get hit by a booby trap. At least you die fighting the enemy. This way, a booby trap, it's such a waste."

The third platoon walked slowly back to LZ Dottie in single file. They had to walk slowly. They were crying. The death of Cox hurt them deeply. The horrible mutila-tion of the others was like rubbing salt into their open wounds.

"On the way back to camp I was crying," remembers West. "Everybody was deeply hurt, right up to Captain Medina.

"Guys were going around kicking sandbags and saying, 'Those dirty dogs, those dirty bastards.'"

Just before reaching Highway 1, the men saw a farmer in the field. Maybe that was the guy who killed Cox. You never could tell the good guys from the bad guys in this nutty war. Not only did everybody wear civilian clothes, but the costume was the same for men and women— black pajamas and a white conical hat. Some of the men fired at the farmer. He fell. They rushed over and began to jump on the body in an insane frenzy (and fire at it again). Then they saw it was a woman. She was dead. They returned to LZ Dottie.

This had become a platoon crazed with fury and frustration and fear; a platoon of a company that could no longer take it—and could no longer be trusted or responsible for its actions.

"Medina came to tell us how sorry he was. The guys were crying. T'Suvas and John Smail were crying with tears in their eyes," Pendleton remembers as his own eyes moisten. "Then Doherty got on his M-60 machine gun and just fired all his rounds. He must have fired for an hour."

Somewhere outside LZ Dottie a hidden VC guerrilla, if he was watching and listening, heard that machine gun chatter. But there was no need to be alarmed. It wasn't firing at anybody. And the guerrilla must have wondered what was happening—a machine gun firing into the emptiness. It was so symbolic of the whole effort of Charlie Company in Quang Ngai Province, of the whole U. S. effort in Vietnam. But the guerrilla couldn't have thought of that; and Doherty couldn't have thought of that. Maybe, thought the guerrilla, these Americans must be crazy wasting all that ammunition. He was so right.

But that lone machine gun, firing into the empty stillness of this God-forsaken place was the funeral dirge of a heartbroken infantry company. It was the lament of an angered, confused, defeated infantryman.

Its meaning was more powerful than the taps of a bugler or the volley of an honor guard at a military funeral. It cleansed a soldier of the blood on his hands, hands not used for killing but for picking up the remains of a close comrade. And it abated the anger and bitterness boiling over in his heart and, since chaplains never visited Charlie Company, it called on God, nay pleaded with the Almighty, for an explanation of the string of tragedies that had been visited upon these men.

"Then we went down for a swim," Pendleton remembers. "T'Suvas got a big bottle of whiskey and the whole platoon got drunk. Then a bunch of kids came out selling things. We chased the kids away. We just didn't feel like being friendly to the kids.

"Hendrickson was such a nice kid. Everybody liked Hendrickson," Pendleton quietly recalled, two years later.

Medina quickly rushed to the hospital after he heard what happened. There was nothing left of Cox to place in that new uniform his wife had sent for the R and R in Hawaii. It fell to Mrs. Medina, still living in Hawaii, and the first sergeant's wife, Reiko Hobscheid, to tell Brigitta Cox there would be no R and R for her husband, that her premonition had come true.

"You've got to visualize an intensive-care unit in a hospital," Medina was recalling, once, long after the event. And as he visualized the intensive-care unit where doctors were trying to save Hendrickson's life, it was almost as if he was back there again.

"What do you do when you walk in and you see a kid with both legs gone and you know him? And he's blind in both eyes and his manhood is gone and one arm is gone and the fingers of the other arm are gone. And when you talk to him, you suddenly realize he is listening and he recognizes your voice." Medina sounded almost helpless.

One lung was also gone from Hendrickson's shred of a

body and a medic was saying, as he held his hand on the kid's chest:

"Breathe, now breathe." The medic is almost shouting the words because much of Hendrickson's hearing was gone too.

"Now breathe in," the medic was pleading.

"Now breathe out," the medic said in relief.

"Now breathe in, yes, good. Now breathe out."

"What do you say to him?" Medina asks. "Do you tell him to stay alive? What for? He didn't even know what was wrong with him." Medina is near tears.

So Medina lies to the kid and he says:

"You'll be all right, kid. You'll be all right, Hendrickson. They got good doctors here. They got good medics, you hear, they got good medics."

And the kid looks at the captain and he realizes it's Medina and he tries to smile gratefully. He had done the best he could for Medina and the company and the Army and the whole fucking country that couldn't care less.

And way down deep inside, Medina is fighting with himself.

"You want to tell him to give up. What's the good of living. What's he gonna be the rest of his life?" Medina remembers what he was thinking. But he tells Hendrickson, "You'll be all right kid. You do as the doctors tell you, hear?" And Medina leaves the hospital. Like what else is there for him to say or do. He has lied enough for the day.

"People don't realize it. They don't understand it. They've never seen it," Medina tries to explain.

Back at Dottie the morale of Charlie Company has hit rock bottom. Too many of their friends are missing. There aren't even any replacements to fill the empty ranks. Bunkers that once were crowded now seem empty. Familiar faces are gone. The bodies have been carried away.

But there is a rumor making the rounds. The company is going back into the field Saturday. They're going to

Pinkville, the rumor says, back to the river where Weber was killed.

Depression becomes mixed with fear. Pinkville was where it started. How many more will be killed there? Pinkville is fear. Is this company doomed to be totally annihilated? Charlie Company, once a group of draftees, of wise guys, of unlucky, reluctant warriors, has become a group of frightened, depressed, sick kids.

The next day, March 15, a chaplain finally came to Charlie Company at LZ Dottie. It was really too late. Where was the goddamned psychiatrist? Charlie Company didn't need a chaplain any longer. The kids were too far gone. Charlie Company was totally demoralized and psychologically destroyed.

Who was the chaplain coming to mourn? Cox or Weber? Bell? Wilson? Rotger? Who else was killed? Maybe Carlson? Reed? Rodgers? Hendrickson?

But the chaplain came and a memorial service was held. And it did no good for the morale of the company. The chaplain came too late; God was dead in Charlie Company.

The service was late that afternoon. A little later Medina got up to speak.

★ ★ ★

CHAPTER XIV

MARCH 15

★ ★ ★ ★ ★ ★ ★ ★ ★ ★ ★ ★ ★ ★

"What hurt most was after it was done and you're sitting loading bodies on the chopper and all the brass came down. Big deal. It didn't really bother the colonels."

FREDERICK WIDMER
A member of Charlie Company

★ ★ ★ ★ ★ ★ ★ ★ ★ ★ ★ ★ ★ ★

It was a badly demoralized company that sat around the bunkers of Landing Zone Dottie late in the afternoon of March 15, 1968.

The chaplain's belated memorial service wasn't helpful for the morale of these men. They wept for Cox who had been good to them, and for Wilson who was everybody's buddy, and for Bell who was so much fun, and for Rotger who had died a hero's death.

And the men mourned Bill Weber, their first loss; and they cried for Hendrickson who had his balls shot off and was probably dead, and for Dyson who lost his legs, and for Van Leer who lost his too, and for White who lost his too and was so respected, and for Foreman who had been carried away raving, and for Carson who lost his toe.

"We missed all of them who got it," Widmer was to remember two years later.

And the men must have wondered, as members of a

family always do, why are the good taken first and what is this Joblike tragedy that is being visited on this company and why are they being put to this horrible test of strength and faith by an angered Lord? For Charlie Company was a closely knit company, and the men believed they were a good company and there was love and comradeship within its ranks; they had come a long way together, they had done their country's bidding and now they were being destroyed.

"As far as I'm concerned," West would later tell the world, "Charlie Company was the best company to ever serve in Vietnam. Charlie Company was a company and not just a hundred-and-some men they call a company. We operated together or not at all. We cared about each and every individual and each and every individual's problems. This is the way that we were taught by Capt. Medina to feel toward each other. We were like brothers."

And now the family was attending its own funeral. What happened to that company, the men wondered, the company that had won all those awards in Hawaii; the company that was handpicked from all the others to go first to Vietnam; the company that had climbed the mountains of the Kahuku range and raced over the hills of Vietnam and done all the bidding of the brass and could do everything they had been trained to do?

That company was being wiped out. Slowly it was being destroyed, and not because of anything it had done wrong.

It could hump the fields better than anybody in the whole Americal Division; it enjoyed the limited number of firefights to which it had been committed; it carried out all the crazy, selfish, ambitious demands of the brass. It slept in the rain and the mud; it got no rest or leave; it did what it was told to do and it never complained.

But still it was being annihilated; slowly it was being killed, maimed, knocked off, and there was nothing Charlie Company could do to forestall the inevitable.

How do you fight mines? How do you fight the very

earth itself when it opens up beneath your feet to take you away, or to take one of your legs or both, or your arms, or your balls?

How do you fight snipers who refuse to face you man to man because they play by rules you had never heard before? How do you fight snipers who hide in the trees or under the ground or between the blades of elephant grass or behind the skirts of their women, or even inside the dirty diapers of their babies. How do you fight people who have committed themselves totally to your destruction; totally, totally, totally, every man, woman, child; yes, even every baby?

Who are these fucking people—these animals, these women who shit in public, who'll screw you for a dirty 500-piaster note, who've got no self-respect—that you've got to help them?

What kind of a crazy war is this anyhow, where our own people are fighting at home, and the rich bastards go to college to get out of this mess, and the smart-asses burn their draft cards or go to Canada, and nobody really gives a shit?

What kind of a war is this anyhow, that us poor dumb bastards got to fight so Col. Beers can become a general and Capt. Medina a colonel, and poor Bobby Wilson is dead? Why are we helping these lousy people who don't want to help themselves except to our money and to our beer and to anything they can get from us? Why doesn't the fucking South Vietnamese Army fight its own battles? You never find them humping the boonies or going where the minefields are.

Why are we stuck with all this shit when back home Sen. Kennedy wants to end this war, and Sen. McCarthy too, and also Sen. Fulbright? Should we die before then? Those guys started this war, now they want to end it. What are we fighting for? Who the fuck gives a shit about Communism? Maybe it would be good for these peasants. They sure as hell don't want us. What the hell can I lose from Communism, except my own life out here?

And at the rate it's going, that'll happen too, because everytime we leave Dottie or Uptight something bad happens. We've had 42 casualties in 32 days. At that rate we'll all be dead in another month or so. We came out here with a company of 176 men. But we never had more than 105 in the field. Now we're down to 75.

Wow!

It's all the fault of these fucking gooks, these shit-eating, slant-eyed slopeheads, that we're here in the first place. There ain't a single one of them worth Weber's death or Wilson's life or Carlson's right toe.

Now soon they say we'll be going into Pinkville again. That's where Weber got it. Which of us will they get this time and who will those chaplains hold a memorial service for—next time they get around to it? You can be sure they won't be holding memorial services for the colonels. They never come down from their helicopters to where a guy can get hurt on the ground.* All they want is the body count—the gook bodies and our bodies.

That's how the men of Charlie Company were thinking and talking the late afternoon of March 15 as they mourned the dead and feared for the living. As Medina put it, the morale of his company "was not at its highest."

The men had heard the rumor that Task Force Barker was planning to storm Pinkville again tomorrow. Charlie Company would have the honor of wiping them out. Again they would try to wipe out the decimated 48th Local Force Battalion which had been giving them so much trouble.

The place to be assaulted, Charlie Company understood, would be the real Pinkville, that built-up area across the inlet from Mylai (1) about 2½ kilometers east of Mylai (4).

---

*Col. Barker did die several months later—in a helicopter accident.

What the men did not know, was that the plans had been changed by Col. Barker on March 15, when he decided to hit Mylai (4) instead.

Carter and Bernhardt, along with another GI, Harry Stanley, had inadvertently overheard a private conversation between Barker and Medina earlier that day. Carter remembers it. He is convinced that higher headquarters wanted to wipe out all the hamlets from Mylai (4) eastward to Pinkville and the sea—but to do it in a way in which nobody could accuse anybody of a willful slaughter.

Carter and Bernhardt believe the overly ambitious brass wanted to score high on the body count. Killing VC was like a contest among Army units in Vietnam at that period. There was no way to tell the difference between a VC or a civilian—alive or dead. One in all liklihood was the other.

"Barker and Medina were gung ho," says Carter. "I believe they did it for the record."

Bernhardt has also expressed the suspicion that the reason Charlie Company had suffered as much as it did before March 16 was because the Army was setting it up for what happened at Mylai (4). He thinks the company was carefully groomed to reach the pitch of anger and madness it achieved by March 16, much as a watchdog is taunted into viciousness.

"Everything miserable that could possibly happen to you over there happened to us, the company. We weren't spared anything," Bernhardt says. "Some units could avoid some things. But we seemed to catch it all. I was wondering what we were being set up for. I thought we were being conditioned for something. I thought they were priming us for something."

At any rate, Carter was at the headquarters section area on March 15 to pick up a supply of tear gas and explosive compound, which he used on operations, as a tunnel rat, to flush out or kill hidden guerrillas. He remembers, and Bernhardt confirms, the conversation the men overheard between Barker and Medina.

"Barker told Medina he was switching plans. Instead of hitting the real Pinkville [Mylai (1)], Charlie Company would assault Mylai (4)," Carter recalls. "But don't tell the men," Carter says he heard Barker order Medina. "We have to keep their fighting spirits up."

Carter is convinced Division Headquarters deliberately planned the annihilation of Mylai (4).

And, adds Bernhardt: "I knew what would happen when Medina gave the order that night."

To the soldiers, Pinkville generally was anything south of the river where Weber had been killed. But some, like Carter, knew the real Pinkville and its general location on the coast.

Low-ranking fighting men, however, never really know the overview plan of a battle, the big picture. All they understand is what they must do; all they know is that nitty-gritty aspect of the battle in which each man is personally involved, in which each man must fight for his own survival. War, of necessity, no matter how complex, must be reduced to its simplest common denominator for the men who fight it.

If rumor said the enemy was in Pinkville and the company was going to Pinkville, then that was that. Where the company would go specifically, the coordinates of its landing zone, is not the problem of the lowly GI. It is left to the higher-ranking officers to decide such technical details. All the company knew was that somewhere south of the river the VC was cornered and the men were going in to fight the enemy.

"If Charlie Company thought it was going to land at another goddamned village full of civilians, they wouldn't want any part of it," Carter remembers.

"I knew and Bernhardt knew and Stanley knew that Barker said we were going to Mylai (4), and then sweep the whole place. But if the men thought Mylai (4) wasn't Pinkville, it would make their morale low," Carter says, and adds:

"The whole company could have sat down and said, 'I wouldn't do it,' if they had known what was going to happen."

Why was the change being made? If Carter's assertion is correct, apparently it was decided to wipe out everything in the Son My complex, which included the region from Mylai (4) to the sea. That entire area, after all, had been a hotbed of guerrilla activity. And guerrillas cannot survive without civilians.

One thing is certain. Charlie Company didn't accidentally land at Mylai (4). Another thing also was apparent. There were enemy troops in this entire area. Task Force Barker had been stopped twice in sweeps around Pinkville. Somebody was killing and wounding those men in Charlie Company.

As Carter was leaving with his supplies, he remembers Barker pointing to Mylai (4) on a field map. Calley was there too, he remembers. "We'll make a clean sweep from Mylai (4) into Pinkville," Barker reportedly told Medina as he swept his finger towards the sea. Then the colonel looked at the captain and winked.

"Barker, that's the man they ought to get," Carter was to recall long afterward. "But they can't get him. He's in a big city in the sky somewhere."

Carter saw Medina go with Barker into a helicopter to reconnoiter the area the company would be assaulting in the morning. They did not fly over the hamlet of Mylai (4), Medina was to recall, for fear of giving away their plans. Carter says he also saw Medina and a major and Barker go into a bunker, presumably to discuss these plans more fully. What was discussed was a secret shared by these three officers.

The company, Bernhardt explains, was in no mood to

just hit another village. They wanted a fight. They wanted revenge. They wanted to get at the guerrillas who were killing them.

To tell the men they would be going into Pinkville, because the 48th was there and the GIs would have a chance to even the score, was a good idea and they would buy it. To tell the men that they were going to seek out the 48th by first landing at a hamlet and then sweeping east for several days would mean another one of those infernal patrols, the walk in the sun that brings casualties to the company and has no effect on the enemy.

One thing about Charlie Company that evening of March 15: they wanted to fight. The company by then had reached a point of despair, frustration, anger, fear and pain that had placed them, at best, just on the borderline of sanity. To have sent them on another routine, fruitless and dangerous search of just another village at this time would have been inhumane, if not impossible.

Perhaps higher headquarters too had reached a point of desperation. Perhaps the whole Army had reached a point of desperation. Perhaps the whole country had reached a point of desperation. One thing was certain. The Viet Cong were not being beaten in the field. The survivors of Charlie Company were living proof of that.

In one respect the operation for March 16 would not be unlike the two previous battles of Pinkville—the one in which Weber was killed on February 12, and the one that began on February 23, two days before Charlie Company was wiped out psychologically. The entire area involved less than two miles in width. There had to be enemy somewhere within this area. Somebody had stopped Task Force Barker those other times. That somebody now had to be stopped.

This time it would be Charlie Company's task on the following morning to conduct the main assault. Bravo Company was ordered to land at Mykhe (4), on the sliver of land about one kilometer south of the real Pinkville.

Alpha Company was to set up a blocking position to the northwest of Pinkville. Naval vessels patrolling the coast would presumably kill or capture any VC fleeing to the sea. Artillery support would come from LZ Uptight and, if the situation became necessary, from the 2nd ARVN division to the southwest.

Thus Charlie Company, harried and harrassed, beaten and bewildered physically and psychologically by the Viet Cong's clever use of booby traps, mines and snipers, would finally be given their chance to get back at the enemy.

For years, the 48th had maintained tight control over this part of Vietnam. Now that it was believed on the run, the time had come to deal the guerrillas a death blow. If Medina, who knew how to handle his men, could pull off this morning assault properly, the VC stronghold in Quang Ngai province would be eliminated once and for all—and Charlie Company could avenge its dead and mutilated—and the colonels might become generals.

After supper, as dusk was falling on March 15, Medina called his men together at LZ Dottie.

"It was real quiet that evening," Terry recalls. "It had reached a point where the guys had had it." The men gathered around, forming a rough horseshoe. They were depressed, hurt, angry and afraid. The memorial service had really hurt. Many men were crying.

The troops knew they were going to Pinkville. Now they would hear it officially. They sat on the ground or on the bunkers as Medina prepared to speak. Barker and some other officers from headquarters were there to listen. They stood behind Medina. It was the first time the brass ever came to a briefing.

A hush fell over the company. There was silence in the ranks except for those who cried.

"It was an emotion-filled scene," remembers Terry. "A couple of the guys were crying and one guy asked the captain when they'd get a chance to fight. And he said that we had a mission coming up where we'd go into this area of Pinkville—we'd been in several times before—we'd go into there the next day and they'd have the chance then. We'd tried to push into Pinkville a couple of times before but they never could make it, and another company lost quite a few guys out there."

Then Medina talked of the mission the next day, remembers Terry. If there was one thing the men didn't want, it was another walk in the sun where more would be killed without a fight. Medina couldn't possibly tell the men the plan called for another patrol, maybe a little more glorified because all the brass was around, but still a patrol. Everybody was charged. The men weren't objecting to fighting. They were begging for a chance to fight. They couldn't take another patrol. Their minds had had it, even if their bodies hadn't.

So Medina began to outline the plan, remembers Bernhardt. He told of the 48th being in Pinkville and of how Charlie Company was going in to get them. He said the company would land at Mylai (4) and would sweep through Mylai (5) and (6) to Pinkville, drawing a rough map in the dirt with a stick, Bernhardt remembers.

But he said the VC would be where the company was going and that a big battle was to be expected. He said all civilians would be gone to the market by the time the company landed.

Die he tell the men that maybe there might be some civilians left in Mylai and to be extracautious or extranice to them? The question is academic. There may have been civilians in the village, but they weren't innocent. There are no innocent civilians in a guerrilla war. If higher headquarters had a plan, who was Medina to challenge it.

These men weren't refusing to fight. These men weren't threatening mutiny. These men hadn't refused to be drafted. These men had heeded the call of their country and the bidding of their superiors. These men didn't like the war but they accepted their responsibility and went.

To ask them to continue walking in the fields and to be picked off like sitting ducks wasn't war. Nor was it sensible. Nor was it reasonable. Nor was it right. Nor was it just.

No one knows for sure what Medina said. Each man had his own interpretation. But whatever Medina said, higher headquarters didn't object. Higher headquarters was standing right behind the captain as he spoke. Barker was there, along with the other officers. There is no indication they protested anything the captain told his men.

And all the men had to do was stare straight ahead to realize the enormity of the pending mission. The fact Barker and the brass were there was a novelty in itself. It was the first time that happened. Everybody was suddenly paying attention to Charlie Company, who until now had felt like orphans. They even had a chaplain come see them for the first time, to help them mourn their dead.

And tomorrow, Medina was telling them, the weapons platoon would be going along, the first time that ever happened. Not only that, there would be demolition teams coming along, something unheard of with Charlie Company. And two intelligence officers and a major from Task Force Barker were coming along with the company. The intelligence officers weren't wearing insignia, but one looked old enough to be a captain and the other a field-grade officer, Carter remembers. And there were going to be interrogation teams too. Man, was this going to be big!

Why they were even going to bring an Army photographer and reporter along to record the great battle. Nothing like that had ever happened to Charlie Company before. There were five hundred civilian reporters in Vietnam, as well as hundreds more in the military, but not one had ever paid attention to Charlie Company before.

Imagine! The folks back home were finally going to learn about Charlie Company. They would soon be heroes. This operation must sure be big; maybe the most important thing that ever happened in Vietnam. Certainly it would be the most important thing that would ever happen to Charlie Company.

Medina continued talking to the men, letting them know it was the 48th that had been plaguing them and soon would be wiped out, and Charlie Company again had been selected to do the honors. And since all women and children would be gone, the area would be a free-fire zone, so that Vietnamese found there would presumably be the enemy.

"One guy tried to pin the captain down," remembers Terry. "Medina left the impression that they could shoot just about anything they saw there that was moving."

Medina has sworn publicly that he did not give orders to kill unarmed civilians. There is no question that he speaks the truth. He didn't have to give such orders. All the men I have spoken with agree that Medina never told them to kill innocent civilians.

But this company was spoiling for a fight. All they needed was the promise of one. And nobody lied when a fight was promised. The trouble was, the company no longer was capable of rational action. Medina apparently sensed this in the way he briefed his troops. The company should have been in helicopters headed for a hospital, not for a combat assault. The men had had too much of Vietnamese combat.

"We lost a lot of guys," Carter remembers Medina telling the troops. "Pinkville caused us a lot of hell. Now we're gonna get our revenge. Everything goes."

"What we had implanted in our minds was that anybody in that village was a VC or a VC sympathizer, and the animals were supplies," remembers Widmer. "That was the impression he placed in everybody's mind. This was not going to be only revenge, but our chance to really meet the enemy."

Then Widmer thinks for a moment and adds rather sadly, "But it didn't turn out that way."

Partsch remembers the men were told all the villages in the area had been warned by loudspeaker of what was to come. This is a ridiculous tactic, as used in Vietnam, since it serves to warn friends and enemies alike that the Yanks are coming. "He told us we were really gonna hit something big. And it might be a good time to get revenge on the guys we lost," Partsch said.

Eager as the men were, they were also afraid. Very afraid. The word Pinkville struck fear in their hearts. They had been bloodied there every time they tried to approach it. Medina had to inspire the men. They were depressed as well as afraid. They had to be put in a fighting frame of mind.

"There's not a man out there wasn't scared. Everybody was scared of Pinkville. Man, I was shaky as heck. Because you know they're waiting. You just know they're waiting," remembers Carter.

Medina spoke for about 45 minutes, both Shivers and West recall. At first they listened quietly because of their emotional state of mind. The memorial service had been too much for men who two years later still couldn't forget the buddies they lost in the war.

In the beginning, the fight was out of them. "If there was a state below depressed, we were in it," remembers Widmer. "During that day we tried to carry on normal activities, but in the evening everybody started getting gloomy and dull. You started to think back to what happened. I was thinking, 'What kind of a war is this? What the hell am I here for? We've taken so many losses and we've never really run into the enemy.'"

Medina kept talking to his men, outlining the plans for the combat assault in the morning and what each platoon was expected to do. He told the men that the huts were to be burned, the livestock slaughtered, the rice, food and other supplies destroyed, the wells and water befouled. The idea was to demolish the base of the 48th VC Battalion, a perfectly sound military tactic.

"He said just like nothing is to be left standing," Carter recalls. And Stanley leaned over and whispered in his ear," 'It's gonna be a slaughter, you watch,' " Carter adds.

Did Medina say slaughter? Probably not. It wasn't necessary.

In the Army, explains Bernhardt, a quick learner, you sometimes don't say what you mean. You hint at it. You wink, maybe, like Barker winked at Medina when he told him there would be a clean sweep from Mylai (4) into Pinkville.

What does a clean sweep mean? Anything you want it to mean. If you're in the Navy and the Boatswain's Mate orders a clean sweepdown fore and aft, he means get rid of every scrap of dirt on deck, and that means everything. If you're in the infantry, a clean sweep may mean get rid of everything in the path of your advance, and that means everything. Nobody remembers for sure what Medina said, but each man had implanted in his mind an interpretation of what was to happen in the morning.

In the Army, continues Bernhardt, an oral order is not explicit. "They can interpret it or you can interpret it," Bernhardt says. "Only written orders are explicit."

Combat commanders have inspired their troops to fight with little speeches made on the eve of battle throughout military history. In essence they have told their men what Patton was reported to have said to his troops once during World War II. The idea of a battle, he said, is not to die for your country but to make "the other son of a bitch die for his." How could any commander be faulted for telling his troops to kill the enemy and try to preserve their own lives.

The men recall that Medina's was a good speech. Nobody could blame him if he inspired his men to fight. Finally, they began to think, they were being given the chance to meet the enemy.

"Capt. Medina told us we might get the chance to revenge the deaths of our fellow GIs," remembers West. But, adds the former sergeant, "Capt. Medina didn't give an order to go in and kill women and children. Nobody told us about handling civilians, because at that time I don't think any of us were aware of the fact that we'd run into civilians.

"I think what we heard put fear into a lot of hearts. We thought we'd run into heavy resistance. He was telling us that here was the enemy, the enemy that had been killing our partners. This was going to be our first real live battle, and we had made up our minds we were going to go in and, with whatever means possible, wipe them out," West recalls.

"We're gonna do him a job to get even, a job he'll never forget," another soldier remembers thinking.

"Until now we were just dying uselessly," Widmer was thinking as he recalled the minefield and the booby traps the men had experienced. "I would rather go out and walk into a whole platoon of NVA myself than get hit by a booby trap."

Widmer could not realize that one day he would win the Silver Star for doing something like that. But that would come after March 16. Now, on March 15, he was thinking that at last he would have a chance to fight.

The evening of March 15, a scared, defeated, tired, angry and shell-shocked company of infantrymen—or what was left of them—were finally being offered a chance to fight back. That's the name of the game called war. You train kids to be infantrymen and, in the final analysis, nothing matters except the clash of opposing forces on the battlefield.

Slowly the spirits of the men rose. They were going to hit the enemy and destroy him. That was what they had been wanting to do. Now they were being given the opportunity. Destroy or die, kill or be killed, that was the lesson of the infantry and now they would put it into practice.

Would they have the nerve to do it? To kill? Tomorrow would be the test. Tomorrow they would be confirmed as men. Tomorrow, Saturday, would be the big celebration when the enemy would die and boys would be turned into men.

"The guys was wanting to get into Pinkville and get into a good fight," Carter recalls. "A good fight," he continues, echoing the philosophical attitude of the combat infantryman who has no alternative, "never hurt anybody. Worst thing that could happen, you could die."

Medina described the feeling of the men that evening as "apprehensive." "I myself had a queasy feeling in my stomach and I was sure that other people had the same feeling," he remembers.

They did.

"Everybody was scared that night," remembers Pendleton. "Capt. Medina's words stuck in my mind. He said that there was gonna be a lot of VC there and we were gonna wipe out this village. He said anybody in the village would be there to fight, including women. That night everybody knew they were supposed to wipe out the village.

"That night I slept with Garfolo. We slept outside the tent. I didn't want to think about the morning too much. I thought 'What am I gonna do about shooting people.' But then I thought I had to do it. Everybody thought we had to do it."

"We knew there was gonna be action and where there's action there's danger, right?" Allen Boyce remembers. "Pinkville meant trouble and trouble scares everyone. Where there's action you're gonna get scared. Everybody was scared that night but everybody tried to hide it. You're scared but you just hold it in.

"Pinkville, they said, was going to be something. There had been a few guys killed around there and it wasn't a good spot. I was nervous. I wouldn't say extranervous, but I was more nervous than any other night.

"I mean, Pinkville, it's just like when you hear a few guys get killed in the streets in New York and the streets are not safe, right? That's how we felt. "I mean you don't go around walking around Harlem at night, right?" Boyce tried to express the feelings he had that night.

"The longer you're there the worse you get. After four or five months you get used to it; but then the shorter you get the more scared you get. You start watching your step. You say, 'I made it this long, I bétter not make a mistake now.'"

Bergthold remembers Medina calling the company together for the briefing. "Just before supper I think it was," Bergthold recalls. "He told us we were going on an operation in Pinkville; to expect lots of action. He said if you see anyone they'd be more than likely to carry a pack or a weapon.

"But he didn't say to shoot anyone. I'm sure he didn't. In my mind I know he didn't. Naturally if you see someone with a weapon, you shoot. We'd heard of some companies that shot snipers out of trees and they turned out to be women.

"But when he said Pinkville, everybody got kind of scared, extrascared. I was real scared."

Shivers, who was the company armorer and never went on patrols, remembers listening to Medina's speech and getting all excited. At first, he recalls, the morale of the company had been very low, but burning within each man was a desire to avenge the death of his buddy.

"Each person had his own reason for wanting revenge. The third platoon lost Cox; the second platoon lost Rotger; the first platoon lost Weber and Wilson."

Psychiatrists tell you that men who survive in combat develop feelings of guilt for living while their buddies are wounded or killed. Shivers, who always had the comfort of the rear-area soldier, had an even greater feeling of guilt. After listening to Medina, Shivers remembers: "I don't know what he did, but whatever it was their spirits were raised. This was going to be a big operation.

"I wanted to go. I had felt so useless since I had been out there. I wouldn't say I wanted revenge or a fight. But why should I be able to sleep on a cot when they couldn't."

In talking about Mylai, 22 months later, young Shivers still caught a lump in his throat when he remembered Bill Weber. Recalling how he felt on March 15, Shivers said: "There hadn't been too many days since Bill was killed that I hadn't thought of him." Then he added hastily, as if embarrassed or feeling guilty: "But I wouldn't say I wanted revenge."

Why not? It's a perfectly normal feeling. Didn't that Army psychiatrist say that in Vietnam men don't fight for mom's apple pie? They fight for their squad and platoon and company—and their buddies.

Psychiatrists also note that firing weapons in combat is a contagious sort of thing. You fire your weapon if you think your buddy is watching you. You don't want to let your buddy down. You do what you think your buddy or your team or your squad expect you to do. Men serve a company, not a country.

It is nice to believe that people are not vengeful. But it is not true. In Norway and Holland today there are still places where people refuse to speak German because of what happened to those two countries during World War II. And there are Jews who will still not buy German products, not even cameras.

The American Indians waited a century or more before they finally took Alcatraz. Negro militancy and hatred today stems from more than a century of mistreatment at the hands of the whites.

Charles De Gaulle built an entire French foreign policy to avenge the bad treatment he felt he suffered at the hands of the British and Americans during World War II. The Greeks and the Turks still refuse to live at peace with each other in Cyprus. Nor can the Jews and Arabs reconcile their differences that started many centuries ago.

It is said a million children died of starvation during the Nigerian-Biafran war, which was a tribal conflict that had its origins in jealousies that go back beyond the white man's intrusion in Africa.

Maybe Jesus said to turn the other cheek. But mere mortal man can't. Why then should a company of shell-shocked kids?

When Medina finished talking, there were one or two questions. How long would the company be in the area, someone asked? "Till we clean it up," was the answer.

Now the men were excited and they began to gather in groups and talk about tomorrow. There was a new grimness and a new hope. The men asked each other what the captain meant, and they were clarifying in their own minds what they would do in the morning.

Shivers remembers some of the guys from the headquarters section had gathered around their bunker and were talking. Then Medina came over and sat down with them. They talked about people and about home and about little things that lonesome, scared and nervous soldiers talk about. And then Shivers worked up his nerve and asked Medina to let him go on the operation in the morning.

Medina looked at this short, likable kid, who had the best job in the company, or certainly the safest, and said with finality, "No, you can't go."

And that was the end, and today Shivers is thankful.

Then the guys started drinking beer and smoking pot. And there was a pornographic movie on that night and they went to watch it. And Carter says there were a lot of beer and pot parties that lasted all night long, so there were a lot of hangovers in the morning.

Charlie Company had been wiped out on February 25. The minds of these men were no longer reasonable. They had become a company of zombies, but somewhere at the top they were being led by selfish, ambitious, indifferent officers, officers who had one year to prove themselves, before retirement.

A company of gaunt, hollow-eyed zombies, their minds torn by the same mines that had ripped their buddies' bodies to shreds, was preparing for a combat air assault in the morning. It would have been better, certainly no worse, if the United States Army planned to send into Pinkville a company of one-legged infantrymen on crutches rather than these men who had been dead for three weeks.

Psychologically they were destroyed, but the Army refused to leave them alone. Sick men were being given false hope as they prepared for their suicidal assault in the morning.

Charlie Company, after three and a half months of defeat on the battlefields of Vietnam, still hadn't learned its lesson. They were on the Viet Cong's turf and the rules of the game were written in a language they couldn't understand. And the people who should have taught them never did their homework.

If there was an atrocity committed at Mylai (4) the next morning, it was on Charlie Company, not by Charlie Company. They were the only innocents on the field of battle on March 16, 1968.

"The American public," Herbert Carter would one day observe, "ought to look at theirself in the mirror."

★ ★ ★

CHAPTER XV

SUMMATION

★   ★   ★   ★   ★   ★   ★   ★   ★   ★   ★   ★   ★   ★

"The atrocity committed was by the military, not by Company C. We only had a half-assed idea of what we were supposed to do."

ROBERT J. VAN LEER
A member of Charlie Company

★   ★   ★   ★   ★   ★   ★   ★   ★   ★   ★   ★   ★   ★

For six months I have immersed myself in the tragedy of Charlie Company, 1st Battalion, 20th Infantry, Task Force Barker, 11th Light Infantry Brigade, Americal Division (numerically known as the 23rd Infantry Division).

I have lived and breathed the history of this tragedy-ridden company until I felt I knew it and its members as well as they knew each other.

I have traveled the length and breadth of this land several times, and have even returned to Vietnam to see Mylai and retrace the ill-fated path of the company in the first twelve weeks of their overseas combat tour.

I have conducted more than 100 interviews in depth with survivors of the company, their parents, families, friends, enemies, psychiatrists, lawyers, critics and defenders.

It was the most difficult and most heartbreaking assignment in more than 20 years of newspapering around the world. There weren't many times when I could laugh with these men. There were occasions when their stories and their simple implied pleas for help brought tears to my eyes.

I began by not believing the story of the slayings at Mylai (4). I quickly discovered it was true. Some of the details told to me and some of the confessions made to me were even more horrible than anything published or related to government investigators.

In the beginning I was repelled by what I learned. I wanted to drop the assignment; to make it go away; to have nothing to do with the people I met who had anything to do with Charlie Company.

How outrageous their actions seemed when viewed at surface level. What right did these people have to embarrass me this way, to embarrass an Army I've always admired, to embarrass a country I've always loved?

Then I thought again of the first few kids I had contacted, of those who had cooperated with me willingly and of those who had given me a bad time. On reflection I realized they weren't bad kids. They weren't cold-blooded murderers—not even those who killed. They were telling me the truth, those who talked. Their stories, gathered in little towns and great cities of America, fit together like pieces of a jigsaw puzzle, forming an entirely different picture than had formerly been revealed. They talked to me because their minds were troubled and their hearts were broken still.

What I had first thought was arrogance and cold indifference really was fear and distrust. These kids were scared and confused. These were frightened children caught up in America's bitterest and most controversial of wars. These kids were pawns in a global game of chess played by brighter minds. And like pawns anywhere, these kids never had any control over their destinies. They were always being moved forward, forward, forward to their ultimate destruction. For a pawn is only used to achieve a crown for somebody else. Then it is eliminated.

They were afraid of me, these men, as they had every right to be. Their experience with the world had always been disappointing. These were the deprived members of our society, deprived on the economic, social, racial and educational levels. These were members of the quiet majority of America's young people, who enjoyed the fewest benefits of the country but served it the most by laying their lives on the line. These were the men who heeded their nation's call and were punished at every turn.

I realized the members of Charlie Company were victims of the worst type of exploitation. The society they served had used and abused their bodies, confused their minds, and now was grasping for their souls.

And I became disgusted with myself for wanting to drop the story. I had begun to assume an air of self-righteous indignation without knowing anything but the superficial facts. That's worse than murder, yet that's what the country and the world were doing to Charlie Company. Was I to become a hypocrite like too many in our nation today?

It would be easy to dismiss Charlie Company as an aberration of our society and go on about our business as before. Those who attempt to do this are exploiting these helpless kids only to justify their own arguments.

Anybody who truly knows war is aware that it is atrocious and brutal, even when it is being waged for justifiable reasons. But, as cynics have pointed out, Vietnam has been used to prove everything, and one wonders whether it has proved anything yet.

In all the words and pictures and transcripts and columns and books about Mylai (4), hardly any mention was ever made about the men, themselves, in the company, and about their experiences in Vietnam leading up to that fateful day.

Perhaps the experiences of Charlie Company are indescribable. Perhaps Widmer was right when he said Americans would never understand Vietnam from radio or TV programs.

"If I tell you I helped load pieces of my buddy's body into a chopper, it wouldn't have the same effect as if you were there helping me load pieces of my buddy's body into a chopper."

Widmer was trying to tell me politely to go out there and face what his company faced and then come back and criticize their reactions.

Seymour M. Hersh, a free-lance writer who has been credited with "breaking" the Mylai story and who has been generally critical of the company, once was asked in an interview in the Miami Herald whether he felt the fact he hadn't gone to Vietnam might detract from his efforts.

He points out, correctly, that the Army had sealed all records on Mylai and that most of the men were no longer there, since the story of what happened didn't come to light until 20 months after the event. Then he adds flippantly, "True I've never been shot at, but neither have most correspondents. I might add that any fool knows that a two-year-old child is not a VC. Perhaps to grasp the dynamics I should have gone. . . ."

He should have gone and got shot at so he wouldn't refer to the members of Charlie Company as being worse than fools.

Widmer's comments echoed the feelings of all members of the company: things are not always as they seem.

When A kills B and that's all we know, then we turn against A and want his blood. When A kills B because B assaulted A in a dark alley for the purpose of robbery and murder, then it is an entirely different story and B deserves what he got.

It is our duty as newsmen to find out not only what happened in that dark alley but why it happened. Unfortunately we in the press don't always do it. It costs money, it takes time, and besides there's not enough room in the paper to discuss the happenings of two anonymous citizens called A and B in their confrontation in a dark alley that nobody ever heard about.

I decided however that this company of men deserved at least one break in their unhappy anonymous history— the right to be heard. Or else I too would join the ranks of the guilt-ridden in our society. For the question that kept running through my mind, the question that nobody as yet had answered, was why, why, why did it happen?

When I decided to go ahead, my publisher wanted to send out publicity announcements but I refused.

He pointed out that two other books were already in the works: one by Hersh and the other by Richard Hammer, a rewriteman for one of the Sunday sections of The New York Times. He said the world ought to know there was a third newsman in the race for the story of Mylai.

I said no publicity. I would not race for first place. Everybody had been racing at Charlie Company's expense. Everybody had been seeking personal glory at Charlie Company's expense.

I wanted to know this story in every detail. These men were facing court trials; some lives were at stake. Worse, even if nothing happened to them, they still would be haunted for the rest of their lives by the charges made against them by a society that didn't have all the facts.

I am glad I made the decision I did. For slowly I have been able to reach the conclusions that I shall detail here with regret. I must make accusations against two institutions that I have always admired and respected: our defense establishment and the American press.

•The United States Army, not Seymour Hersh, broke the story of Mylai (4), to save its own neck by sacrificing the lives and the futures of Charlie Company.

•There was no massacre of innocent civilians in Mylai (4) on March 16, 1968. What happened there was a terribly unfortunate accident of war. It was less serious than the human or mechanical error that causes an artilleryman to fire a round short so that it kills friendly troops. It was no more serious than the failure in calculation of a bombardier who misses his military target and hits a residential area.

We allow for human error and the malfunction of machinery. When will we accept the fact that human minds sometimes go awry too?

•At Mylai (4) an undetermined number of enemy suspects were killed inadvertently by an irrational company of men no longer psychologically capable of controlling their acts. The failure at Mylai was caused by bad Army intelligence, faulty leadership, inadequate troop indoctrination, poor judgment and a questionable counterguerrilla policy.

Army policy, at that time, was to seek out and destroy the enemy. This meant that the homes of Viet Cong suspects were to be demolished and that guerrillas were to be killed. To make sure the policy was followed, each army unit encouraged its troops to maintain high body counts. "Kill, kill, kill" and "burn, burn, burn," were the orders of the day.

It is not within my competence to determine whether this policy is correct or not, therefore, I will not judge the Army's military thinkers. It became obvious to me, however, that whatever the Army sought to accomplish was not motivated by a racist attitude. The South Vietnamese Army pursued a similar policy. South Vietnamese permission was granted for the assault on Mylai. And when the story broke in all its fury, the least critical was the South Vietnamese government. Saigon knew right from the beginning what happened at Mylai (4).

It would be unfair, indeed ignorant, to compare the United States Army with the German Nazis and their abhorrent racial and religious policies of World War II. But the fact remains that the Army pursued a policy of searching for and killing the Viet Cong, and destroying their homes and their supplies. Charlie Company adhered to this policy. It had no choice.

And when the brass bungled, it followed that Charlie Company suffered the consequences. It had no choice.

To understand what happened to the company, one must first accept the fact that guerrilla warfare in Vietnam cannot be compared to the large scale battles of the first and second World Wars and of Korea. The enemy in Vietnam is fighting a very clever psychological guerrilla-type war in which it uses the press, propaganda, fear and frustration with better effect than we use our thousand-pound bombs or rapid-fire rifles.

Charlie Company was fighting the VC on the enemy's turf. The Viet Cong set the rules of war. That is a fact that the company never quite understood, and possibly neither did the Army.

The Viet Cong policy of hit and run, fight and fade, sneak and snipe was so devastating that Charlie Company was defeated in battle the day it lost Bill Weber. It was wiped out in the enemy mine field for all practical and effective purposes, and its remains should have been removed from Vietnam then.

But the Army insisted on flailing a dead horse. It was short of men at that period because of the Tet offensive and the siege at Khe Sanh. Dissension at home precluded bringing more troops to Vietnam. The military leadership at the higher levels were overly ambitious but poorly equipped to fight the war they were facing. (President Johnson later sent 10,500 more men to Vietnam, but it was too late for Charlie Company.)

That is why the Army is embarrassed. It had taken a calculated risk at Mylai (4) with a company of sick infantrymen who went berserk. It lost.

Now everybody knows what happened. But for 20 months the Army sat on the story, although it was an open secret in Vietnam. While an average of 500 newsmen are accredited in South Vietnam at any given time, not one learned the story that the whole Army was talking about.

The Americal Division commander, the 11th LIB commander and Task Force Barker's commander all had flown overhead during the operation and listened to what was happening. And if there was any doubt that this story was known at the highest level, it should have been cast aside when Gen. William C. Westmoreland, then in command in Vietnam, gave Charlie Company a letter of commendation for its effort at Mylai (4).

The company was credited with killing 128 Viet Cong and capturing 3 rifles. Westmoreland is a 4-star general. A corporal would know that if you kill 128 enemy soldiers and come close enough to count them you should find more than 3 rifles.

But nobody was objecting. The Army reporter and photographer assigned to the Mylai mission did a story that was carried in The Stars and Stripes and The New York Times, telling of the great battle. Widmer sent a copy of the Times story home to his mother, and he observed dryly: ". . . Boy did the paper ever build that up. All we encountered was one sniper. I guess it was bloody for Charlie. However, it was no battle."

An investigation was begun by the Americal Division, and Charlie Company was made to disappear. Right after the Mylai affair it was sent into the field for 60 days. Bernhardt says sometimes he thinks the Army was trying to get rid of the company.

They probably were. Maybe the Army hoped the company would be wiped out in an ambush. More than likely, however, the Army tried to keep the company out of contact with the rest of the world for fear the story would be reported back.

But nothing happened, or at least the Army thought that nothing was happening.

Then in June 1968, Col. Barker was killed in a helicopter accident. Since he was in charge of the Mylai affair, he was an integral part of the investigation. To continue the probe now might have meant casting aspersions on a dead officer who could not defend himself. Besides, the press, by June, still had not made any inquiries. The South Vietnamese government didn't care either. After all, Mylai (4) was an enemy stronghold and if its victims weren't enemy, they were enemy sympathizers, relatives or collaboraters.

So the investigation was dropped.

But just to make sure the affair was kosher, a helicopter pilot was given a medal for rescuing some children at Mylai (4) on March 16. The medal was for bravery. He was brave. But the "enemy" he faced was a berserk company of American infantrymen. This was not mentioned in the citation.

Now the case of Mylai (4) was closed, the Army thought. But what it didn't know was that something had been happening. It began in April 1968 when Ronald Ridenhour, the young GI who was not with the company, first heard about Mylai when he rejoined the Lurps.

Ridenhour spoke to members of the company, collected every scrap of information he could, in the service and afterwards, and by March 1969, one year after the event, he sat down to write his famous three-page letter.

In the mimeographed letter, Ridenhour named names, places, dates; he even gave the coordinates of Mylai, although he was a little off on this, but not much.

Then on March 29, 1969, he sent copies of the letter to Congressmen and other government officials in Washington. Among the people to whom the letter was sent were President Nixon, Ridenhour's own Congressman from Arizona, Morris K. Udall; as well as the peace-warrior senators Edward M. Kennedy, J. William Fulbright and Eugene J. McCarthy.

Letters also went out to Secretary of Defense Melvin R. Laird, Chairman of the Joint Chiefs of Staff Gen. Earle G. Wheeler and Chairman of the House Armed Services Committee L. Mendel Rivers.

Ridenhour's letter could easily have been dismissed as

kooky, and apparently it was by the peace warriors, who never answered it. But Udall grabbed it, perhaps because it was from a constituent. However, it was well written, articulate and intelligent. Not only that, but it was accurate, as everybody in the military establishment knew.

I would have liked to be a fly on the wall when that letter passed through the inner sanctum of the Pentagon.

Here was a story the Department of Defense thought had been buried and forgotten. Now here was a kid outlining the facts as the Army knew them to be. A check would indicate Ridenhour was no dope. His war record was outstanding, both as a helicopter door gunner and as a Lurp. Each is a combat-type duty, so he couldn't be faulted on that.

Then Udall must have contacted the Pentagon, which maintains an office of Congressional liaison where all letters go when GIs complain to their congressmen. That's where the answer is made up.

There must have been panic in the Pentagon the day Ridenhour's letter was brought to the attention of the top hierarchy of the military establishment. The Army is afraid of Congress and a civilian public, particularly a critical one. The only civilians it can handle are draftees and government employees. It also fears the press and not without justification. The press has been rough on the Army, particularly over the Vietnam controversy.

The Defense Department must have wondered who else Ridenhour had contacted. So it immediately dispatched an investigator from the Army's Inspector General's office (IG), Col. William V. Wilson, to go see Ridenhour. Ridenhour not only confirmed what he knew, but asked the Army to keep him informed on what it planned to do about this affair. This kid was persistent too; it looked like he was going to hang on like a leech.

So an investigation was launched against Lt. Calley, one of the people named in the Ridenhour letter. The Army had to work fast because Calley was due for discharge on September 6, 1969. And the Army must have begun wondering how it would handle the public. For the Army hierarchy knew the tragedy at Mylai was not the fault of Charlie Company.

By the summer of 1969 the Army was plunged into still hotter water. Eight Green Beret officers were being charged with murdering a Vietnamese double agent. This strange case was creating a great public outcry. A particularly perplexing question was why the Army was making an issue out of the slaying of an espionage agent. One explanation seemed to be that the Army was trying to deflate the reputation of the Green Berets, which had become an elite organization in the public mind. The regular Army frowns on elitist groups in its ranks.

Another explanation might have been that the Army was upset because it knew it had a far more awkward case on its hands: Charlie Company. And if professionals like the Green Berets allegedly commit murder, how could anybody blame amateurs like a company of draftees.

It was a long hot summer for the Army, which must have begun to think seriously about how to get itself off the hook and how to handle the inevitable press corps that was sure to charge in screaming. One good way to get out of it was to put Charlie Company back on the firing line.

This had already begun. CID investigators were going all over the country, questioning former members of the company. The few still in the army were really trapped. At Ft. Benning, where Calley was stationed, I was told that professional Army officers were angered at this lieutenant since they felt he had blackened their name. Ft. Benning is the home of the U. S. Infantry. There was even a plan among some officers to bring charges against Calley in case it would be decided to stop the investigation at a higher level.

But late that summer it was decided there was enough

evidence to charge Calley with killing 109 civilians and to
have him court-martialed. Charges were preferred
against him on September 5, one day before he was
due for discharge. It isn't often that an officer is court-
martialed in the U. S. Armed Forces. The Army may have
thought this would placate the public and show that it can
cleanse its own house and would not tolerate incidents
such as Mylai. Shortly after that, charges of assault with
intent to kill were filed against S. Sgt. David Mitchell, a
member of Calley's platoon.

I believe the Army was prepared to sacrifice a lieutenant, a sergeant and maybe a few privates if it could prove
to the world that Mylai was unique and intolerable. It
isn't a great sacrifice in terms of the casualties coming
weekly from Vietnam.

The Mylai tragedy, as everyone now knows, may have
been the largest incident of its kind, but it wasn't unique.
Since the Mylai story, there have been many reports and
some courts-martial involving servicemen accused of
murdering Vietnamese civilians—usually in the heat of
guerrilla combat.

Now that the open secret of Mylai was about to come
out, the Army must have turned its attention to how it
would handle the story publically—how to get to the press
before the press got to it. An old rule of thumb in the
public relations business says that if there is a skeleton in
your client's closet and the press has a whiff of the smell,
don't try to hide it any longer. Volunteer the information
and you might get your own point of view across. If you
keep hiding it from a persistent press, they will become
antagonized, find it anyway and will make you look worse
than you are.

I don't know if the Army followed this solid rule. It
ceased being cooperative with me after it learned I was
sympathetic to Charlie Company and was more interested in the why of Mylai rather than the what. But I must
say, if the Army planned to guard its own flanks, it

couldn't have picked a better ally than Hersh, despite the fact the two are incompatible.

Hersh is a critic of the Army and vice versa. In everything he has written about Mylai he has been highly critical and shown little sympathy to the men involved. He referred to GIs in an article in the Columbia Journalism Review as "notorious liars," and he referred to the defendants in the Mylai case as "these guys are murderers and killers. What they did was scandalous." And this before the trial.

The Deadliner, a publication of the New York Chapter of Sigma Delta Chi, a professional journalism society, wrote that Hersh told a luncheon meeting of newsmen "he has not been reporting on the case as an impartial observer but as someone who is committed." Hersh told the New York newsmen, "I happen to hate war." He undoubtedly does since he once was the public relations man for Sen. McCarthy, whose opposition to the Vietnam War drove President Johnson from office.

If the Army was out to sacrifice Charlie Company, it needed a public story that would discredit Charlie's members. I think the Hersh book does a good job of that. Politics sure do make strange bedfellows.

According to all the publicity, Hersh has been credited with "breaking" the Mylai story. Actually that is not correct. Ridenhour is the man who first broke the story. The Army pressed its investigation only because Ridenhour was on its tail. But there were many newsmen who got the tip long before Hersh that an officer was being held at Ft. Benning on charges of killing lots of Vietnamese civilians. The tips were coming from higher-level government, military and civilian officials.

The first tip came on September 4, 1969, one day before Calley was charged. It arrived in the form of an anonymous phone call to Charles Black, a highly regarded military editor of the Columbus, Georgia, Enquirer. The Enquirer services Columbus and the sprawling Ft. Ben-

ning Army post. The tipster told Black there was a lieutenant being held on post who was charged with killing
Vietnamese civilians. He said the lieutenant was being
kept in service to answer murder charges that "sooner or
later is going to tear the Army apart."

Black tried that day to get a confirmation, but could not.
The next day, the Enquirer got another anonymous call.
The City Editor, John Dunn, took this. Black, ever the
newsman, was in Columbus covering a bank robbery complete with running gun fight.

That night Black checked the second tip with the Ft.
Benning public information officer at his home. The PIO,
remembers Black, already had a prepared statement to be
read to any newsman making inquiries on the Calley
case.

The Enquirer ran 14½ inches on Page One of September 6, a Saturday, reporting the Mylai affair. Black, thus,
was the first newsman to break the story.

Since the Enquirer was a member paper of the Associated Press in that area, it passed the story on to the
wire service. AP cut it down to 190 words and ran it September 6 around the country. UPI followed less than one
hour later. Now the story was out. It was up to the nation's
press to pick it up and run with it. The story was ignored.

On September 9, 1969, Robert Goralski, the Pentagon
correspondent for the NBC Television News network was
frantically covering the Green Beret case, when he got a
tip. This was not from a military source but from the
highest level of the South Vietnamese government in Saigon, Goralski recalls, and the tipster asked, in effect,
"What the hell are you worrying about the Green Berets
when there is a lieutenant at Ft. Benning being charged
with the murder of 100 civilians."

The South Vietnamese government was always aware
of what happened at Mylai.

Goralski called Ft. Benning and the story was
confirmed. The story was reported on the Huntley-Brink-

ley television newscast on September 10, 1969. Nobody picked it up.

Sometime in early September, retired Col. Robert D. Heinl, Jr., the military analyst for the Detroit News, stumbled on the Mylai story while investigating the Green Beret case. Heinl was getting ready to go to the Middle East but he tried to get confirmation. He couldn't. He passed his information on to the Detroit News Washington Bureau Chief, Jerry ter Horst, who tried unsuccessfully to get confirmation. Then ter Horst dropped the story. He too was busy with the Green Berets case. Also the peace moratorium was coming up.

Later in September or October, ter Horst remembers, he heard more "rumblings" of a mass killing in Vietnam. He says all arrows pointed south. The story of Mylai was being spread everywhere. It was the topic of conversation at cocktail parties in Washington, particularly in military circles. The Washington Post and The New York Times also got wind of the story and began checking it out.

Late in October, Hersh got his tip. As soon as he heard the story he grabbed the ball and ran with it. Everybody in the country had had a chance with the story. Hersh was the only reporter who took it and began a thorough investigation of the Mylai affair.

The Times, however, also was tracking the story. And in November ter Horst finally was able to get confirmation, but he didn't have the details Hersh had. However, ter Horst broke the big story first. It appeared on Page One of the Detroit News on November 12, one day before the Hersh story appeared, reporting that Calley was being charged with murdering 109 Vietnamese civilians.

Another paper that got the story November 12 was the Montgomery, Alabama, Journal.

The Hersh story appeared November 13 in more than 30 newspapers across the country. That same day the New York Times came out with its story. The main thrust of all the stories was that a company of American soldiers massacred a village of innocent civilians. Nobody bothered to explain why, and the anger of the press was directed at the company. When Calley came to Washington, for example, to appear before the Peers committee, a newsman shouted at him: "Hey, Lt. Calley, how many kids did you kill?"

Now the race had begun to get all the details of March 16. The Army couldn't be happier. If the story had to come out, better Charlie Company be discredited than the Army. Everybody wanted to know what happened to "poor innocent civilians" on March 16. Nobody wanted to know what happened to Charlie Company that brought them to the breaking point on March 16. All the Army had to do was point to Calley and Mitchell and say, "They did it."

The clincher came a short time later when Paul David Meadlo, a former member of the company, appeared on the Mike Wallace CBS television show and told how he and his company killed large groups of civilians. He was grilled as if he were an accused murderer. Nowhere in the interview was a serious effort made to understand what happened to boys like Meadlo.

His lawyer, John A. Kesler, later said Meadlo was conned into coming to New York. He had been sold to CBS by Hersh for $10,000, the lawyer said; Meadlo got a free trip from Indiana and a lunch.

"He did it out of misguided patriotism," Kesler told me. "They led him to believe he was making a great patriotic gesture." Then, commenting on Hersh, the lawyer said, "He ruined Meadlo's life."

After everything about the March 16 incident was revealed in minute detail in the nation's press, and the company had been cast in the role of a villain, the Army stepped in to say it would investigate the Mylai affair. That's like allowing the Mafia to conduct an investigation into organized crime in America.

The first thing the Army did was clamp a lid of secrecy on the Mylai affair, under the pretense that the defendants of Charlie Company could not get a fair trial if there was too much publicity surrounding the case. The only trouble was there had already been too much publicity, and all of it unfavorable to the defendants. With the lid of secrecy sealed tight by the Army, members of the company had no chance to say anything in their own defense.

The Army thought it had this thing sewed up.

But some former members of the company were angry. They felt Calley was being used as a scapegoat. They knew the blame for Mylai went much higher, members of the company told me. At least one sought out his local paper to protest that Calley was a scapegoat, and to wonder publicly why Captain Medina wasn't being charged with anything.

The Army knew that if it charged Medina, then the whole service would be blasted. For in his defense Medina would have to incriminate his superiors in the task force, brigade and division.

But Ridenhour sat down and wrote a second letter. This one was not publicized. In it he demanded to know why Medina wasn't being prosecuted and outlined reasons why the captain should be.

"These enlisted men were victims, just like the inhabitants of Mylai (4) were," he told me. "Somebody up the chain of command was much more responsible."

The letter was sent to Udall, who bucked it to the Pentagon, where they must really have panicked.

But the Army acted. Charges of murder were brought against Medina. Shortly after that, 2 generals and 12 other officers, Medina among them, were charged with military violations ranging from false swearing to dereliction of duty.

This thing had gotten out of hand. The Army must have felt the sacrifice of an infantry company plus a fistful of other officers, including two generals, would be a cheap price to pay for protecting its own image. But the truth was still being suppressed. And the truth is that Charlie Company should never have been sent into Mylai, because of its mental condition. It had already lost the psychological war to the VC.

I cannot understand why this has not been brought up before. And I do not understand why anything that may be favorable to the company has received such scanty public attention.

Hersh, for example, has been telling the world how he traveled thousands and thousands of miles and interviewed so many members of the company. Yet in his book he devotes two chapters to the morning of March 16 and one paragraph to the disaster in the minefield on February 25. If the story of February 25 had been properly reported, there would be no story of Mylai.

Hersh must have had this information. Everybody to whom I spoke in the company talked about the minefield. The men will never forget it.

He makes other charges in his book that in all fairness must be questioned. In outlining the assault itself, Hersh says that Medina and his company, numbering 75 men, attacked Mylai (4), where intelligence indicated there would be 250-280 enemy.

Hersh says he has been told by tacticians that an invading force must outnumber a defending force, and the situation here was reversed. So he question's Medina's judgment. He chooses deliberately to omit the fact that three companies were participating in the assault: the three companies that made up Task Force Barker. The VC were believed in the general area; 280 soldiers don't congregate in one hamlet. Even a fool would realize that.

With attached units, including demolition teams, Charlie Company had a strength of 125 men on the assault. Multiply that by the three participating companies and the invading force now totals nearly 400 men.

It is correct that an invading force should outnumber a

defending force, assuming all other things are equal. But all other things were not equal at Mylai. The enemy had no artillery or air support. The Americans preceded the assault with an artillery barrage and an attack by helicopter gun ships. The invading force and its superior firepower were sufficient to handle the anticipated enemy.

Hersh relates a story about a firefight in which the company was involved before Mylai. The company came under attack and Hersh tells how a family of four were caught in a crossfire. One of the four, the baby, was killed. Hersh neglects to mention the company was green and nervous. He leaves the reader with the uneasy thought that the baby was deliberately shot and the GIs are cold-blooded killers.

If they were cold-blooded killers, why didn't they shoot the rest of the family? And if the Viet Cong had respect for their own people, why did they fire on the company when they too saw that family?

More tragic than the death of the baby was the indifference of the parents. Did the death of their infant mean so little that they would make no effort to remove the body? What were they doing in the field when there were VC nearby preparing to fire on the Americans? Why didn't the VC warn the family to get out? Apparently the VC were willing to lay the life of a Vietnamese baby on the line in order to win a firefight with the Americans.

What undoubtedly happened was that the platoon fired in response to the snipers, and then realized its error. Ideally, a soldier shouldn't fire first before studying the consequences. But, according to Bernhardt, the Army teaches its infantry recruits to react automatically by firing their weapons, and then asking questions.

Another item that is disturbing, and that I think serves to point out what I feel has been a deliberate attempt to malign the company, is the story Hersh relates about the death of Sgt. Cox.

Hersh charges the platoon just robbed and killed as

they returned to LZ Dottie following Cox's death. He neglects to mention the men were heartbroken, indeed crazed by now, actually crying as they headed back to the base. After shooting a suspected Viet Cong, the men raced forward and stomped on the body. No normal person would do that.

There is another book on Mylai about which I wish to comment in passing: Richard Hammer's collection of newspaper and magazine articles that he rewrote and called a book. Hammer was racing Hersh for first publication, and as a result his research adds nothing new to the Mylai affair. Since he must have felt he had to contribute something, he came up with the ridiculous assertion that Charlie Company hit the wrong town, because Mylai (4) is really called Xom Lang by the local residents.

He tends to confuse the reader entirely. Apparently he is completely unfamiliar with military maps, which identify localities through the use of coordinates. If his logic were carried to the extreme, then Brooklyn isn't really Brooklyn because it is known officially as King's County.

The army hit Mylai (4) because it wanted to hit Mylai (4), regardless of what it is called locally.

On Army maps all hills are numbered, for example, and are not always referred to by their names. The number indicates the height of the hill in meters. But it doesn't matter. It is still where it belongs geographically.

In his book Hammer also defends the Viet Cong. Conceding they practice a policy of terror and atrocity, he excuses it on the grounds that they represent a totalitarian government.

The tragedy of Charlie Company was that it was defeated long before Mylai (4), and really died in the minefield on February 25. But the army refused to bury it, and now society won't even let the bodies rest in peace.

When I visited the bodies I found frightened, conscience-stricken, terrified kids. Tears still welled in their eyes as they talked of the deaths of Weber and Wilson,

Bell and Rotger and Cox. Van Leer, who had developed a stutter after his experiences in the minefield, had overcome this problem after settling down in civilian life. But it became worse than ever when the story of Mylai broke in the press. Another psychological hangup he developed in the rice fields was an unnatural fear of people coming up behind him. This too he thought he had conquered, until the Mylai affair was publicized. The problem got so bad he once almost hit his wife when she playfully came up behind him to kiss him.

Van Leer was one of the men the company sought to avenge at Mylai. He feels grateful for their thoughtfulness but he feels terribly guilt-ridden for what they face because of what they did. Van Leer is lucky: he is married, he works and he goes to school. Many of the men I visited two years or more after Mylai are not that fortunate. They still run. Their slaughter in the minefield and the horror at Mylai have scarred the minds of these boys for life.

Most still didn't have the patience for school or for work when I visited with them. Fred Widmer has been on and off jobs since his discharge. Richard Pendleton hasn't been able to find work. James Bergthold was earning $60 a week as a truck driver's helper when I met him.

Tom Partsch went off to school, but gave it up. He can't concentrate. Joseph Konwinski was having the same problem. One veteran of Mylai is a garbage man; another an apprentice mason. Another has reportedly become a drug addict. Two have had nervous breakdowns.

One of these two is Herbert Carter, who still sees bodies in front of his eyes at night—bodies of Americans, bodies of Vietnamese. The Army that used him dropped him, and for two years Carter got no help from anyone. He was entitled to a pension for his war wounds, but nobody ever helped him get it.

Carter served honorably in Vietnam. His buddies and his commanding officer speak highly of him. But he has

been abused by the press ever since the story appeared
that he shot himself in his foot. He didn't. And those who
know him don't believe he did. He knows the story was
wrong and made it appear as if he let down his company.
He didn't.

But the nation he served let Carter down. One story
about him insinuated he was attempting to profit from
his experiences by asking money for his story. What was
ignored was that Carter was working as a menial laborer
in Texas for $1.60 an hour, when he could find jobs. He
was ashamed to go home because he had nothing. When
his stepfather lost his right arm at the shoulder in an
accident, Carter was the only member of the family who
couldn't get home. He couldn't afford it.

Everybody has been after Carter. Nobody has offered
him anything. Ossie Brown, who is David Mitchell's lawyer, called me to ask how to get in touch with Carter.
Brown said he wanted to help the youngster. Carter later
told me the real story. He said Brown told him to get out
of town, and didn't even offer him the cost of a ticket out.
Carter was scheduled to be subpoenaed by the Army to
testify against Mitchell.

The prosecuting attorneys have also been to see Carter,
to review the testimony they wanted him to give against
Mitchell and Calley. Carter has refused to cooperate.

All of these kids have been haunted. If they weren't
haunted by the past, then they were haunted by the FBI
and the CID and pesty newsmen like myself. Gary Garfolo's grandmother begged me to leave her grandson
alone. She complained that Hersh parked in front of Garfolo's house all day, then grabbed the ex-GI and interviewed him into the wee hours of the morning. Her
grandson can't take it anymore, she told me. The press did
the same to Pendleton. His mother complained they surrounded his home, waiting to talk to him.

Everybody has been after Charlie Company for reasons

of politics, profit or publicity. Everybody has always used Charlie Company.

I asked George W. Latimer, a prominent attorney, for an interview with his client, William L. Calley, Jr. Latimer asked me how much I would offer. I said, "nothing." I didn't get the interview. But there must be big money in Calley. The American Legion has announced it is raising $200,000 to show its support for Calley. It is unclear who gets the money.

Ronald Haeberle, an army photographer who saw his first action at Mylai, after one year in Vietnam, reportedly earned $40,000 for the pictures he took of Charlie Company. Charlie Company has been good to everyone.

One mother told me, when I tried to reach her boy by phone, "Leave my son alone. He did his duty for his country. Now why don't you all leave him alone." And she was right, and she was wrong. I left him alone. But society won't.

The CID crisscrosses this country like an army of busy ants, bugging these kids over and over and over again— literally. Twice I went to Tom Partsch's house, calling him beforehand. And twice a CID agent interrupted me, so that the kid thinks I'm a spy.

I'm not a spy, Tom. The CID has your phone bugged. And when I called they interrupted. They knew what I wanted: your diary. And you didn't trust me, but you gave it to them and you let them xerox it. They promised you it would be kept in confidence. Don't you know they will have to make it a matter of public record sooner or later.

The Army has banked on the GI's traditional fear of the brass to intimidate the company. None of the former members of the company could be compelled to go to Washington to appear before the Peers Committee that was investigating the Mylai affair.

The Army had no power of subpoena, but the kids came running anyhow.

No other proof is needed as to the questionable judgment and intelligence of these former infantrymen than the fact they went to Washington to testify against themselves and their buddies.

Many who talked did not even have benefit of an attorney.

A high-ranking officer in the Pentagon was asked how the Army got these ex-soldiers to come and testify, and he answered with sarcasm: "They're getting a free trip to Washington." One kid went because it was a chance to take his mother on a tour and the army agreed to pay him a car-mileage allowance. More than 400 witnesses appeared before the Peers committee. Most were given free plane tickets, plus $25 a day while they were in Washington. When Carter, who was broke, said he didn't have the price of a cab fare to the airport, the Army in Houston, Texas, arranged to chauffeur him there.

Many of the ex-GIs apparently believed they could no longer be prosecuted and they cooperated with the Army in the mistaken notion that they were doing the right thing.

One kid, talking to his buddy, long distance, said, "Don't forget. We're under orders not to talk." What orders? He was a civilian. A ranking Pentagon official said studies were being made between the Justice and Defense departments to find a way to prosecute the civilians. "We'll get them too," he told me confidently.

I remember when I tried to see Howard Holland. His mother brought him to me, but he wouldn't talk. I guess I can't blame him. I tracked his mother down to a little wooden frame house near the railroad track, where she lived. I knocked and knocked until she had to answer. She was a poor woman, with tired eyes, and she was afraid, and I guess she was like most mothers of infantrymen. "I want to see your son," I told her, when she finally opened the door. She looked at me carefully and studied me for the longest time, it seemed, and she said, almost in anguish, "Do you mean him any harm, mister?" And I said, "I mean your son no harm, Mam." And she studied me some more and maybe felt she could trust me. Then she said, "There have been so many people to see my son from the government."

But her son didn't trust me. The Army told him not to talk and, although he was a civilian, he obeyed. I guess I don't blame him.

The guy I remember most, I guess, was Richard Hendrickson. The Army wouldn't cooperate with me in helping to find him. They said he was dead. They said a man with the wounds I described couldn't be alive.

Hendrickson had one leg gone and the other going. He had lost the use of one arm. He was blind and there were only red slits where his eyes once had been. He was nearly deaf, but could still hear a bit. His face was still blackened from the powder burns. His nose and mouth were scarred, and he had lost his sense of taste so he didn't eat much. That's why he was rather thin.

He had a hole in his chest left by something that had gone in and come out on his left side. Part of his right lung was removed. He had scars on his throat from a tracheotomy, and had undergone open-heart surgery three times, for three times doctors said he was dead. He had a hole in the back of his head, and at one time his intestines protruded from his side to facilitate bowel movements. That was when they had placed a tube in his penis, which along with his testicles had been wounded. His teeth still rattled and were loose, two years later.

Mostly he stays indoors, for he cannot move around, and when I finally found him he was lying on a couch "watching" a television set. His doctors say he wants to live and he told me he was glad to be alive. He wanted to talk about Charlie Company, to which he belonged until Cox was blown up.

I told him he was one of the men whom the company sought to avenge at Mylai. And I asked him what he thought.

He didn't answer right away. And then he said: "I'm glad something was done, but I'm sorry they're in trouble. I wish I could have been there in Mylai.

"If I was there I don't know what I'd have done. But I probably would do the same as Calley. Nobody likes to see his buddies wiped out without being able to do anything."

I asked him how he felt about the war, considering the wounds he had suffered. "I'm not at all bitter," he said. "I just take it as part of life. I'm not a very religious man, but I believe there is a reason for everything that happens. I'll find it."

In a way I was glad he couldn't see me. I was crying.

A nation had sent its children to a war it didn't approve and taught them, in the words of the drill instructor, to "Kill, kill, kill." And now that they did, the nation is preparing to punish them.

The Army threw Charlie Company into the field for 60 days in the hope it would disappear. But it didn't. Therefore the army is preparing to sweep Charlie Company under the carpet so America can feel clean again.

"If you give a kid a shotgun and tell him to shoot a sparrow," Carter said to me once, "don't spank him afterwards for it."

INDEX

★ ★ ★ ★ ★ ★ ★ ★ ★ ★ ★ ★ ★ ★